Generating Inequality

GENERATING INEQUALITY

Mechanisms of Distribution in the U.S. Economy

LESTER C. THUROW

BASIC BOOKS, INC., PUBLISHERS

NEW YORK

TO EMILY

For her iron determination
in the face of
overwhelming odds

Library of Congress Cataloging in Publication Data

Thurow, Lester C.
Generating inequality.

Includes bibliographical references and index.
1. Wealth. 2. Income—United States. 3. Wealth,
Ethics of. I. Title.
HB821.T47   330.1'6   75-7264
ISBN 0-465-02670-2
ISBN 0-465-02668-0 pbk.

CONTENTS

INTRODUCTION:
THE ECONOMIC GAME

IMAGINE watching a chess game without knowing any of the rules of chess. Complicated moves are being made; players are being captured; games are being won. Without being able to ask questions, how long would it take you to deduce the complete rules of chess from simply watching chess games? How many times would you make mistakes and postulate rules that later observations would disprove?

Now imagine a more complicated game in which some of the moves are random events not determined by the explicit rules of the game. Accidents occur. The game is also being played by players who do not always act in accordance with the rules. They make mistakes. In such a game, constructing the rule book would be a monumental task. Yet it is just such a game that economists are trying to dissect. What are the rules of the economic game? How are economic prizes distributed? What determines the actions of individual players?

Ultimately, the purpose of knowing the rules of any game is to be able to explain how the game works, to predict the outcome of the game, to play the game better, or, perhaps, to design a better game. The starting point, however, is our knowledge of the outcome of the current economic game—a game played for life-and-death stakes. We can observe this game directly by looking at the distributions of earnings and wealth. These are the prizes that the economy has distributed. Once we know the distribution of economic prizes, we can begin the task of working backward to understand the process whereby prizes are generated and distributed.

Suppose an outside observer had familiarized himself with the data on the United States distributions of earnings and wealth but then decided to retreat to the library to look up the rules for distributing economic prizes. What would he find? If he were to look at introductory textbooks in economics, he would find that economic prizes are supposed to be awarded in accordance with the marginal-productivity theory of distribution. In its simplest form the marginal-productivity theory of distribution springs from a game played according to strict rules—perfect competition, perfect knowledge, perfect rationality, and so on.

In a market system, supply and demand determine both product and factor prices. The demand curves for factors of production (land, labor, and capital) are, however, "derived" demand curves that spring from each factor's marginal contribution to economic output—its marginal physical product—and the price at which output can be sold. As cost minimizers, entrepreneurs select factor combinations that produce the desired output at the least costs. To do this they compare each factor's market price with its marginal revenue product (marginal physical product times output price). If the market price of a factor exceeds its marginal revenue product, producers reduce their use of that factor and substitute other factors until factor prices and factor marginal revenue products are brought into equilibrium. Conversely, if a factor's marginal revenue product exceeds its price, the factors will be substituted for other factors until price and marginal revenue products are once again brought into equilibrium. As a result, when in equilibrium all factors will be paid an amount equal to their marginal revenue product. In such a world economic prizes are being awarded in accordance with the rules of the marginal-productivity theory of distribution.*

Once our observer had proceeded beyond introductory and intermediate micro-economic texts, he would find that the marginal-productivity theory of distribution fades into the background. It ·is a theory often assumed to exist but seldom analyzed. Economies do not meet the rigorous conditions necessary for the existence of perfect competition; yet the implications of these deviations for marginal productivity are seldom investigated. What one means when one claims to be an adherent to the marginal-productivity theory of distribution is left amorphous.

This amorphousness makes it very difficult, if not impossible, to prove or disprove the marginal-productivity theory of distribution: it simply has not been spelled out in sufficient detail to be provable or disprovable. If anyone attempts to spell out a detailed theory that is susceptible to disproof, he can always be accused of setting up a straw man. He is disproving something, but not what is really "meant" by the marginal-productivity theory of distribution.

Various drafts of this book have contained a critique of conventional marginal-productivity analysis, but each time I have been accused of setting up my own straw man that could easily be knocked down. As a result, this book makes no attempt to disprove the conventional wisdom. It is so amorphous that I have been unable to say what it is. Instead, Appendix A—a do-it-yourself guide to marginal productivity—outlines a series of detailed determinations that must be made if marginal-

---

* Since the marginal-productivity theory is taught in every basic economics course, the reader is assumed to be familiar with its basic postulates. If he or she is not, any standard text on micro-economics will quickly fill the gap.

productivity analysis is to be made into an operational theory of distribution. Each reader is encouraged to skip to the appendix and make these determinations for himself. Construct your own theory of distribution and then decide whether your own variant of marginal productivity is more or less persuasive than the theories that I shall attempt to propound. But be fair! Your theory must be spelled out at the same level of detail. What facts can be explained; what facts cannot be explained? If it is a true operational theory, there will be some facts that cannot be explained. To be able to explain everything with an amorphous theory is ultimately to explain nothing.

The problems do not revolve around the words "marginal productivity." From some perspectives what is to follow is a marginal-productivity theory of distribution. The problem is to describe a theory of distribution that can actually explain the existing distributions of economic prizes. To do this the book begins with an overview of the existing distribution of economic prizes. Who gets what? How is the economic pie divided? The analysis then begins with an examination of each of the lenses necessary to give us a binocular view of the distributions of earnings and wealth. Under what conditions is a distribution of economic prizes *efficient?* Under what conditions is a distribution of economic prizes *equitable?* Equity and efficiency are the two alternative ways of judging distributional mechanisms.

Since the 1950s, economic analysis has focused almost entirely on efficiency and has ignored equity. Economists have implicitly assumed that it is possible to think economically (i.e., objectively) about the efficiency of any distributional mechanism, but it was not possible to think objectively about the mechanism's equity. In this view equity questions can only be settled by force—can I club you into agreement with my position?—or must be left to some other discipline (political science, philosophy, theology, etc.).

As we shall see, efficiency analysis is not value free. Economic efficiency and economic equity stand upon exactly the same foundations, be they rock or quicksand. In both cases it is necessary to accept an underlying set of value judgments before analysis can commence. Once the value judgments have been accepted, it is possible to think economically about either problem.

Although it might be appropriate to ignore equity problems in many economic studies, it is clearly inappropriate in a book on the processes for distributing earnings and wealth. Efficiency and equity are both essential ingredients in judging whether any distributional mechanism is good or bad and in determining how the mechanism ought to be modified. To talk about distributional mechanisms without thinking about their equity properties is to miss at least half of the problem. That is why this book investigates at some length the problems of making statements about economic equity.

Once the foundations of efficiency and equity have been understood, the analysis moves on to examine some of the empirical problems that require an enrichment of simple marginal-productivity models. Over time, economists have added a wide variety of ad hoc additional hypotheses to the simple marginal-productivity model to explain these deviant observations. This book will attempt to show that many of these explanations are mutually contradictory and that others are unlikely. Many of them take the form of ad hoc "market imperfections."

One of the basic tenets of this book is that nothing should be labeled a market imperfection without close analysis. If something is a market imperfection, there are always profits to be made by eliminating it. If markets are basically competitive, someone will sooner or later discover a way around the imperfection. Thus, there is a reasonably high probability that any long-lasting "market imperfection" plays some kind of a functional role in the economy. Or at least this possibility should be extensively investigated before the situation is labeled a market imperfection. If markets are not basically competitive, then the imperfections are permanent features of the economic game and need to be built into the distributional mechanism. In that case conventional marginal productivity cannot apply, and some alternative distributional mechanisms must be constructed based on the market imperfections that actually exist.

Proceeding on the premise that any long-lasting feature of the economy is apt to be functional, the intellectual problem is to construct consistent mechanisms for explaining the observed distributions of earnings and wealth with as little resort to market imperfections as possible. Each deviant observation must be examined to see if it plays a functional role in the economy. In the process two theories of distribution will be constructed and examined. The "job-competition" model will be advanced as an explanation of the distribution of earnings, and the "random-walk" model will be advanced as an explanation of the distribution of wealth. I shall argue that many of the factors that are "market imperfections" from the point of view of simple marginal productivity are actually at the heart of the process of achieving dynamic efficiency in our economy. From the perspective of the job-competition model and the random-walk model, they are not imperfections.

The analysis of earnings and wealth are separated, since the distributional mechanisms do not seem to be the same. The job-competition model springs from the observation that the labor market is not the conventional bidding market where people meet to buy and sell existing skills. Since most people acquire their skills through informal on-the-job training from one worker to another, the labor market is primarily a market for allocating training slots. As we shall see, the characteristics necessary to construct an efficient training market are very different from those necessary to allocate existing skills efficiently. Many implications flow from this observation, but one of the principal ones concerns the usefulness of wage flexibility. Analysis will show that although wage flexibility is an efficient mechanism for clearing skill markets, it is an inefficient mechanism for clearing training markets. As wage flexibility rises, training falls.

The random-walk model shows that most large fortunes are not created via a patient process of earnings, savings, investments, reinvestment, and accumulation at market rates of interest. Instead, large fortunes are created in a matter of a few years, although they may be passed on from generation to generation. Compared to the conventional model of wealth accumulation, they are instantaneous fortunes. To understand instantaneous fortunes it is necessary to understand the distributional implications of the random-walk hypothesis, which argues that there are persistent disequilibriums in the real capital markets (the markets for real plant and equipment) that are capitalized into equilibrium in the financial markets. This process of capitalizing disequilibrium into equilibrium leads to a lotterylike process with equal *ex ante* expected returns but an unequal *ex·post* array of returns. Different individuals making the same types of investments with the same expected rates of return will actually earn enormously different returns. This unequal *ex post* array of returns leads to the random-walk process of distributing wealth.

In both the job-competition and random-walk models, the world is not as deterministic as simple marginal-productivity models would imply. As far as the individual is concerned, he or she is subject to large stochastic shocks in his or her earnings and wealth. Although these shocks are random as far as the individual is concerned, they are an integral systematic part of achieving an efficient economy.

In the United States the basic mechanisms for distributing earnings and wealth are overlaid with discrimination against women and various minorities. The problem is to understand how discrimination interacts with the basic distributional mechanisms of the economy to produce the observed distributions of economic prizes for those who suffer from discrimination.

Existing theories of discrimination are inadequate, since they are unable to explain the persistence of discrimination against minorities and the existence of sex discrimination. Strong economic pressures should exist to eliminate discrimination against minorities, yet it lasts. Maximizing physical or social distance (the analytical heart of existing theories) just does not make sense when thinking about women. From the perspective of the job-competition model, however, it is possible to build up a theory of "statistical" discrimination that explains both the persistence of discrimination against minorities and the existence of discrimination against women. Although the effects cancel out in the aggregate, statistical discrimination is also a factor in the distribution of earnings among adult white males—the group least subject to prejudice.

Finally, the policy implications of the job-competition and random-walk models are examined. If these theories are correct, what economic policies should be altered or put in place? As the analysis will show, substantial changes would be required. The current calculus for deciding whether or not to invest in education is inappropriate. Equalizing the distribution of human-capital investments will not necessarily lead to a more equal distribution of earnings. Conventional recommendations for increasing the rate of growth of productivity are apt to be counterproductive. Efforts to improve capital flows across real capital markets become important in controlling the distribution of wealth. Without eliminating statistical discrimination, it will be impossible for individuals or groups to escape the impacts of discrimination.

When examined, these and other conclusions indicate that it is important to know which distributional mechanisms are at work in the economy. Depending upon the answer, very different policies will be adopted to accomplish exactly the same objectives. In the end it is not possible to be an agnostic about the distributional mechanisms if you wish to design effective economic policies for accomplishing your objectives. To be an agnostic is to support current economic policies and the distributional mechanisms upon which they are implicitly based.

The original work for substantial parts of this book was financed under research grants from the U.S. Department of Labor's Manpower Administration and from the Carnegie Commission for Higher Education. These institutions are not, of course, responsible for the conclusions. I would also like to thank various seminars at M.I.T. and elsewhere that have contributed to the verbal refining of this product. Hopefully, the arguments are better because of their efforts.

Generating Inequality

1

THE OUTCOME OF
THE ECONOMIC GAME

IF AN OUTSIDE observer were to look at the distribution of economic prizes in the U.S. economy, what would he see? In 1972 (the latest year for which complete data are available) he would have seen that 122 million Americans were income recipients. They had a mean income of $6,375 and a median income of $4,713, but these averages were merely summary measures of a widely dispersed distribution of income (see Table 1). Two and one-half million Americans had incomes in excess of $25,000 per year, while almost 11 million Americans had incomes between $0 and $500 per year.

Average incomes grow as the economy grows (the median income was only $1,787 in 1947), but changes in the dispersion of income are much smaller. An examination of the economic prizes captured by different quintiles of the population in the postwar period indicates that the fourth quintile has made small gains at the expense of the first, second, and fifth quintiles (see Table 2). Or to put it another way, the upper middle class is gaining at the expense of the rich, the lower middle class, and the poor.

TABLE 1
Money Income in 1972

INCOME	PERCENT OF INCOME RECIPIENTS
$0–999	15.2
$1,000–1,999	12.2
$2,000–2,999	9.6
$3,000–3,999	8.0
$4,000–4,999	7.0
$5,000–5,999	6.5
$6,000–6,999	5.8
$7,000–7,999	5.5
$8,000–9,999	8.9
$10,000–14,999	13.4
$15,000–24,999	6.0
$25,000–49,999	1.7
$50,000 and up	0.3
Median	$4713
Mean	$6375

U.S. Bureau of the Census, *Current Population Reports: Consumer Income 1972* (Washington, D.C.: Government Printing Office, 1973), p. 108.

TABLE 2
Percentage Share of Aggregate Income
Persons 14 and Over

	1947	1972
Lowest fifth	2.5%	2.0%
Second fifth	8.3	7.2
Third fifth	14.8	14.8
Fourth fifth	21.6	25.6
Highest fifth	52.8	50.4
Median Income (1972 $)	$1,833	$5,144

Source: U.S. Bureau of the Census, *Current Population Reports: Consumer Income 1972* (Washington, D.C.: Government Printing Office, 1973), p. 118.

Note that the data in Table 1 and 2 measure the distribution of income among persons rather than the more common data on families. As the data in Table 3 indicate, income is dis-

TABLE 3

Family Incomes Shares

	1947	1972
Lowest fifth	5.1%	5.4%
Second fifth	11.8	11.9
Third fifth	16.7	17.5
Fourth fifth	23.1	23.8
Highest fifth	43.3	41.4
Top 5 percent	17.5	15.9
Median Income (1972 $)	$5,665	$11,116

Source: U.S. Bureau of the Census, *Current Population Reports: Consumer Income 1972* (Washington, D.C.: Government Printing Office, 1973), pp. 34–35.

tributed much more equally among families than it is among persons. This is partly because family data ignore 17 million unrelated individuals and partly because family incomes include the incomes of more than one individual. The process of sharing individual incomes makes family incomes more equal than individual incomes.

One of the major factors leading to a more equal distribution of family income is the pattern of female labor force participation. Since males with low incomes are more apt to have working wives than males with high incomes (see Table 4), working wives serve to increase the aggregate income shares of the poorest families.

Family incomes have received most of our attention, since they are relevant data when studying economic welfare.[1] Since families consume as families, a family's consumption possibilities are determined by its family income. Families are less interesting, however, when discussing the factors that determine the distribution of economic prizes, since, with the exception of government transfer payments, economic prizes are almost

5

TABLE 4

Husband–Wife Earnings

HUSBAND'S EARNINGS	PROBABILITY OF WIFE WORKING (PERCENT)	MEDIAN EARNINGS OF WORKING WIVES (DOLLARS)
$0–$1,000	34.9	2,519
$1,000–$2,000	36.0	2,000
$2,000–$3,000	46.0	2,363
$3,000–$4,000	45.7	2,302
$4,000–$5,000	48.5	2,503
$5,000–$6,000	46.3	2,853
$6,000–$7,000	49.2	3,134
$7,000–$8,000	47.2	3,155
$8,000–$10,000	44.9	4,621
$10,000–$15,000	37.6	3,205
$15,000–$25,000	30.7	2,941
$25,000 and up	19.2	2,968

Source: U.S. Bureau of the Census, *Current Population Reports: Consumer Income 1969* (Washington, D.C.: Government Printing Office, 1970), p. 56.

never awarded to families as families.[2] Prizes are awarded to individuals who then may choose to share them with others. Since this book focuses on the prize-awarding process and not the sharing process, the focus of the analysis will be on individual incomes and not on family incomes.

The most striking fact to our outside observer would be the variance or dispersion in incomes. Enormous differences exist both between and within groups. The data in Table 5 provide an illustration of the dispersion by sex, race, and degree of work effort. The time devoted to work rather than to leisure is an important element in determining earnings, but, as the table indicates, it does not by itself solve the problem of why workers earn different amounts. Average income declines as work effort diminishes, but the variance around these averages is substantial. Some individuals earn high incomes with little work effort; others earn low incomes with great work effort. In 1972, 6,234 American men earned over $25,000 even though they worked only part of each week and less than fourteen weeks

TABLE 5

Work Experience and Total Money Income in 1972 by Race and Sex

TOTAL MONEY INCOME	FULL-TIME, FULL-YEAR JOBS (35+ HOURS, 50-52 WEEKS)				PART-TIME, PART-YEAR JOBS (LESS THAN 35 HOURS, 13 WEEKS OR LESS)			
	MALES		FEMALES		MALES		FEMALES	
	WHITE	BLACK	WHITE	BLACK	WHITE	BLACK	WHITE	BLACK
Less than $999	1.3%	1.0%	1.5%	2.4%	71.5%	81.9%	84.4%	75.2%
$1,000 to 1,999	1.0	2.6	2.3	4.8	10.8	10.1	7.7	13.9
$2,000 to 2,999	1.3	2.6	4.0	7.2	6.0	2.2	3.3	4.1
$3,000 to 3,999	2.2	6.9	9.4	14.7	3.6	1.9	1.6	0.9
$4,000 to 4,999	3.3	10.9	14.8	16.8	2.1	1.5	1.3	2.1
$5,000 to 5,999	4.9	11.1	15.5	14.7	1.3	–	0.5	0.7
$6,000 to 6,999	6.3	10.3	13.8	11.3	1.6	1.3	0.4	1.1
$7,000 to 7,999	7.3	12.1	11.9	9.4	0.7	–	0.3	–
$8,000 to 9,999	16.3	17.6	13.5	10.1	1.1	–	0.3	–
$10,000 to 14,999	33.0	20.1	10.9	7.3	0.9	–	0.1	–
$15,000 to 24,999	17.2	3.9	1.9	1.1	0.1	–	0.1	–
$25,000 and up	5.8	0.8	0.3	0.3	0.3	–	–	–
MEDIAN	$10,918	$7,373	$6,172	$5,280	$ 433	$360	$353	$422
MEAN	$12,167	$7,809	$6,625	$5,692	$1,268	$627	$637	$764

Source: U.S. Bureau of the Census, *Current Population Reports: Consumer Income 1972* (Washington, D.C.: Government Printing Office, 1973), pp. 130–131.

TABLE 6

Occupation of Longest Job in 1972—Civilian Workers 14 Years Old and Over, by Total Money Earnings in 1972, by Sex and Work Experience

(Persons 14 years old and over as of March 1973)

OCCUPATION	NUMBER WITH EARNINGS (THOUS.)	PERCENT DISTRIBUTION								MEDIAN EARNINGS (DOLLARS)	MEAN EARNINGS (DOLLARS)
		LESS THAN $1,999	$2,000 TO $3,999	$4,000 TO $5,999	$6,000 TO $7,999	$8,000 TO $9,999	$10,000 TO $14,999	$15,000 TO $24,999	$25,000 AND OVER		
MALE year-round full-time workers											
Total	38,184	3.1	4.1	9.7	15.0	16.8	31.2	15.2	4.8	10,202	11,304
Prof., technical, and kindred wkrs., total	5,773	1.1	1.8	2.7	8.4	12.0	33.8	29.5	10.6	13,542	15,192
Self-employed, total	556	3.6	1.8	2.4	5.2	3.9	12.8	24.3	46.0	23,351	25,463
Physicians and surgeons	103	1.5	1.5	–	2.9	–	7.1	19.1	67.9	25,000+	33,271
Salaried, total	5,217	0.9	1.8	2.7	8.7	12.9	36.0	30.1	6.9	13,187	14,098
Engineers, technical	936	–	0.3	0.5	3.4	3.5	36.6	49.7	5.9	16,124	16,113
Physicians and surgeons	134	–	–	2.5	2.2	6.7	19.6	30.4	38.7	21,287	26,375
Teachers, primary and secondary schools	804	0.6	2.4	2.3	14.4	18.9	43.5	16.1	1.8	11,310	11,471
Farmers and farm managers	1,333	27.2	15.4	14.7	12.6	8.7	12.8	6.4	2.1	5,060	6,220
Managers and administrators, exc. farm total	6,224	2.6	2.5	4.0	9.0	11.3	29.6	27.2	13.8	13,486	15,299
Salaried	5,071	0.7	1.3	2.7	8.0	11.2	31.5	29.8	14.8	14,146	16,250
Clerical and kindred wkrs. total	2,673	1.4	3.2	9.9	16.2	22.4	38.3	8.0	0.6	9,716	9,750
Sales workers, total	2,251	1.8	3.2	8.3	14.0	12.8	30.3	20.4	9.1	11,610	13,298
In retail trade	638	2.7	5.7	15.1	24.6	14.8	23.4	9.3	4.3	8,254	10,338
Craftsmen and kindred wkrs., total	8,356	1.3	2.7	7.9	15.5	19.2	38.7	13.7	0.8	10,413	10,494
Foremen	1,228	0.2	1.4	4.7	12.8	17.6	43.9	18.3	0.9	11,497	11,502
Craftsmen	7,127	1.7	3.0	8.5	16.0	19.4	37.8	12.9	0.8	10,196	10,320
In construction	1,496	2.1	2.4	9.2	14.9	19.0	33.3	18.3	0.9	10,367	10,658
Other craftsmen	5,632	1.5	3.1	8.3	16.3	19.6	39.0	11.4	0.8	10,157	10,282
Operatives, including transport, total	6,748	1.9	4.0	14.7	20.8	22.9	30.5	4.8	0.4	8,747	8,835
Manufacturing, total	3,810	1.5	2.8	14.6	21.5	25.5	30.5	3.4	0.2	8,754	8,792
Durable	2,505	1.5	2.5	12.5	20.7	26.7	31.7	4.2	0.2	8,954	9,002
Nondurable	1,306	1.5	3.4	18.5	22.1	23.1	28.3	2.0	0.2	8,311	8,388

Service wkrs., exc. pvt. hshld.	2,507	4.1	7.2	18.9	24.5	16.2	22.8	5.6	0.6	7,630	8,175
Farm laborers and foremen	442	16.1	23.8	25.4	16.7	10.3	4.3	2.9	0.4	4,615	5,335
Laborers, exc. farm	1,870	3.7	9.4	22.0	20.9	21.8	20.0	1.8	0.5	7,477	7,620
FEMALE year-round full-time workers											
Total	16,675	4.9	15.2	31.4	24.8	12.4	9.7	1.4	0.3	5,903	6,287
Prof., technical, and kindred wkrs., total	3,041	1.6	4.9	9.8	23.9	26.5	28.9	3.9	0.6	8,744	8,851
Salaried, total	2,993	1.2	4.8	9.8	24.1	27.0	29.1	3.7	0.5	8,758	8,871
Teachers, primary and secondary schools	1,447	0.6	4.7	6.2	28.6	27.9	29.5	2.4	0.1	8,706	8,748
Farmers and farm managers	115	27.6	28.1	20.8	8.3	–	5.1	–	–	3,129	3,048
Managers and administrators, exc. farm total	1,111	7.1	8.6	19.9	24.4	13.8	19.4	5.6	1.0	7,024	7,720
Self-employed, total	211	28.3	15.2	14.0	14.6	6.6	12.6	7.2	1.5	5,170	5,760
In retail trade	147	25.5	15.6	14.1	14.6	8.5	11.2	8.3	2.1	5,412	6,277
Salaried	900	2.2	7.1	21.3	26.7	15.5	21.0	5.2	0.9	7,369	8,178
Clerical and kindred wkrs. total	6,349	2.0	9.2	37.8	33.0	11.7	5.6	0.4	0.2	6,054	6,275
Sec., steno, and typists	2,573	1.1	7.8	34.3	36.7	14.3	5.2	0.4	0.2	6,341	6,514
Sales workers, total	684	6.5	33.3	37.0	12.9	5.2	2.8	1.8	0.2	4,445	4,935
in retail trade	516	7.2	39.4	37.6	10.3	4.3	0.6	0.6	–	4,137	4,317
Craftsmen and kindred wkrs., total	276	4.4	18.3	34.4	29.4	7.7	5.9	–	–	5,545	5,627
Foremen	94	3.0	19.1	28.3	35.4	11.1	3.1	–	–	5,972	5,750
Craftsmen	182	5.0	18.0	37.4	26.3	5.9	7.3	–	–	5,317	5,563
Operatives, including transport, total	2,306	3.2	22.7	43.1	21.0	7.2	2.7	–	–	5,004	5,206
Manufacturing, total	1,986	2.5	20.4	45.0	21.9	7.1	3.0	–	–	5,114	5,308
Durable	876	2.6	10.6	43.5	27.8	11.2	4.4	–	–	5,709	5,861
Nondurable	1,110	2.4	28.2	46.2	17.3	4.0	2.0	–	–	4,690	4,871
Private hshld. workers	305	40.9	35.5	12.4	4.2	0.5	1.6	–	–	2,295	2,619
Service wkrs., exc. pvt. hshld.	2,308	9.8	30.4	36.8	15.2	5.3	2.0	0.3	0.1	4,483	4,628
Laborers, exc. farm	114	9.1	25.6	41.2	14.7	6.6	2.7	–	–	4,633	4,746

Note: – Represents zero.

Source: U.S. Bureau of the Census, Current Population Reports: Consumer Income 1972 (Washington, D.C.: Government Printing Office, 1973), pp. 136–138.

per year. At the other end of the spectrum, 458,376 American men and 250,590 women worked over thirty-five hours per week and fifty to fifty-two weeks per year but earned less than $1,000 for their effort. Why this dramatic difference?

Black males earn less than white males for the same degree of work effort, but the differential sharply diminishes as weeks and hours of work fall. In the part-time, part-year labor force, blacks make almost as much, or in a few cases even more, than whites. Among females the earnings differentials for each work effort class are much less than those for males. But females of either race make much less than males who are contributing the same work effort. Why do men earn more than women? Why are earning differentials sharper among men than women? Why do black-white differentials diminish as work effort declines?

The simplest explanation for earning differentials is human skills. Yet within occupation groups there still are enormous differences in earnings. Table 6 presents data on male and female earnings for full-time, full-year workers in different occupations. Although the occupations in these tables are broad aggregations of different specific skills, the same dispersions exist when one looks at the detailed occupational titles in the U.S. Census. To illustrate the problem, look at two relatively homogeneous occupations. The mean year-round, full-time, self-employed male physician and surgeon earned $33,271, but 6 percent of this group earned less than $10,000. Conversely, 22 percent of all common non-farm male laborers earned more than $10,000. How can common unskilled laborers earn more than M.D.s when both are working full-time, full-year?

If our observer looks at the male-female differences, he will note that female earnings are lower but that there are also different earnings differentials between different skills. Male salesmen earn more than male clerical workers, but female clerical workers earn more than female saleswomen. After eliminating differences in work effort, why do women earn less than men with the same skill? Why are skill wage differentials different for men and women?

Data such as that presented in Tables 5 and 6 and in the more detailed tables of the U.S. Census and the U.S. Census Bureau's *Consumer Income Reports* constitute only part of the empirical reality that needs to be explained. Basically, they yield data on the distribution of earnings even when income rather than earnings is being reported.

For example, in 1972 wages and salaries accounted for 77.5 percent of total Census income, self-employment income accounted for 8.3 percent, and indirect labor earnings (mostly public and private pensions) accounted for another 8.9 percent—making a total of 94.7 percentage points attributable to labor earnings. Of the remaining 5.3 percentage points, public welfare programs accounted for 1.0 percentage points, with the remaining 4.3 percentage points coming in the form of dividends, interest, rents, income from estates and trusts, and other forms of capital income. By contrast, capital income accounted for 23 percent of the Gross National Product in the same year. This does not mean that the Census made a mistake and did not conduct an accurate Census. It merely reflects the fact that the Census definitions of income are designed to capture earnings and do not attempt to measure all forms of capital income. Since Census data do not adequately measure capital income, whenever possible data will be reported on earnings rather than income. But now we are left with the problem of ascertaining the distribution of physical wealth or capital income.

The Distribution of Physical Wealth

To determine the distribution of wealth in the United States, it is necessary to measure wealth directly. Capitalizing those few forms of capital income that appear in U.S. income statistics gives a very poor measure of the actual distribution of wealth.

TABLE 7
Net Worth of Consumers Within Specified Groups, December 31, 1962

GROUP CHARACTERISTIC	ALL FAMILIES	PERCENTAGE DISTRIBUTI(					
		NEGATIVE	0–$999	$1,000–4,999	$5,000–9,999	$10,000–24,999	$25,0 49,9
All families	100	8	17	17	14	24	1
1962 income:							
0–$2,999	100	12	31	16	15	17	
$3,000–4,999	100	15	22	22	12	17	
$5,000–7,499	100	7	14	21	17	28	
$7,500–9,999	100	3	5	19	16	37	1
$10,000–14,999	100	1	3	9	13	34	2.
$15,000–24,999	100	(1)	(1)	2	8	18	3
$25,000–49,999	100	1	(1)	(1)	1	2	
$50,000–99,999	100	(1)	(1)	(1)	(1)	(1)	
$100,000 and over	100	(1)	(1)	(1)	(1)	(1)	(1

(1) Less than 0.5 percent.
Source: Dorothy S. Projector, "Survey of Financial Characteristics of Consumers,"
Federal Reserve Bulletin 50 (March 1964):285.

Empirical techniques for measuring earnings and wealth spring from the nature of the markets for labor and capital. Since it is illegal to sell human capital, the labor market is a market for renting and not for selling. Measures of earnings (rental prices) are much more accurate than direct measures of human wealth. The latter do not exist. Conversely, the capital market is primarily, but not exclusively, a market for buying and selling capital. Buying and selling prices are more prevalent and accurate than rental prices. Often the latter do not exist. The difference in the nature of the markets for labor and capital leads to a situation in which human wealth is best estimated by capitalizing measured earnings and income from physical capital is best estimated by annuitizing measured capital.

This dichotomy between the two markets and the distinct measurements of earnings and wealth that flow from it is fortunate, since it allows us to analyze the processes for gen-

MILIES, BY NET WORTH						
$0,000–9,999	$100,000–199,999	$200,000–499,999	$500,000–999,999	$1,000,000 AND OVER	MEAN (DOLLARS)	MEDIAN (DOLLARS)
5	1	1	(1)	(1)	22,588	7,550
1	(1)	(1)	(1)	(1)	8,875	2,760
3	(1)	1	(1)	(1)	10,914	3,320
4	1	(1)	(1)	(1)	15,112	7,450
5	2	(1)	(1)	(1)	21,243	13,450
11	4	1	(1)	(1)	30,389	20,500
26	7	7	1	(1)	74,329	42,750
20	31	30	5	3	267,996	160,000
3	13	37	27	20	789,582	470,000
(1)	1	4	61	35	1,554,152	875,000

erating earnings and wealth separately. As we shall see, these processes are fundamentally different. The motivations, constraints, and market interactions that lead to the distribution of earnings are not the motivations, constraints, and market interactions that lead to a distribution of physical wealth.

The United States has voluminous annual and comprehensive decennial data on earnings, but the data on wealth are sparse. The last direct comprehensive measurement of the distribution of wealth was carried out by the U.S. Federal Reserve Board in 1962. Since they collected income as well as wealth data, the lack of symmetry between income and wealth is extremely clear. As the data in Table 7 show, individuals in the same income classes have very different amounts of physical wealth. Although most of the families with incomes of less than $3,000 had little wealth, 1 percent had net assets between $50,000 and $99,999 and another 7 percent had assets between $25,000 and $49,999. Conversely, those with incomes over $100,000 per year had mean assets over $1.5 million, but over 66 percent of this group had less than $1 million in assets. Thus, no assessment of the distribution of economic prizes is complete if it examines either income or wealth alone.

According to the Federal Reserve Board study, the distribution of wealth is much more skewed than the distribution of earnings (see Table 8). If we look at relative shares, we will

TABLE 8

U.S. Distribution of Family Wealth in 1962

PERCENT OF TOTAL FAMILIES OF WEALTH	PERCENT OF TOTAL FAMILY WEALTH
Lowest 25.4	0.0
Next 31.5	6.6
Next 24.4	17.2
Top 18.7	76.2
(Top 7.5)	(59.1)
(Top 2.4)	(44.4)
(Top 0.5)	(25.8)

Source: Dorothy S. Projector, "Survey of Financial Characteristics of Consumers," *Federal Reserve Bulletin* 50 (March 1964):285.

see that the rich have a much larger fraction of physical wealth than they do of earnings. According to the Federal Reserve Board, the poorest 25 percent of the population has no net assets. By contrast, the top 18.7 percent of the population has 76.2 percent of total wealth and the top 0.5 percent of the population has 25.8 percent of all of the privately owned physical assets in the United States.

Although no direct measurements of wealth are available for the period since 1962, it is possible to gain more current data by estimating the distribution of wealth from estate-tax data. Estates must be evaluated at death. Using these evaluations and statistical techniques, it is possible to generate a distribution of wealth for the living. Because some forms of wealth, such as trusts, escape estate taxation and are not evaluated, estate-tax data are not as good as direct measurements of wealth, but they are all we have for more recent years.

Calculations based on estate-tax data indicate essentially the same distribution of wealth for 1969 as for 1962. But because estate taxes are only collected from those with estates in excess of $60,000, they only represent a statistical sample of the top 7.4 percent of the population, or about 9 million people. Looking at this data (Table 9) and the previous data yields three surprising results. First, just $60,000 in net assets is enough to place an individual in the top 7.4 percent of the population. Second, the top 7.4 percent of the population owns almost 60 percent of all of the wealth in the United States. Third, within the wealthiest 7.4 percent of the population, most of the wealth is owned by the *very* rich. The wealthiest 8 percent of this top 7.4 percent (0.6 percent of the total population) owns 42 percent of all of the assets of the top 7.4 percent, or 25 percent of all the assets of the entire population.

Analysis of estate-tax data over time indicates little change in the concentration of wealth in the post–World War II period. Between 1953 and 1969 the share of total wealth held by the

TABLE 9

Distribution of Wealth in 1969

NET ASSETS (IN DOLLARS)	PERCENT OF POPULATION WITH GROSS ASSETS OVER $60,000	PERCENT OF TOTAL ASSETS OF THESE WITH GROSS ASSETS OVER $60,000
Under 50,000	20.1	6.0
50,000–100,000	38.8	19.1
100,000–150,000	18.2	14.1
150,000–300,000	14.4	18.6
300,000–1,000,000	7.1	21.8
1,000,000–5,000,000	1.2	13.4
5,000,000–10,000,000	.07	2.8
over 10,000,000	.04	4.2

Source: Internal Revenue Service, *Statistics of Income, 1969: Personal Wealth,* Publication 482 (10–73) (Washington, D.C.: Government Printing Office, 1973), p. 19.

top one-half of 1 percent of the population varied between 20 and 24 percent of total wealth, and the share of the top 1 percent varied between 25 and 29 percent.[3]

Human Wealth

Some economists like to capitalize earnings and use this as a measure of human wealth. Theoretically, it is then possible to add human and physical wealth together to get an aggregate measure of the distribution of personal wealth. Although there is nothing technically wrong with this procedure, it adds nothing to our understanding over and above what was already available in the data on earnings and wealth.[4] It does, however, point to a gap in our knowledge. To capitalize earnings it would be necessary to know all future as well as current earnings. Obviously, we do not have data on individual future earnings, but unfortunately we also do not have historical data on lifetime incomes.

Thus, it is possible to have inconclusive arguments as to whether the lifetime distribution of earnings is more or less equal than the annual distribution of earnings. Those who argue for more equality maintain that individuals who earn little at one age are high earners at other ages. Those who argue for the same or a greater degree of inequality maintain that individuals who are low earners at one age are low earners at every age and that cross-sectional data on different individuals at different ages may underestimate lifetime inequalities. Without actual data no one can say which of these two arguments is more correct.

What is clear, however, is that earnings inequalities cannot, as some have suggested, be explained by the process of acquiring human skills. According to this argument, many low-earnings individuals are thought to be in the process of investing in their human capital through on-the-job training. Being willing to work for low wages is simply the way that they pay their employer for this type of training. Once they complete their training their wages will rise, the distribution of earnings will become more equal, and as a consequence the lifetime distribution of earnings must be more equal than the annual distribution of earnings. But if this were true, we would expect to see a more equal distribution of earnings among older workers who have completed their human capital investments. In fact, however, the distribution of income among older workers is more unequal than the distribution of income for males as a whole (see Table 10). Thus it is not possible to use human-capital investments as an explanation of the dispersion in annual earnings, and we are left to speculate about the relative degrees of inequality in lifetime and annual earnings.

While data limitations prevent us from calculating an actual distribution of human capital or lifetime earnings, aggregating human wealth and physical wealth is a mistake for many purposes even if it could be done. Although they can be denominated in the same terms (dollars), the economic characteristics of human and physical wealth are really very different.

Since human capital cannot be sold (even self-imposed slavery is illegal), human capital is not fundable (liquid) in the

TABLE 10
Distribution of Male Income (1971)

PROPORTION OF MALES BY INCOME	PERCENT OF MALE INCOME	
	ALL MALES 25 AND OVER	MALES 45 TO 54
Lowest Fifth	4.8	4.2
Second Fifth	11.8	13.1
Third Fifth	17.8	17.6
Fourth Fifth	24.8	23.7
Highest Fifth	40.8	41.4

Source: U.S. Bureau of the Census, *Current Population Reports: Consumer Income, 1971* (Washington, D.C.: Government Printing Office, 1972), pp. 112–113.

same sense that physical capital is liquid. Being illiquid, the risks associated with human capital are substantially higher than those for physical capital. Physical wealth represents potential purchasing power in a way that human capital does not. Physical wealth can always be sold and converted to consumption goods or other investment goods, but human capital can only be rented and it cannot be exchanged for alternative types of human capital. For most purposes $1 million in human capital is not equivalent to $1 million in physical wealth. If, for example, potential control over economic resources is desired, this is better measured by adding current earnings to wealth rather than by capitalizing earnings and then adding human wealth to physical wealth.

The two types of wealth differ in an even more fundamental way, for it is possible to separate a human being from his physical wealth but not from his human wealth. The individual always needs to accompany his human capital wherever it is employed. This means that a whole spectrum of personal benefits and costs (often called psychic income) becomes relevant in determining where to employ human capital. Personal benefits and costs are much less relevant in physical investments, since an individual can invest in an area without having to accompany his investments physically. This means that it makes much more sense to treat man as a money income maximizer when considering physical investment than to treat man as a money earnings maximizer when considering human investment.[5] Since the investment calculus differs in the two areas, it normally makes sense to keep track of earnings and physical wealth separately.

Conclusions

Although more data on the distribution of earnings and wealth will be presented throughout the rest of this book, our outside observer already has a flavor of the problem. What mechanisms generate the distributions of earnings and wealth that we have been observing? How can the wide variances of dispersions within productive subclasses be explained? These are the questions that must ultimately be answered. But before moving on to examine mechanisms, it is necessary to think about the problem of economic equity. What characteristics make a mechanism for distributing earnings and wealth fair or unfair? Indeed, what characteristics make a given distribution of earnings and wealth just or unjust?

These questions are important because they ultimately form part of the basis for designing economic policies to alter the distribution of economic resources. To design economic policies it is necessary to understand how earnings and wealth are generated and distributed, but it is also necessary to know whether the current distributions of earnings and wealth and the current mechanisms for distributing economic resources are equitable or inequitable. If the current situation is equitable, then there is no need to design economic policies to change the system. If the current situation is inequitable, then there is a need to design an economic system that will generate equity. Economic policies ultimately depend on being able to combine both efficiency and equity skills.

As we shall see, the degree of intellectual rigor that is necessary to develop equity skills is at least as high as that necessary to develop efficiency skills. In both cases there is a lot of hard analysis to be completed before it is possible to say what should be done.

2

ECONOMIC EQUITY

AN OUTSIDE OBSERVER of the economic game can ask two major questions. First, he can ask whether the economic game is an equitable game. What is the distribution of economic prizes across the population? Is the distribution of prizes fair or unfair? Is the mechanism by which prizes are distributed just or unjust? Second, he can ask whether or not the economic game is an efficient game. How large is the average prize? Could the game be reorganized to generate a larger economic prize?

With the death of traditional welfare economics in the 1950s, economic analysis has come to focus almost exclusively on the efficiency questions. Problems of equity are mentioned as important, but they are then treated as too difficult to be discussed or as not the proper area for economists to investigate. Either equity questions are regarded as the province of someone else—philosophers, political scientists, theologians, citizens— or it is assumed that they can only be settled by force.

Concentration on efficiency is justified on the grounds that, unlike equity, efficiency analysis can be value free. The basic argument can be seen in the parallel that is often drawn between efficiency-equity concepts and means-ends concepts. Equity decisions concern the ends of the economy—who should get what?—and ends inevitably involve value judgments. Efficiency decisions, on the other hand, concern the means used to achieve the economy's ends. Given some end, the goal of efficiency is a desirable property of whatever means are used to accomplish this end. Incomes (benefits or prizes) should be generated with the least effort (costs). A larger aggregate income can always be redistributed to give more to everyone. Since efficiency is universally desirable, it is value free and noncontroversial.

Even if this common perception of efficiency as value free were correct, which it is not, it would still be impossible to avoid the concept of equity in an analysis of the mechanisms of income distribution. Means and ends are hopelessly scrambled. Often our value judgments attach more importance to the means by which incomes are distributed (fascism, communism, capitalism, welfarism) than to the ultimate distribution of prizes. The means are in fact ends in themselves. For many, anything produced by the desired mechanism is fair.

Equity judgments may be value-laden and controversial, but they are also unavoidable. In market economies individual preferences determine market demands for goods and services, but these individual preferences are weighted by economic resources before they are communicated in the market. An individual with no income or wealth may have needs and desires, but he has no economic demands that he can communicate to the market. To make his personal preferences felt, he must have economic resources. If income and wealth are distributed in accordance with equity (whatever that might be), individual preferences are properly weighted and the market can efficiently adjust to an equitable set of demands. If income and wealth are not distributed in accordance with equity, individual preferences are not properly weighted and the market adjusts to an inequitable distribution of purchasing power. Technically, the market may be equally efficient in either case, but in the second case it is normatively inefficient just as a street-sweeper sweeping the wrong street is inefficient regardless of its technical street-sweeping ability.

Since market economies generate a distribution of factor payments to capital and labor in the process of satisfying demands for goods and services, an inequitable initial distribution of income will produce a set of demands that will lead to an inequitable distribution of factor payments or incomes in the next period even if the market economy is certified as a fair method for distributing economic prizes. At least once, a market economy must be certified as having a fair distribution of income and hence demands. Thus, even when an individual is willing to define justice entirely in terms of a mechanism by which economic prizes are distributed, it is necessary to make value judgments, at least once, about the fair distribution of prizes.

Not only are equity judgments logically necessary but they are practically unavoidable. Failure to make an overt equity judgment merely leads to the de facto certification of the current market distribution of income and wealth as the equitable distribution of income and wealth. One way or another, each society is forced to reveal its collective preferences with respect to the "justice" of its distribution of economic prizes.

It is not at all obvious what equity means in a mixed economy such as that of the United States. Americans often use the words *equity* and *equality* as if they were synonyms, but they are not. Equity has to do with the just distribution of economic resources. Justice may or may not require equality. If one looks at the actual actions of our society (our society's revealed preferences), they seem inconsistent. Progressive and regressive taxes coexist. Equal opportunity is often used to specify equity, but equal opportunity is itself left unspecified. Does it mean 100 percent inheritance taxes or does it merely mean the absence of overt discrimination?

Since an understanding of equity is necessary to judge both the outcome of the economy (the ultimate distribution of income and wealth) and the means by which that output is distributed, the equity issue cannot be postponed or avoided. No one can demonstrate that a particular distribution of income and wealth is equitable, but there are intelligent and unintelligent statements to be made about economic equity just as there are intelligent and unintelligent statements to make about economic efficiency. Only by wrestling with the difficulties inherent in economic equity and by understanding the strengths and weaknesses of previous attempts to specify equity is it possible to reach a clearer understanding of one's own concept of economic equity.

In this effort there are several directions from which one can attempt to specify economic equity.

1. Reliance can be placed on process and procedures—that is, an economic game is specified as fair or equitable when individuals agree on the rules of the game, and any outcome of that game is considered just.
2. Individual preferences can be made the key criterion—that is, if the outcome of an economic game is in accordance with the individual preferences of the citizens of a country, it is regarded as equitable. Equity is achieved when society reaches the distribution of economic resources that generates the most agreement.
3. Merit, however defined, can be used to specify equity—that is, equity occurs when resources are distributed in the same manner as merit. In nineteenth-century liberal economic thinking, this would mean rewarding everyone on the basis of his or her marginal product as determined in a free marketplace. The person who contributes most gets most.
4. Equity can be related to the common good, however defined— that is, equity corresponds to that distribution of economic resources that maximizes the common good. Substantively, the problem then becomes one of determining the common good.

Obviously, any actual specification of economic equity can, and probably will, have elements of all four of these facets of equity. At the same time, there are problems with using any and all of these techniques for specifying a just distribution of economic resources. To clarify some of the issues surrounding the problem, I shall outline the fundamental reasons that led economists to abandon their search for economic equity and examine some of the intellectual escapes that have been proposed.

Can Economic Equity Be Discussed?

One often hears it said that although there are economic statements to be made about efficiency, there are no economic statements to be made about equity, only personal prejudices. In fact, equity statements stand on the same foundation as efficiency statements. Neither is value free. Both depend upon an underlying set of discussable value judgments. Once these value judgments have been made, there are technical studies to be done on economic equity just as there are technical studies to be done on economic efficiency.

Modern analysis of economic efficiency depends upon the acceptance of Pareto optimality: State A is better than State B if at least one person is better off in A and no one is worse off. A person is better off in A if he prefers to be in A rather than in B. In a weaker version of the same principle, State A is better than State B if those who are better off in State A could adequately compensate those who are worse off in State A. An economy moves toward Pareto optimality in its weaker sense when scarce resources are used in such a way as to maximize potential output. There are more economic prizes to be distributed. With an improvement in efficiency there is a larger bundle of goods and services (including leisure) that individuals can choose among. More is better.

All analysis of economic efficiency depends upon these postulates, which are all thoroughly ethical in nature. Thus, a value judgment is made that each individual is the best judge of his or her own happiness, and that more choice is always better than less. If productivity goes up, society has a wider range of choices among goods and leisure. It is better off. Without such value judgments, "efficiency" ceases to have any meaning in modern economics.

Paretian efficiency values were easily absorbed into economics because they seemed to be universally held. They are, after all, the values of a liberal-individualistic society. The invocation of universally held value judgments has been the traditional way to avoid discussing values. This occurs partly because we believe what is universally held does not need to be discussed, but also because values that are in fact universally held seem to be intuitively true and are often held to be facts rather than values. To many "more [choice] is better" is a fact and not a value. But it is easy to see alternative postulates. On a survival hike, less is better. The fewer material aids you start out with the more you have achieved in your survival. Many societies are, and have been, founded on the principle that collective judgments dominate individual judgments. A person is better off in State A if the *group* decides that he is better off.

We may all share Paretian postulates, but this does not alter the fact that they are value judgments or elevate them beyond the realm of analysis. Take the inviolability of consumer preferences. Given the nineteenth-century belief in the existence of innate wants within the individual, the inviolability of consumers' preferences seemed sensible. Given modern sociology and psychology, the postulate of innate wants is no longer so plausible. We now perceive that every society or culture generates the "wants" of its population. Moreover, as our knowledge of how "wants" are generated improves, the activity of generating wants increasingly falls within the domain of deliberate policies. Indeed, a debate on whether our society should try to generate traditional economic "wants" or other life styles is currently under way.

As this example illustrates, various types of beliefs about matters of fact—especially psychological and sociological matters of fact—can force alterations in values. Similarly, many economic beliefs about matters of fact can affect values. Take such statements as, "Income equality is bad because it leads to less work," or, "Socialism is good because it stops an individual from acquiring economic power over other individuals." Before going to the barricades over either of these statements, a lot of hard empirical economic research and tough economic analysis must be done. Does income equality lead to less personal effort? Is economic power less concentrated under socialism? When does the adverse work effort effect set in? How should economic power be measured?

If "more is better" and the "inviolability of consumers' preferences" are the values underlying any analysis of traditional economic efficiency, what are the values underlying the analysis of economic equity? The problem depends in the final analysis upon whether you subscribe to Rousseau's belief that all men are by nature equal or the Greek belief that men are by nature unequal. It also depends upon how you proceed to define these beliefs more precisely.

To say that men are by nature equal is not to say that men are in fact equal. They are not. It is merely to say that men are equal until they prove themselves unequal. The burden of proof is on the side of those who maintain that two men are unequal. Conversely, if you subscribe to the Greek belief that men are by nature unequal, the burden of proof lies on the side of those who maintain that two men are equal. Men born into different classes are unequal until proven equal.

Assigning the burden of proof may seem trivial, but it is not. A society that distributes economic resources equally except in those cases where men can be shown to be unequal has a very different distribution of economic resources than a society that distributes resources unequally except in those cases where men can be shown to be equal. The distinction is the same as that made with respect to guilt and innocence in our system of criminal justice. Is a man guilty until proven innocent or is he innocent until proven guilty? A different set of men will go to jail under the two rules.

A belief in the equality of men means that social and economic differences must be based on the conviction that such differences contribute to the common good. In other words, such differences must be justified as *functional*. They must be shown to lead to something else of merit that legitimates a departure from the norm of equality. Since American society is founded on Rousseauian beliefs rather than Greek beliefs, equality is the norm. Departures from that norm must be justified.

It is at this point that economic analysis becomes relevant to questions of equity. What departures from equality are economically functional? The answers are not obvious. They depend upon probing more deeply into the concepts of economic equity and into the mechanisms by which the economy actually distributes economic prizes. Only in this manner is it possible to determine the appropriate degree of inequality.

A Fair Economic Game

Traditionally, the norm of equality has been phrased in terms of "equal opportunity." The economic game should be so constructed that every individual has an equal chance to win. In a fair economic game men are equal until they prove themselves unequal. Americans may subscribe to "equal opportunity," but this still leaves two fundamental problems. What are the rules of a fair economic game and what is the optimum structure of economic prizes? This involves two different determinations. Playing a free-enterprise game does not, for example, say anything about the optimum structure of economic prizes. Depending upon the initial distributions of income and demand, markets can be adjusted to yield very different distributions of prizes.

But what constitutes a fair game? Do we let consumers' preferences determine the economic merit of an opera company or do we create, through education, a public demand for operatic performances? Is a fair game a game in which each person has an equal chance to win? If chances of winning are to be equalized, do we handicap those born with advantages or compensate for those born with disadvantages? What constitutes an equal start? Should every individual be subject to the same initial budget constraint? Consider inheritances. Is there any difference between the individual who inherits $1 million and the individual whose athletic talents will earn him the same lifetime income? As these questions indicate, the rules of the lottery are not intuitively obvious.

The traditional test for determining the validity of specific rules has been their capacity for being universalized. This test springs from Kant's categorical imperative (my actions are moral if I "can will that my maxim becomes a general law"), but it has antecedents at least as far back as the golden rule (do unto others as you would have them do unto you). The idea is to perform a mental experiment in which you place yourself in the position of every other person. If you would be willing to live with your suggested rule in all conceivable circumstances, then the rule is a fair rule and can be used to construct a fair economic game.

The problem with this procedure is that there are two types of relevant circumstances: factual states and preference states. It is easy to say that each individual should test his suggested rules in all possible factual states, but what is he to do about different preference states? To take an extreme case, consider the preferences of a masochist. Clearly, a masochist will be willing to specify universal rules that others will not consider fair. Kant specifically recognized this problem when he wrote that rules were to be universalized based on the preferences of a "rational" man, but this only leads to the problem of specifying the preferences of a "rational" man. What preference states can be ruled out? Unfortunately, no satisfactory answer has been found to this question.

The latest attempt to specify a fair economic game is embodied in the work of the Harvard philosopher John Rawls.[1] He uses the Kantian framework to establish both the natural equality of men and the optimum distribution of economic prizes. As in Rousseau's philosophy, the natural equality of men comes from a social contract in which each man's signature is as necessary and important as anyone else's. Men simply would not join societies unless they were assured natural equality. Unlike Rousseau, Rawls sees the structure of economic prizes as also being determined in the process of signing the social contract.

Imagine that you were to be asked to establish rules for distributing economic prizes. The easiest way to envision yourself in the position of everyone else in society is to imagine a giant lottery. You can set any distribution of prizes, but you do not know what prize you yourself will receive. You might get the largest prize or you might get the smallest prize. As far as each person knows, he has an equal chance of landing at the top or middle or bottom of the social order. Perform the mental experiment. What distribution of prizes would you establish if a giant lottery were going to be used to determine your position in life?

Rawls argues that there is only one structure of prizes that everyone would be willing to accept. This is a prize structure that maximizes the minimum prize (maximin). In economists' terms Rawls is asserting that every individual is (or should be) absolutely "risk averse." Everyone acts on the assumption that he will be getting the smallest prize and thus wants to maximize the smallest prize. No one thinks about anything else.

Rawls' universal rule becomes: "In each economic activity men must act in such a manner as to maximize the minimum economic prize." Although maximizing the minimum prize seems egalitarian and Rawls believes it to be so, it need not be. Under this rule I can undertake any project that raises my income by any amount as long as it also raises the income of the poorest man—no matter how little. Rawls believes that the trickle-down effect is so large that it would be impossible to design economic activities that concentrate income gains among high-income groups, but this is clearly a matter for economic analysis. Are there economic activities with marginal amounts of trickle-down? To be really egalitarian, social rules would have to state that individuals must choose those economic activities that have the largest trickle-down effect. But this would infringe on the liberty of everyone except the poorest man. Should we force one man to work to raise the income of another? Rawls does not want to do this, but maximizing the minimum prize clearly calls for such an infringement. If we do not force men to work, what universal rule do we postulate to justify this exception to maximin? Liberty? Once we have two clashing universal rules, liberty and maximin, we are in trouble. How do we delineate the domain of the two rules? Once again there is no satisfactory answer.

As Rawls' specification of economic equity indicates, a great many assumptions about preferences must be made to generate his desired distribution of prizes. Thus, for Rawls the gambling man's preferences are illegitimate. Given that the economic lottery is a game in which some prize is necessary to survive, the idea of a minimum prize makes sense (although there probably are some people who would be willing to take a chance on their own starvation); but maximizing the minimum prize is something else again. Empirical evidence would seem to point toward the viability of lotteries that do not maximize the minimum prize; people are clearly willing to bet a small part of their current prize on a very small chance for a very large payoff.

Rawls is also forced to rule out the envious man. Suppose the worst-off man were envious. In this case anything that lowers the incomes of better-off people faster than it lowers the income of the worst-off man maximizes the minimum prize. If envy is not ruled out, maximizing the minimum prize can easily lead to zero incomes for everyone.

As the envy problem indicates, the distinction between factual states and preference states creates problems for Rawls as it has for other philosophers. His golden rule is "do unto the worst-off man as he would be done unto." To some extent the worst-off man will be the man with the least economic resources; but to some extent he will also be the man with the preference structure that is hardest to satisfy. To what extent should the distribution of economic prizes take into account the personal usefulness (utility) of those prizes? Should the man who is relatively inefficient in processing economic prizes—the man who gets less satisfaction out of his income than do others with the same income—get larger prizes because of his inefficiency?

Perhaps Rawls could convince us that a willingness to take risks or an interest in other things than one's own income are perverse preferences in the same sense that masochism is a perverse preference. But it is not obvious that this is the case. And Rawls certainly cannot persuade us that maximizing the minimum prize constitutes economic equity unless it involves something other than the process of signing a universalizable social contract.

When maximin is considered carefully, it runs into a host of problems. What do you do about saving? Since this generation is going to be poorer than the next generation, maximin would call for the end of all saving. If this generation saves for the next generation, a perverse transfer will take place from the relatively poor to the relatively rich. Yet if no generation saves, real standards of living can rise only slowly. Similarly, there are a host of what Rawls calls micro-situations in which maximin does not seem ideal. Must a teacher give all of his students A grades? Maximin would seem to call for such a rule, yet it vitiates the whole idea of grading and feedback. As a result of these factual states and a host of other situations in which maximin does not seem ideal, Rawls argues that maximin is only applicable in what he calls macro-situations.

The whole problem here is that there is no simple way to define a macro-situation in which the ethical maxims of maximin are applicable. Conventionally, macro-economics concerns itself with those economic activities that primarily affect the level of output rather than the composition of output, and micro-economics deals primarily with the composition of output (i.e., some particular sector). When we are talking about economic justice, however, it is not possible to make a distinction between level and composition: the level of economic justice is directly dependent upon the composition (distribution) of economic output.

As this critique of Rawls indicates, it is no simple matter to specify a set of universalizable rules for the economic game. True, Rawls has sought to isolate two important ingredients in a specification of economic equity: A belief in the natural equality of man (no matter how established) leads to the conclusions that *deviations from economic equality must be shown to be beneficial, placing the burden of proof on those who advocate inequality* and that *some minimum economic prize is an essential ingredient in economic equity* once one assumes that a rational man is risk-averse enough to avoid economic suicide. The net result, however, is that it is not yet proven possible to deduce workable specifications of economic equity from philosophical axioms (the natural equality of man, universalizability, etc.) upon which we might all agree. These attempts add something to our understanding of economic equity, but they do not solve the problem.

Aggregating Preferences

Although philosophers have sought to specify equity in universalizable principles, the basic thrust of the economics profession has been to seek specification of economic equity in the aggregation of individual preferences rather than in universal values. Unfortunately, the process of aggregating preferences ran into an intellectual dead end and came to a halt in the 1950s. Although the dead end is real, the attempt to find economic equity in individual preferences illuminates the concept of economic equity. There may also be an escape.

The aggregation approach starts with individual utility functions. Each individual has a utility function that expresses the satisfaction (utility) that he derives from any factor (goods, services, friends, beauty, etc.).[2] The second ingredient is the individualistic social-welfare function. This function expresses the relationship between social welfare and the utility of each individual in society.[3] The name "individualistic social-welfare function" springs from the fact that social welfare depends upon individual utilities. Each person determines the amount of utility that flows from his income. No one gets to impose his preferences on anyone else. Social welfare is found by aggregating individual utilities. Since no one is given a zero or negative weight in the social-welfare function, every time an individual is better off (i.e., has more utility) and no one else is worse off, social welfare must increase (even if only a little).

Given a social-welfare function and knowing individual utility functions, economists would be in a position to pronounce on the equity or inequity of any economic change. Anything that makes the social-welfare function go up is good; anything that makes the social-welfare function go down is bad. The obvious economic goal is to maximize social welfare. Equity has been transformed into a maximization problem like that of efficiency. Economists liked the transformation of equity problems into maximization problems since it enabled them to apply to equity all of the economic tools they had developed to deal with efficiency. Unfortunately, both theoretical and empirical problems intervened.

How, for example, is one to specify the social-welfare function? In the case of individual utility functions, it is possible, at least in principle, to analyze personal preferences and choices. A skilled analyst would ask the individual to tell him when he was better off and when he was worse off. How much income would he be willing to give up to get one more friend? In theory there is an answer to such questions, and we are all crudely involved in making such trade-offs every hour of our lives. But what is the social analogue? What trade-offs do we look at to determine social values?

What weights do we use to add one person's utility to another person's utility? A variety of weighting schemes have been suggested. The simplest is to add individual utilities and to use total utility as a measure of social welfare.[4] But this form of the social-welfare function leaves open the possibility that there might be a miser who so loves money that most of the country's resources must be given to him if social welfare (total utility) is to be maximized. The rest would be left with nothing.

Others, wishing to eliminate this unfortunate logical possibility, have suggested the multiplicative social-welfare function. Instead of adding, utilities are multiplied, with social welfare becoming the product of all individual utilities.[5] This eliminates the possibility that anyone can be left with a zero income and zero utility (any number multiplied by zero is zero), but it also has a definite empirical implication. If, for example, utility is a simple function of income and if everyone has the same utility function, then a completely equal distribution of income is required to maximize social welfare—i.e., reach economic equity. Or more realistically, if individuals have different utility functions but you do not know what individual has what function, a completely equal distribution of income is necessary to maximize the expected value of social welfare.

These are just two of many possible social-welfare functions. All implicitly embody a specification of economic equity. But which is the right social-welfare function? How do you choose among the possibilities?

The problem turns around the fact that some rule is necessary to weight individual utilities but some rule is also necessary to determine how utility weights are to be determined. Thus, theoretically there is an infinite regress: rules are needed for weighting rules for weighting rules. The only answer is to continue the regress until either a weighting rule is found that will command universal assent or, lacking this, a weighting rule is imposed. But this brings us right back to the problems of universal rules that we have already examined. No one has yet found a universal social-welfare function that will command unanimous assent.

The same perverse preference problems arise in aggregating preferences as in finding universal values. Suppose utility depends on relative rather than on absolute incomes. People are envious. Their utility goes down more when their relative incomes fall than when their absolute incomes rise. In that case utility maximization may call for very low incomes for everyone. Just as with universalization, preference aggregation requires rules to eliminate perverse preferences. Fundamental philosophical problems remain.

At a still more basic level, the whole "utility function" approach is suspect in a world without innate preferences. The social-welfare function is the place where society is supposed to make interpersonal comparisons, yet the individualistic social-welfare function lets each person determine his own importance in social welfare if he can control his own preferences. Even if preferences are fixed, an aggregation problem arises. How do you determine when two individuals have the same level of satisfaction (utility)? For any one person it is possible to ask him whether State A is better than, equal to, or worse than State B. You simply ask about the relationships or observe his decisions. But how do you and I determine that we are equally happy, or, even more difficult, how do we determine that two other people are equally happy?

For a long time utility theory has been searching for its Archimedean point. If there were some observable point at which we knew that individuals were equally satisfied, it would be possible to use this point and each person's revealed preferences to build up comparable indexes of utility.[6] For example, suppose you knew that every person was equally happy when he was spending the same proportion of his income on food or when he first started to save some of his income. Each individual could then construct his own (cardinal) utility index relative to this point (when I have an income of $10,000, I might, for example, be twice as well-off as when I have an income of $7,000), and these could be compared. The only problem is to find the Archimedean point.

Lacking the Archimedean point necessary to quantify cardinal utilities, economists shifted to the analysis of choice (ordinal utility). Here, no attempt is made to quantify utility. We simply try to determine whether individuals prefer State B to State A. Individuals rank order different states of the world. For a time economists thought that great progress could be made by shifting from cardinal to ordinal utility, but the vision was shattered by Kenneth Arrow.[7] He was able to show that there was no social decision rule, such as majority voting, that could in all circumstances lead to social orderings from these individual orderings without violating the following four seemingly mild and reasonable conditions: (1) the social welfare function must be capable of handling *all* logically possible sets of individual offerings; (2) if everyone prefers X to Y, then society must prefer X to Y; (3) the choice between X and Y should not depend upon how individuals rank these states vis-à-vis other irrelevant third states; and (4) the social-welfare function should not be dictatorial—everyone's preference should count.

The problem can be illustrated by the well-known paradox of majority voting. Suppose there are three voters (A,B,C) rank ordering three possible states of the world (X,Y,Z). A prefers X to Y to Z. B prefers Y to Z to X. C prefers Z to X to Y. Clearly, there is a 2 to 1 majority for X over Y, a 2 to 1 majority for Y over Z, and a 2 to 1 majority for Z over X. This leads to the situation for which there is no determinate solution. If voters started in State Z, they would vote to move to State Y. Then they would vote to move to State X, but this would lead to a vote to move back to State Z. Unfortunately, every democratic decision rule seems to lead to similar problems. There is no perfect way to get social rankings from individual rankings. As a result, economists abandoned the search for a social-welfare function. They could not specify cardinal utility functions and they could not aggregate ordinal utility functions in social-welfare functions. What they were left with was Paretian efficiency—more is better than less.

But within the constraints of Paretian efficiency, it *is* possible to say something about equity. More is better than less, but certain distributions are also better than others. This situation arises because individuals will *voluntarily* give some of their incomes to other individuals. We know that the second distribution of income is preferred to the first distribution of income because individuals voluntarily give some of their income away. Such voluntary redistributions of income are called Pareto equitable, since they depend upon the arbitrary initial distribution of income. Only those who have income that they wish to give to others can affect the distribution of income. Since all gifts are voluntary, no one can be worse off as a result of the gifts. They are Pareto optimal.

Individuals undertake Paretian redistributions because they raise their own utility by doing so. Each person maximizes his own satisfaction subject to his initial budget constraint, and in the process a new distribution of income is generated. The equity problem is identical to the efficiency problem: given some income, how do I allocate it across goods and services, private charities, and public taxes for transfer payments in such a manner as to maximize my utility?

Paretian redistributions can occur for a number of reasons. First, individuals experience satisfaction from giving gifts.[8] Gifts thus appear in an individual's utility function. Presumably, this is the motive behind private charity. Since one person's gift is another person's income, the distribution of income differs before and after the gift.

Second, individuals may have "interdependent" utility functions.[9] My satisfaction may partially depend upon your satisfaction or utility. I may be happier if my neighbors are well-off and not in poverty. In this case I take satisfaction not from the process of giving a gift but from the fact that other persons are well-off. To achieve this result I may prefer to give them my money impersonally through the tax structure rather than personally through private charity. Presumably, such interdependencies also explain why Americans like to live in homogeneous suburbs with other persons at approximately the same income level. Our level of satisfaction is higher than it would be if we were forced to live in a heterogeneous neighborhood. As a result, I have two economic options with which to satisfy this source of personal satisfaction. I can either transfer some of my income to generate compatible neighbors or I can move to a neighborhood where my neighbors have the income that makes me most happy. The option I choose depends upon relative costs. In the first option my income is reduced to pay transfer payments; in the second option equivalent housing may cost more.

Third, there may be social externalities that flow from the distribution of economic resources.[10] If social unrest, crime, riots, and similar social phenomena are caused by maldistributions of economic resources, I may choose to give some of my income away as a method of eliminating crime, unrest, and riots. In this case the noneconomic goods in my utility function are affected by the distribution of economic resources. To purchase less crime I allocate some of my income to others in the form of public transfer payments. The exact amount to be allocated will depend on the importance I attach to the social factors affected by the distribution of economic resources and the extent to which these factors are determined by the distribution of economic resources.

Fourth, the distribution of income may itself appear in my utility function.[11] I want to live in a society with a certain kind of economic lottery, and I am willing to contribute some of my own income in order to get the right structure of prizes. The final structure of prizes will, of course, depend upon how much I and others contribute. This case differs from the interdependent preferences in that I have no preferences about which individual is rich or poor. I am simply interested in the number of individuals who will be rich and poor.

Fifth, public income redistribution schemes may be a form of insurance—minimum-income insurance. If society uses its transfer payments to guarantee a minimum income, then my own income cannot fall below some level regardless of the unfortunate events that might afflict me. To buy minimum-income insurance for myself, I must be willing to make tax payments that will be used to make transfers to those who now fall below the minimum-income line. In the process of buying minimum-income insurance, I voluntarily alter the distribution of income. No one can fall below the designated floor.

There is thus a class of Paretian equity statements that corresponds to the class of Paretian efficiency statements. Equity State A is better than Equity State B if there is someone in State B who is willing to give some of his own income to someone else to transform Equity State B into Equity State A. Equity State A is Pareto optimal if there are no further voluntary income transfers to be made. Paretian equity thus depends upon on how much income each person is willing to contribute to charity, to having income-compatible neighbors, to eliminating social externalities, to living in a society with different degrees of inequality, and to purchasing minimum-income insurance.

Yet Paretian redistributions are not substitutes for the social-welfare function approach, since they depend upon an arbitrary initial distribution of income. They also do not consider the preferences of those with no initial income to transfer. These individuals have no economic votes to use in defining economic equity—they have been assigned a zero weight in the decision rules for preferences weighting—just as they have no economic votes in determining the efficient demands for goods and services.

Paretian equity, therefore, seems too limited to serve as a general specification of economic equity. This brings us back to the individualistic social-welfare function and the intellectual dead end that it represents. One possible escape is visible in the central problem of determining the appropriate interpersonal weights. Adhering to the spirit of the individualistic social-welfare function, individual preferences should play a role in determining the weights or functional form of the social-welfare function. This leads, however, to individuals with two different levels of preferences. They have preferences about what yields them utility and they have preferences about the appropriate weights to assign to different individuals in the social-welfare function. The failure to recognize this distinction leads to many of the failures of the individualistic social-welfare function.

Individuals have different levels of preferences. They have preferences about the rules of the economic game and the distribution of prizes that it should generate; but they also have preferences about maximizing their own position in the current economic game, no matter how much they like or dislike the economic game they are forced to play. The distinction can be clearly seen in the area of speed limits. There is nothing self-contradictory, for example, in driving at the speed limit of 75 mph yet believing that a lower speed limit would be better and save lives. An individual decision to drive at 55 mph when the speed limit is 75 mph and others are driving at this limit increases accidents rather than reduces them. Similarly, there is nothing self-contradictory in seeking to become extremely wealthy and powerful in our current economic game yet believing that in a better economic game there would be no "extremely wealthy" economic prizes to be had. A personal limit on accumulation would not produce the more egalitarian society that is desired. There is nothing logically self-contradictory in these two preferences, since they simply do not exist in the same domain. To distinguish these two levels of preferences I will call the one *individual-societal preferences* and the other *private-personal preferences*.

Distinguishing these two levels of preferences makes it possible to avoid the intellectual dead end implicit in the individualistic social-welfare function. Individual preferences can be separated into those that concern the ideal rules of the economic game (communism, capitalism, etc.) and the optimum distribution of economic prizes (social-welfare function weights, etc.) and into those that concern maximizing personal utility within any given economic game or distribution of prizes. Societies can, if they wish, discuss what constitutes economic equity without worrying about individual differences in the efficiency with which people process economic goods. A preference such as envy is ruled out, not because it does not exist and not because it does not affect private-personal preferences —it does—but because society chooses not to take envy into account in its social rules, even though each one of its members may be envious. In their individual-societal preferences, individuals decide to rule out their private-personal preference of envy, since collectively it can lead to absurd results.

Individual-societal preferences also make it possible to solve the Archimedean point problem. As we have seen, you cannot have an individualistic social-welfare function unless utilities can be added together. To compare utilities, you need some "objective" criteria that will tell us when two people are equally well-off. Utility theory has been searching for such an Archimedean point for a long time without success. In a world comprised solely of private-personal preferences, the search is futile. It is, however, also unnecessary. Although the Archimedean point cannot be derived from private-personal preferences, it *can* be specified on the basis of individual-societal preferences. Socially, we simply decide that individuals are economic equals —i.e., that they are equally "happy"—under certain circumstances. Thus, the specification might say that individuals are economic equals when they have the same income, wealth, and family size. But whatever the conditions, the Archimedean point is clearly specifiable by an act of social judgment.

In a similar manner the optimum distribution of economic resources is socially specifiable even though it is not derivable from any aggregation of private-personal preferences. This is because the distribution of economic resources may itself be a focus of individual-societal preferences. Individuals may want to live in a society in which economic prizes are distributed in a specific manner, even if they live (and express their private-personal preferences) in a society with a different scheme of distribution.

Although cardinal utility functions are not subject to Arrow's impossibility theorem, the distinction between individual-societal and private-personal preferences does not solve the aggregation problem in a more fundamental sense. Cardinal preferences can be added together theoretically, but they are not going to be determined in fact. Individual-societal preferences are always going to be added together with the imperfect specification of any democratic voting procedure. Some element of coercion must exist when any social decision is made. Perfect aggregation of preferences is only a theoretical construct that may serve as a useful yardstick with which to measure actual systems of aggregation.

Rewards According to Merit

Merit has historically been approached from two alternative vantage points: that of the producer and that of the consumer. The standard economic perspective is that of the producer. Here, the discussion concerns the marginal productivity theory of distribution both as normative theory of what should be and as positive theory of how incomes are actually distributed in a market economy. Consumer merit is discussed with a different set of linguistic conventions. Here, wants and needs rather than productivity become the focus of the discussion.

The economist's concern with producers' merit springs from his interest in efficiency. Economic efficiency exists when there are no changes that could be made that would make some people better off without making others worse off. If every factor is paid in accordance with its marginal contribution to the total supply of economic goods and services (its marginal product), and if marginal products are determined by competitive supply and demand conditions, then economists can show that a market economy is efficient, or Pareto optimal. Any attempt to pay people other than their marginal products will lead to a situation in which it would be possible to make changes when some were better off and no one was worse off.

The adequacy of the marginal-productivity theory of distribution as a positive explanation of how incomes are distributed will be discussed extensively later. Here our concern is with the normative aspects of marginal productivity. As a normative theory of equity, marginal productivity is inadequate. The distribution of marginal products depends directly upon the structure of market demands for goods and services. But market demands in turn depend upon the distribution of income. As a result, the distribution of marginal products is a direct function of the initial distribution of money incomes. A classic chicken-egg problem arises. The distribution of marginal products (market incomes) directly depends upon the initial distribution of money incomes, but market money incomes are also dependent upon marginal products.

Even if you are willing to argue that distributing incomes in accordance with marginal products is a fair or equitable rule for the economic game, there is still a need to certify that the initial distribution of income is a just distribution of income. Such a certification must be made at least once to get the economic game started. But it is just this problem of determining equity that we are currently confronting. Thus, the marginal-productivity theory of distribution does not solve the ethical problem of achieving equity even though it may keep you in a state of equity once that state is achieved. The ethical problem must be solved before marginal productivity can be invoked.

The concept of consumers' merit (wants and needs) has often been suggested as a technique for specifying economic equity. At least since Marx, there has been a widely held belief that it is not necessary to specify a just distribution of rewards. This belief is based on two related doctrines: the doctrine of "super-abundance" and the doctrine of "satiated needs."

According to the doctrine of superabundance, equity decisions need not be made, since it is assumed that the problem will wither away as we get richer. Economic wants will be satiated, each of us will have everything he wants, and no one will care what someone else has or does not have. Since all personal preferences will be satisfied, it will not matter that individuals have different preferences. With superabundance and satiated wants, Marx thought that both nation states and personal budget constraints would wither away and that equity problems would gradually become irrelevant.

Conservatives often subscribe to this solution of the equity problem, but they usually add a subsidiary proposition. To eliminate the problem of economic equity, society should concentrate on economic growth without worrying about the current distribution of economic resources. Do everything possible to hasten the day of satiated wants. Today's inequalities are then justified in terms of their contribution to economic growth and tomorrow's achievement of satiation.

Unfortunately, our demonstrated ability to create new wants has eliminated the possibility—for both Marxists and conservatives—of ever being able to satiate everyone's wants as long as we embody Western society's process of social-want creation. Other societies—the East, primitive cultures, medieval society—have succeeded in satiating wants, but insatiable wants are almost the trademark of our culture. As long as these insatiable wants are with us, the problem of specifying economic equity is also with us.

According to the *doctrine of satiated needs,* wants cannot be satisfied but needs can be. Thus, economic equity is achieved when the minimum economic prize is large enough to satiate the poorest man's needs. The doctrine of satiated needs refers to physiological needs, as opposed to wants that are artificially generated by society or wants that do not serve some physiological need. What is the minimum amount of income a person (or family) would need to have a perfectly balanced diet and to have as long a life expectancy as is medically possible? This is the basic question. But problems arise, since the answer to this question suggests a very low poverty line. Consider the cheapest medically balanced diet. By combining soybeans, lard, orange juice, and beef liver (edible, cheap, nutritious, but hardly enjoyable foods), a medically balanced diet can be created that costs less than $154 per person per year (in 1974 prices).[12] Medically speaking, it would be a better diet than most of us now eat. But are we ready to compel people to eat it? Similarly, how much housing space per person is necessary to live to a ripe old age? The answer is: very little. Are we then prepared to ignore the housing wants of poor people? And what does society do about poor families that are ignorant, inefficient, or stubborn? Does a family have an unmet need if it does not know the cheapest way to have a medically balanced diet, if it does not want the diet that it knows it should have and can afford, or if it simply refuses to eat an unappetizing or unusual diet?

Since the United States has very few people in poverty when poverty is based on such a definition of physiological "needs," the OEO's poverty lines were specified in terms of need. But need itself was defined in a relative manner, i.e., in terms of "wants." Given that a family is going to want to eat as other American families eat (and given it is going to manage its resources in the same inefficient manner), how much income does it need to get a medically balanced diet (in spite of itself, as it were)? Given that it is going to want to consume something like the same amount of space per person, how much housing does it need? But the minute "needs" are defined in terms of "wants," the concept of need loses its concreteness. Wants become necessities whenever most of the people in society believe that they are in fact necessities. Anything to which we have grown accustomed and that is generally available becomes a necessity. Needs, thus defined, grow right along with average incomes. Like satiated wants, satiated needs will not occur as long as our current culture exists.

This phenomenon can be seen in Gallup polls that asked, "What is the smallest amount of money a family of four needs to get along in this community?" The responses represent a rather consistent fraction of the average income prevailing at the time at which the question was asked, but the sum grows in absolute terms. As Lee Rainwater has shown, the answers to this question in the post–World War II period have indicated that families estimate their own needs to be a little more than half of the average family consumption of the day.[13] Similarly, when Rainwater asks individuals to categorize people as "poor, getting along, comfortable, prosperous, or rich," they rather consistently do so relative to average incomes.

No matter how economic equity is specified, it is clear that the problem is not going to disappear in economic superabundance and satiated wants or needs in our society. The net result is that the problem of specifying economic equity will not wither away. Relative economic scarcity will exist as long as our culture exists. Thus, neither producers' merit (marginal productivity) nor consumers' merit (wants and needs) provides an escape from the need to specify economic equity. Like the proverbially poor, equity questions are always with us. Or at least they are with us as long as our basic culture remains the same.

The Common Good

The common-good approach attempts to specify economic equity by isolating those distributions of economic prizes that contribute most to other social goals. Political arguments among liberals and conservatives often revolve around the types of social externalities that flow from alternative distributions of economic resources. Liberals often argue that social unrest, crime, riots, and other such phenomena are caused by maldistributions of economic resources and could be cured with alternative distributions of economic resources. But in this case the evidence, or lack of evidence, seems to be all on the side of the conservatives. There is little or no empirical evidence (economic, sociological, or psychological) showing such a connection. Thus, disagreements over equity cannot be buried in agreements over social externalities.

But there are other social considerations in a political democracy. Limits on economic inequality may be necessary in order to preserve political equality, if economic power can be translated into political power. Given the techniques for financing political campaigns in the United States, it would be hard to argue that a considerable amount of political power does not come out of the end of a dollar bill. But this does not automatically lead to arguments for economic equality. It is possible to design political democracies (such as the United Kingdom) where there is much less opportunity to translate economic power into political power. If the basic aim is political equality, the preferred technique presumably would be to isolate political and economic power so that economic power does not yield political power. As Keynes once remarked, the best argument for capitalism is that it allows individuals to tyrannize their bank accounts rather than other individuals. If separation is not possible, however, the goal of political equality may be an argument for limited economic inequalities.

For conservatives the common good is often taken to be a higher Gross National Product. Current inequalities in the distribution of economic rewards are justified as necessary to promote incentives and growth—more income for everyone. This idea is closely connected with the concept of producers' merit (marginal products) and paying everyone so as to maximize economic output. As we have seen, the need for growth to solve the equity problem is based on unsupported assumptions about the possibility of satiating wants. But even if wants could be satiated, the common good of growth cannot be used to justify the current inequalities in the distribution of income. Remember that a belief in the natural equality of man means that inequalities must be shown to be necessary for economic growth if they are to be justified. The natural state is equality and inequalities must be proven beneficial.

In the 1950s economists studied the interconnections between economic growth and inequalities (economic incentives) extensively. These studies revolved around an investigation of the impact of the high progressive federal income tax rates then in existence on work effort and personal savings. Although the empirical studies of work effort and savings yielded similar results, only the work-effort studies are relevant to the problem at hand. Economies, after all, can and do grow without personal savings. Saving is done collectively either by corporate businesses or by government. Governments simply collect more taxes than they need for public consumption and invest the remainder.

Personal work effort, on the other hand, is a real constraint on economic growth since collective work cannot be substituted for individual effort. Empirical studies are necessary, however, since it is not possible to determine theoretically the degree to which high progressive taxes might affect work effort. High taxes give rise to lower after-tax wage rates, leading theoretically to less work and more leisure (the substitution effect); but they also lower after-tax incomes, leading theoretically to more work and less leisure (the income effect). Much to the surprise of the initial investigators (several were employed by the Harvard Business School), empirical studies indicated that high taxes either did not affect work effort or might even increase work effort among executives and professionals. This result has been found in every succeeding study.[14] People work as hard or harder to restore their previous incomes or to obtain their income goals.

With the current interest in the negative income tax, a series of studies have been commissioned on the work-effort effects of transfer payments in a system of negative income taxes. Most of these studies are not yet completed, but in the experiment in northern New Jersey that has been completed little significant difference was found between those receiving aid and a control group.[15]

Thus, high progressive tax rates at the top and a negative income tax transfer system at the bottom both seem compatible with the current level of economic growth. The present degree of inequality cannot be justified as functionally necessary to promote economic growth. Substantial equalization could occur before growth would be adversely affected. Although the goal of economic growth may conflict with egalitarian desires at some point, it currently is not a constraint. The distribution of economic prizes could be substantially equalized before conflicts would emerge, if at all. In any case we have already seen that economic growth is not a "solution" to the problem of making equity judgments.

Conclusions

Not surprisingly, after examining the four approaches to specifying economic equity, equity remains unspecified. Some general principles have been suggested (the need for a minimum economic prize, placing the burden of proof on those advocating inequalities, etc.), but no particular distribution has been advanced as an equitable distribution. This is almost unavoidable, however, since any specification of equity requires substantial amounts of empirical information. The best method by which to gain some of the necessary information is to analyze the process whereby earnings and wealth are generated and distributed in the United States. As the current economic game is being dissected, the reader should be investigating his own conceptions of economic equity and thinking about his own specifications for a "just" economic game. What should the rules of the game be? What distribution of prizes should the economic lottery produce?

3

DEVIANT OBSERVATIONS
IN THE LABOR MARKET

JUST AS archaeologists have two sources of information on ancient civilizations—artifacts and primitive writings—so our observer has two sources of information on economic prizes. He can look at the observed distributions of economic resources or he can look at what has been inscribed in the economic literature on the process of distributing economic resources. If our observer were to look at the literature on earnings or wages, he would notice a peculiar phenomenon. Neoclassical micro-economics, macro-economics, and labor economics all have different theories explaining what occurs. Often, these theories are mutually inconsistent.

Micro-economics treats the labor market as if it were any other market in which price is the short-run market clearing mechanism. Individuals buy and sell skills in a bidding framework in which the equilibrium price clears the market so that there are no unsatisfied buyers or sellers. In the long run, cost minimization on the demand side and earnings maximization on the supply side determine shifts in supply and demand curves. Investments in laboring skills are equivalent to investments in plant and equipment, with the same investment calculus being relevant. Individuals invest until the rate of return on both human and physical investments is driven down to the market rate of interest. Prices clear markets in the short run and provide investment signals in the long run. The marginal-productivity theory of distribution is applicable.

Instead of treating the labor market as an equilibrium phenomenon, macro-economics treats it as a case of fundamental disequilibrium. At least since Lord Keynes, money wages are assumed to be rigid. Wages (prices) do not shift to clear markets in the short or medium run. Unemployment is the visible sign of disequilibrium. To minimize disequilibrium in the labor market, governments must use macro-economic policies to raise or lower the aggregate level of demand in such a manner as to clear the labor market or to hold the disequilibrium within tolerable limits.

In the econometric models that are used to represent the economy in macro-economics, the demand for labor depends upon total output, not upon the wage rate for labor. Careful calculations are made of the amount of labor that will be absorbed or disgorged when aggregate output goes up or down. Similarly, the equations used to represent the supply of labor depend upon long-run demographic trends and job availabilities. Wages typically do not appear in either participation functions or hours-of-work functions.

In labor economics the mode of analysis once again takes an abrupt shift. There, inter-skill or inter-industry wage differentials become the focus of analysis, and discussions revolve around wage contours and the links between different occupations and industries. The 1974 Economic Report of the President states, for example, that 1973 was a year of moderate wage increases because "wages in different industries seemed in good balance." [1] The *structure* of wages becomes paramount. Except for analyses of how inequities in the structure of wages influence the level of wages, aggregate wages or their rate of increase are ignored. Instead of looking at the determinants of individual marginal productivity, the analysis focuses on social or group decision making.[2] In many respects the analysis of the labor economist is closer to the sociologist's analysis of relative deprivation than it is to the analysis of the micro-economist. Interdependent preferences and norms of industrial justice influence wages.

One of the problems with these three different perspectives is that they are often mutually inconsistent. If the micro-economic approach is correct, the macro-economic problem cannot exist. Or at least it cannot exist in its present form (see below). Wages are not exogenously set, and the labor market is not in perpetual disequilibrium. Conversely, if the macro-economic approach is correct, micro-economics is wrong and economics is left without a theory of wage determination. Wages are determined in some unknown manner that is exogenous to the economic system.

Labor economics has a theory of the wage *structure*, but it does not have a theory to explain the growth of average wages. Labor economics and micro-economics are also thoroughly inconsistent. The interdependent preferences, relative deprivation, norms of social justice, and the wage contours that labor economists work with are not the factors that determine labor's marginal productivity. A structure of wages set in accordance with the axioms of marginal production is not a structure of wages set in accordance with the labor force's patterns of interdependent preferences. Something is clearly wrong with our analysis if it is necessary to have three inconsistent intellectual approaches to explain what is occurring in the labor market. Alternative approaches exist when there are a variety of movements being made by the players of the game that cannot be explained by any one approach. Although it may be impossible to eliminate the need for mutually inconsistent theories, all of the labor market observations that are deviant with respect to one or an-

another of these three theories should be examined to see if some consistent rules of the economic game can be found.

Deviant Observations

Someone once remarked that Newtonian theories of celestial motion would never have been discovered if Newton and his contemporaries had the modern computer. Deviant observations kept being made that did not fit into the existing epicycle theory of heavenly motion, but each deviant observation could be explained with the addition to the system of another epicycle. Given enough epicycles, all patterns were theoretically explainable. Eventually, however, the computational difficulties of adding new epicycles forced Newton to rethink the theories of heavenly motion to obtain a simple, calculable set of results. With the modern computer Newton would never had been forced to look for a simpler theory, since he never would have gotten bogged down in computational problems. The computer would have done all of the necessary geometry.

Similarly, computational difficulties will never drive economists to seek alternative theories of wage determination. At some point, however, it is necessary to examine the weight of the evidence to see the extent to which the labor market is or is not working in accordance with our theories. Like celestial motion at the time of Newton, deviant observations keep being reported in the labor market. Each of these deviant observations can be explained. Some particular market imperfection is hypothesized to explain what is going on. But each of these market imperfections has an *ex post ad hoc* epicycle quality that is ultimately unsatisfactory. Some of the dissatisfaction springs from an understanding of micro-economic theory itself. Whenever market imperfections exist, profit opportunities exist for someone to exploit. If some price is being held above equilibrium to yield high profits, someone else can slightly undercut that price and earn the extra profits unless there are structural impediments.[3] In exploiting the profit opportunities, the market imperfection is eliminated. Ultimately, the process of undercutting prices leads the price back to its equilibrium level. As a result, market imperfections are transitory in competitive markets. Yet many of the deviant observations have a long history.

An observer of the economic game should be extremely reluctant to label anything that has existed for long periods of time a "market imperfection." If the phenomenon has survived, the chances are high that it is an integral part of the game and not a market imperfection. Or at least, this possibility should be seriously investigated and each of the deviant observations should be examined to see if they can be explained in some consistent manner that does not rely on *ex post ad hoc* market imperfections. In the process we will also see that many of the suggested explanations are inconsistent with each other when the deviant observations are examined as a group.

UNEMPLOYMENT

Unemployment is the most important deviant observation that cannot be explained by a simple marginal-productivity (micro-economic) view of the labor market. Macro-economic theories sprang from the need to explain it. When unemployment occurs, unemployed workers should exert a downward pressure on wages, since more labor is being supplied than demanded at current wage rates. As the unemployed bid to obtain jobs, wages fall, the quantity of labor supplied is reduced, the quantity of labor demanded is increased, and unemployment is eliminated. In fact, the hypothesized process does not occur. Wages fell during the Great Depression, but unemployment was not eliminated. In the post–World War II recessions there is no evidence that wages fell in response to unemployment. Wages seem extremely rigid downward. There are three standard explanations for rigid wages: (1) a monopoly explanation, (2) a Keynesian explanation, and (3) a simple denial of the facts.

1. The first explanation argues that unions are a monopoly element in the economy that prevent wages from falling. This argument suffers from a severe defect. It is hard to argue that the 20 million union members can, or do, exercise monopoly power for the 70 million American workers who are not members of unions. Wages do not seem more flexible in the nonunion sector than they do in the union sector. Analytically, there is no reason why nonunion wages should be rigid simply because unions can exercise monopoly power and prevent their own wages from falling. Indeed, union monopolies should have exactly the opposite effect in the nonunion sector of the economy. Rigid wages in the union sector should result in a larger decrease in wages in the nonunion sector, since all of the competitive pressures to reduce wages in order to eliminate unemployment are now localized in this sector rather than spread across the entire economy. Unions could create rigid wages in their own part of the economy, but this would not prevent falling wages from eliminating unemployment in the economy.

2. The Keynesian explanation provides an answer to why falling wages may not eliminate unemployment, but it does not even attempt to explain rigid wages.[4] Keynes simply worked with a model in which rigid wages were taken as an exogenously given fact that he did not attempt to explain. As Keynes pointed out, falling wages will not eliminate unemployment if the reduction in aggregate demand induced by falling wages (and incomes) is large enough to cause the derived demand curve for labor to fall at the same (or greater) rate than wages. Lower wages lead to less demand for goods and services; less demand for goods and services leads to a smaller demand for labor and hence to a lower equilibrium wage. Depending upon the propensity to consume and the elasticity of the supply curve of labor, it is easy to construct a system that does not

reach equilibrium. Wages keep falling, but demands for labor fall as much or more and wages never succeed in restoring full employment. As a result, in a Keynesian world one can systematically explain the coexistence of falling wages and unemployment, but it is not possible to explain rigid wages and unemployment. Rigid wages must be brought into the Keynesian system as an exogenous hypothesis.

3. A simple denial of the facts argues that what is observed as unemployment is really voluntary unemployment rather than involuntary unemployment. The unemployed will not work at the current wage rate but are seeking higher wages than those available. There are two major problems with this explanation.

First, it is necessary to explain why the willingness to work at current wage rates fluctuates over time. Why was 3.5 percent of the population unwilling to work at 1969 wage rates while 5.9 percent of the population was unwilling to work at the higher wage rates of 1971? Even if you think that there is a residue of voluntary unemployment, it is hard to argue that cyclical unemployment is caused by exogenous shifts in the willingness to work at current wage rates.

Second, you must explain why those who are unemployed accept periodic periods of employment at the current wage rate. The unemployed are not a group of persistently unemployed people but a group with recurring periods of employment and unemployment. If voluntary actions explain their unemployment, why do their attitudes change? At one moment they are willing to take a job at the current wage rate; at the next moment they are not.

In sum, none of the various ad-hoc explanations of why wages are rigid downward and why they do not fall in an attempt to eliminate unemployment is very convincing. The downward rigidity of wages is one of the central observations that must be explained in any satisfactory theory of wages.

Closely linked to the downward rigidity of wages is the overall rigidity of the wage structure as average wages grow. Higher productivity leads to higher wages, but the wages of different occupations change very little relative to the average over long periods of time. A rigid structure of wages has been a general characteristic of the economy since World War II. For example, if the relative wages for 148 occupations are compared between 1959 and 1969, 94 percent of the variance in 1969 relative wages can be explained by knowing 1959 relative wages.[5] Yet over the same period the economy grew by 52 percent, with substantial shifts in the relative proportions of different types of workers. Just as the economic observer must explain why wages are rigid downward, so must he explain why the structure of wages is rigid as wages increase.

WAGES DURING WORLD WAR II AND THE GREAT DEPRESSION

The last major shift in the distribution of earnings occurred during the Great Depression and World War II. Compression occurred at both the top and bottom of the income distribution. The share of total income going to the bottom 40 percent of United States families rose from 12.5 percent to 13.6 percent between 1929 and 1941, and then to 16.0 percent by 1947. The top 20 percent of the families saw their income going from 54.4 percent to 48.8 percent between 1929 and 1941, and to 46.0 percent by 1947. The top 5 percent of the population saw its income fall from 30.0 percent to 24.0 percent to 20.9 percent over the same time periods.[6]

It is not surprising that demands for capital and high-skill (earnings) factors of production should fall more during the Great Depression than the demand for labor and low-skill factors. What is surprising is that the demand curves did not move back to their old positions when the economy moved back to low unemployment rates during and after the war.

World War II is even more interesting from this perspective because narrowing of income differentials was the result of deliberate public policies rather than market pressures. An over-

58

whelming consensus existed during World War II that the economic burdens of the war should be shared relatively equally. Thus, the federal government undertook to use its wage and labor controls to implement this consensus and equalize market wages. Once again the puzzle is not that such wage differentials were imposed during the war but that they were maintained in the market wage structure after the controls were eliminated.

If these wage changes are to be explained from the perspective of marginal productivity, it is necessary to argue that the relative supply and demand curves just happened to shift so that the wage differentials caused by high unemployment and government fiat were exactly the right market differentials after the war. Although such a possibility cannot be definitively ruled out, the probability of its occurrence is low. To believe that such is the case requires a major act of faith. It also requires the belief that demand curves were shifting to reduce wage differentials during World War II and the Great Depression but suddenly started to increase wage differentials in the postwar period (see pp. 61–66).

(see pp. 61–66)

A SKEWED DISTRIBUTION OF EARNINGS

The skewed distribution of earnings has long served as a deviant observation that needs to be explained. Although all innate unaugmentable abilities (IQ, height, weight, etc.) are commonly thought to be normally distributed, earnings are not normally distributed. There is an upper tail of earnings not present in the normal distribution and concentration of low earnings that is not consistent with the proportion of the population with low abilities (see Chart 1).

Nor is the shape of the distribution of earnings consistent with the shape of the distribution of augmentable human capital or at least that part of it reflecting education. Once again there are more low-income individuals than would be predicted from the

CHART 1

Distribution of Income, Education, and Intelligence (IQ)
of Males Twenty-five Years of Age and Over in 1965.

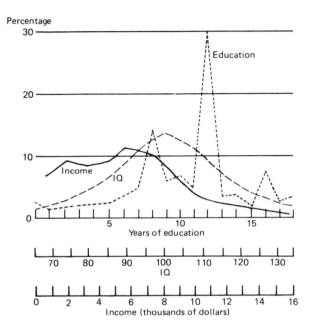

Note: Data scaled to equalize standard deviations from the mean.
Sources: Income data from U.S. Bureau of the Census, "Income in 1965 of Families and Persons in the United States," *Current Population Reports*, Series P-60, No. 51, (1967), p. 34; education data estimated from U.S. Bureau of the Census, *Statistical Abstract of the United States: 1967*, p. 113; IQ data from David Wechsler, *Wechsler Adult Intelligence Scale Manual* (New York: Psychological Corp., 1955), p. 20.

number of low-education individuals, and the upper tail of the earnings distribution extends several standard deviations beyond the upper tail of the education distribution.

Racial and sexual discrimination can be used to explain part of the concentration of individuals in the lower tail, but the same problem exists if one looks solely at adult white males—a group that does not suffer from discrimination. Something must be added to discrimination to explain what needs to be explained.

A variety of ingenious explanations have been offered for this paradox, but the standard explanation is to postulate the existence of some unobservable non-normally distributed ability. The usual candidates are the willingness to accept economic risk or the motivation to earn money. Since both of these qualities are difficult, if not impossible, to measure, this possibility is hard to refute. But it is also hard to confirm. Such unsupported assertions are the economic equivalent of epicycles. They could be true, but they can be used to explain any and all deviations from the predicted results.

Another explanation revolves around the interaction of augmentable and innate human skills. Possessing both characteristics may lead to a very different income than the sum of the two characteristics evaluated separately. This possibility could explain a wider dispersion in the distribution of earnings than in the distribution of either innate or augmentable human skills (those with high innate skills acquire more augmentable human capital than those with smaller innate skills), but the different shapes of the upper and lower tails still must be explained. Something else must be invoked.

The something else could be a nonlinear interaction equation that produces the desired results. Algebraically, there is always some equation that will produce the observed distribution of earnings from the observed distribution of innate abilities and human capital just as there is some epicycle that will explain every movement in the heavens. The real question has to do with the independent proof for the existence of such an equation.[7]

CHANGES IN THE DISTRIBUTION OF EDUCATION AND EARNINGS

A related problem can be seen in the post–World War II change in the distribution of education and earnings. The distribution of education (human capital) has become more equal, and the distribution of earnings has become more unequal. Much of the increase in earnings inequality, however, can be traced to the increasing prevalence of women, teenagers, elderly, and minorities in the work force. As a result, it is difficult to determine what fraction of the inequality is caused by factors, such as discrimination, that are peculiar to these groups and what fraction is determined by the normal distribution mechanism of the economy. To isolate the basic distribution mechanism from discrimination, it is necessary to look at the changes in education and earnings for white males twenty-five to sixty-four years of age—a group that does not suffer from discrimination or variations in participation rates.

As the data in Table 11 indicate, the distribution of education

TABLE 11

Distribution of Education and Earnings
Among White Males 25 to 64 Years of Age

	PERCENTAGE SHARE OF MAN-YEARS OF EDUCATION		PERCENTAGE SHARE OF INCOME	
	1950	1970	1950	1970
Lowest 5th	9.2	9.3	6.1	6.1
Second 5th	15.1	18.5	13.0	13.3
Middle 5th	19.2	20.7	17.5	17.7
Fourth 5th	24.4	22.7	22.0	23.6
Highest 5th	32.1	28.8	41.4	39.3

Source: U.S. Bureau of the Census, *U.S. Census of the Population: 1950* (Washington, D.C.: Government Printing Office, 1952), vol. 2, *Characteristics of the Population*, pt. 1, "U.S. Summary," Tables 115 and 139; *U.S. Census of the Population: 1970* (Washington, D.C.: Government Printing Office, 1972), vol. 1, *Characteristics of the Population*, pt. 1, "U.S. Summary," Tables 199 and 245.

has become more equal for white males twenty-five to sixty-four years of age between 1950 and 1970. During that period, the bottom three quintiles increased their share of the group's man-years of education by 5 percentage points, yet they made no significant gains in their share of the group's earnings. In the distribution of earnings, the only changes occurred among the top two quintiles. The fourth quintile increased its share of total income at the expense of the fifth quintile.

Using marginal-productivity analysis, an economist would have expected the equalization in education to be matched by an equalization in earnings. There should have been a powerful three-pronged equalizing effect. First, an educational program that transforms a low-skill person into a high-skill person raises the earnings of the person receiving education and training. Second, it reduces the total supply of low-skill workers leading to an increase in their wages. Third, it increases the total supply of high-skill workers leading to a decrease in their wages. The net result is a more equal distribution of earnings combined with a higher average income. (The worker given the increased education has a higher productivity.)

Black-white income gaps reveal the same education-earnings problem. Between 1952 and 1968 the mean education of black male workers rose from 67 percent to 87 percent of white male workers, yet median wage and salary incomes only rose from 58 percent to 66 percent. Most of this increase can also be traced to mobility from the South (with its low relative incomes for blacks) to the North and West (with its higher relative incomes for blacks). As a result, education does not seem to be equalizing black and white incomes in the manner that marginal productivity would hypothesize.

One explanation is to argue that earned incomes are composed of two types of income: income earned by pure human labor (innate ability or effort) and income earned by human capital. Equalizing the distribution of education should equalize the earnings from human capital, but it does not necessarily lead to a more equal distribution of total earnings. As long as the variance (dispersion) in the returns to human capital are larger than the variance in the returns to pure labor income, increasing the quantity of human capital (education) may increase the variance in total income. If, for example, pure labor incomes are absolutely equally distributed, additions to human capital, and hence to the share of human capital income in total income, increases the dispersion of income even if human capital income is becoming more equally distributed. Pure labor income (the equally distributed portion of total income) becomes a smaller and smaller fraction of total income. Total income becomes more unequally distributed even though pure income is equally distributed and human capital is becoming more equally distributed. Eventually, however, as human capital income becomes a larger and larger fraction of total income, total incomes will once again start to equalize. According to this argument, if earnings are not becoming more equal, the United States simply hasn't reached the point at which equalization begins to occur.

Although logically possible, such an argument is not in accordance with the empirical evidence. First, if the earnings of laborers with zero years of education are used as the measure of pure labor earnings, over three-fourths of the earnings of college graduates are a return to their human capital rather than a return to their pure labor. As a consequence, the United States has already reached the point at which education should have entered into the equalizing phase of its impact. Second, the variance in returns to pure labor are, if anything, greater than the variance in the returns to human capital. In 1950 the coefficient of determination (variance/mean) of earnings for those with zero years of education was 1.26; the coefficient of determination for those with a college education was 0.86. As a consequence, a more equal distribution of education should have led to a more equal distribution of income (as measured by the coefficient of determination). Using the actual income coefficients of determination for different educational classes in 1950, the actual postwar changes in the distribution of education should have led to an 11 percent reduction in the overall coefficient of determination in earnings for adult white males by 1970. In fact, the coefficient of determination rose by 1 percent over the period. Even taking the interaction between pure labor earnings and human capital earnings into account, education has not been having the equalizing impact that marginal productivity would predict.

An alternative explanation is to postulate exogenous shifts in the derived demand curves for labor with different educational qualifications. Demand curves have been moving in such a manner as to offset the predicted impacts of the observed changes in supply. The distribution of education is becoming more equal, but wage differentials between educational classes are becoming larger. Similarly, adverse shifts in the demand curves for blacks have overwhelmed favorable shifts in their supply curves—i.e., discrimination against blacks *increased* from 1952 to 1968 in such a manner as to more than offset the improvement in their relative education.

Exogenous shifts in demands constitute a tautological explanation for any and all observed movements, but they cannot be ruled out definitively. They may have occurred even if they go against the conventional wisdom in the case of blacks. Ultimately, the acceptance or rejection of this hypothesis must depend upon whether it is possible to find another explanation that is both more persuasive and more consistent with other observations in the labor market. The hypothesis of an exogenous shift in demand leading to greater relative demands for highly educated labor is, however, inconsistent with the standard explanation of another phenomenon.

During the post–World War II period, man-years of education have been added to the labor force at an increasing rate. The growth in years of education per member of the labor force accelerated from an 8 percent increase in the decade of the forties, to a 13 percent increase in the fifties, to over 16 percent in the sixties.[8] Given more human capital per worker, productivity should also have accelerated over this period. If wage differentials have also been widening (as they were hypothesized to be to explain the absence of predicted wage equalization), then the predicted acceleration in productivity should be even greater than that indicated by the acceleration in man-years of education. Higher wage differentials indicate that productivity differentials have grown between different types of workers under the rules of marginal productivity. Therefore, human capital (productive power) has grown more rapidly than data on raw man-years of education would indicate.

Yet the aggregate rate of growth of productivity seems to be at, or maybe even slightly below, its long-term trend of 2.9 percent per year. Productivity should have responded to the acceleration in employed human capital, but it has not. The easiest way to explain this epicycle is to argue that productivity (wage) differentials have fallen between different classes of workers. Therefore, human capital has not been growing as fast as data on man-years of education would warrant. Although this may be true, it is exactly the opposite argument of that used to explain the absence of wage equalization.

INTRAGROUP VARIANCE IN EARNINGS

In a micro-economic world competition among buyers and sellers of labor serves to equalize wages. Each individual with the same characteristics is paid the same amount. Perhaps what is most perturbing about this vision of the world is the observation that satisticians are unable to find the homogeneous wage groups that are predicted by marginal productivity. Corrections can be made for education, occupation, industry, region, age, race, sex, hours of work, IQ, and a variety of other factors; yet there are still substantial variances in the observed distributions of income. Typically, the variance within any group is 80 to 90 percent as large as the variance for the population as a whole.

The reader can best verify this observation for himself or herself by looking at the detailed data in the annual Census Bureau publications on incomes or the decennial census.[9] As an illustration of the phenomenon that will be discovered, look at the distribution of earnings for male physicians forty-five to fifty-five years of age who worked full-time during 1969, or at the distribution of earnings for male automobile mechanics thirty-five to forty-four years of age who worked full-time during 1969 (see Table 12). Similar results will be found for all occupations even though there are over two hundred detailed occupations in this particular tabulation and the data has been corrected for work effort, age, and sex. An alternative expression of the same problem can be seen in the econometric literature on individual earnings functions. Typically, these functions explain only 10 to 20 percent of the earnings variation of the population to which they are fitted. Very occasionally someone can explain 40 percent of the variance in his sample, but most of the variance of any group is left unexplained.

There are two alternative explanations for intragroup earnings variance. Some relevant characteristics may not have been measured, or the existing classifications may not be detailed enough to reach identical working skills. If the data were avail-

TABLE 12

Earnings in 1969 for the
Experienced Civilian Labor Force

	FULL-TIME MALE PHYSICIAN 45 TO 54	FULL-TIME MALE AUTO MECHANIC 34 TO 44
$0 to $1,999	1.1%	2.4%
$2,000 to $3,999	1.0	5.1
$4,000 to $5,999	1.2	16.0
$6,000 to $6,999	0.6	11.4
$7,000 to $7,999	0.8	14.5
$8,000 to $9,999	1.5	23.7
$10,000 to $14,999	6.2	22.2
$15,000 and up	87.5	4.7
Median	$25,000+	$8,050

Source: Bureau of the Census, *U.S. Census of Population: 1970* (Washington, D.C.: Government Printing Office, 1972), vol. PC(2–7A), *Occupational Characteristics.*

able, additional corrections could be made for physical appearances, verbal skills, willingness to take risks, or desires to earn money.

Additional corrections can always be made, but it is also possible to go too far in correcting observed distributions of earnings. Earnings data and earnings equations are often corrected for both industry and geographic location, but should they be? Wage payments in a marginal-productivity world are supposed to be made on the basis of the skills supplied and not dependent upon the industry or region of use. Yet industry and geographic variables are significant in individual earnings functions.[10] Without them, the equations would explain much less of the total variance in earnings. This significance, itself, constitutes a deviation from the norms of a competitive market. It vitiates the idea of pools of laborers with identical skills competing against one another and in the process producing equilibrium wage rates for each skill class.

A similar problem emerges if you look at the distribution of earnings by education level. Instead of finding narrow non-overlapping earnings distributions, the ranges of these distributions are wide with considerable overlap. This means that at the very least the standard human capital calculation (i.e., the rate of return on obtaining a college education) needs to be augmented with an estimate of the risks associated with that investment. Although it would be necessary to have data on lifetime distributions of earnings for individuals to estimate precisely the risks attached to investments in a college education, the nature of the problem can be seen in the aggregate data that are available.

In 1972 the median adult white male with a high-school education (twelve years) had a money income of $10,182, and the median adult white male with a college education (sixteen-plus years) had a money income of $14,385. This would seem to yield a good gross rate of return on going to college. But approximately 28 percent of those with college educations had in-

TABLE 13

Money Income of White Adult Males in 1972
(25 and over)

INCOME (IN THOUSANDS)	12 YEARS OF EDUCATION (PERCENT)	16 OR MORE YEARS OF EDUCATION (PERCENT)
$0–1	1.5	1.2
1–2	1.8	1.5
2–3	3.0	2.2
3–4	3.2	2.2
4–5	3.7	2.4
5–6	4.7	2.4
6–7	6.2	2.9
7–8	7.1	3.8
8–10	17.5	8.5
10–15	34.7	26.1
15–25	13.7	31.1
25 and over	2.9	15.7
Median	$10,182	$14,385
Mean	$10,694	$16,531

Source: Bureau of the Census, *Current Population Reports: Consumer Income, 1972* (Washington, D.C.: Government Printing Office, 1973), p. 124.

comes below the median high school income (negative gross rates of return), and approximately 21 percent of those with high school educations had incomes above the median college income. The net result is a 49 percent chance that obtaining a college degree lowers an individual's gross income. Since substantial costs are incurred in going to college, the probability of a negative net rate of return is even higher. If the opportunity costs of going to college are $28,500 ($12,000 in direct college costs and $16,500 in lost wages) and college loans can be obtained at a 6 percent interest rate, the probability of a negative net rate of return rises to 58 percent.

If the normal adjustments are made for differences in ability, family background, on-the-job skills, motivation, etc., the overlapping nature of the two distributions becomes even more pronounced. Some of the higher college incomes are attributable to these factors and not to a college education. Making such corrections raises the risk of negative and low rates of return. Why is there such a high degree of risk (variance) associated with obtaining a higher education?

If the variance problem is to be reduced, it is necessary to argue that there is some systematic factor creating earnings that is *not* correlated with the amount of education a person receives. The only problem is to think of such a factor. On-the-job training is another source of earnings, but it is thought to be correlated with education.

If intragroup variance in earnings is taken seriously, it leads to a radical set of policy prescriptions such as those reached by Christopher Jencks in his book on *Inequality*.[11] Since the intragroup variance in earnings exists and cannot be explained on the basis of human capital models, very little of the total variance in incomes can be eliminated by equalizing personal characteristics such as education, training, etc. Most of the variance is caused by some unknown phenomenon (Jencks calls it luck). Before retreating to random luck or accident, however, it is worth thinking about alternative formulations that might be able systematically to explain the intragroup variance in incomes.

DIRECT TESTS OF MARGINAL-PRODUCTIVITY
THEORY OF DISTRIBUTION

The marginal-productivity theory of distribution is subject to one direct test. Wherever there are estimates of capital and labor stocks, production functions can be estimated econometrically. These production functions can then be differentiated with respect to capital and labor in order to determine the marginal products of capital and labor. The estimated marginal products can then be compared with the observed payments to capital and labor in order to see if they are identical or similar.

TABLE 14

Marginal Products and Factor Payments for Capital and Labor in 1965

PRODUCTION FUNCTIONS FOR PRIVATE ECONOMY	MARGINAL PRODUCT OF CAPITAL	ACTUAL RETURNS TO CAPITAL	MARGINAL PRODUCT OF LABOR	ACTUAL RETURNS TO LABOR
Cobb Douglas with embodied technical progress and disembodied technical progress	18.2%	29.3%	$7,236	$4,536
Cobb Douglas with only disembodied technical progress	19.3%	29.3%	$6,727	$4,536
Cobb Douglas with economies of scale	90.0%	29.3%	$19,003	$4,536
Cobb Douglas with all embodied technical progress	19.0%	29.3%	$7,605	$4,536
CES with elasticity of substitution of 0.75	13.1%	29.3%	$8,043	$4,536
CES with elasticity of substitution of 1.25	21.2%	29.3%	$6,578	$4,536
Cobb Douglas functions with disembodied technical progress				
Manufacturing	11.8%	38.5%	$9,239	$7,336
Farming	15.9%	29.3%	$2,353	$1,331
Non-Farm, non-manufacturing	21.9%	25.8%	$6,105	$3,723

Source: Lester C. Thurow, "Disequilibrium Under Alternative Production Functions," in *Unfashionable Economics: Essays in Honor of Thomas Balogh*, ed. Paul Streeten (London: Weidenfeld and Nicolson, 1969), pp. 335–336.

When such tests are applied to American data,[12] the marginal product of labor exceeds its actual returns and the marginal product of capital is less than its actual returns (see Tables 14 and 15). Marginal products and actual returns are

TABLE 15

*Median Earnings and Marginal
Revenue Products*

OCCUPATION	MEDIAN EARNINGS	MARGINAL REVENUE PRODUCTS
Managers	$8,189	$ 4,035
Sales	6,136	2,324
Professionals	6,007	5,343
Craftsmen	4,875	13,942
Operations	3,797	8,598
Clerical	3,640	5,804
Laborers	3,154	5,804
Service	2,871	5,804

Source: Peter Gottschalk, "An Empirical Comparison of Marginal Productivity and Income by Occupation," mimeographed (1974), p. 12.

not consistent with respect to either levels or patterns of movement over time. Discrepancies arise for a wide variety of production functions, for different levels of aggregation, for different industrial classifications, for different areas, for different time periods, and for different occupations.

The defender of marginal productivity can at this point go on the offensive. Problems inherent in the nature of production functions may make it impossible to use production functions to test marginal productivity. The basic problem is one of aggregation. Different plants have different production functions, and it may be misleading to represent the economy, or any subsector of the economy, as if it were the result of a statistical production function.[14] The size of the empirical errors introduced by the aggregation problem remains in doubt, but if the errors are large, then there is no valid direct test of the marginal-productivity theory. Until this issue is resolved, we are left with a questionable, but negative, conclusion as to the validity of marginal productivity.

MICRO-ECONOMIC SURVEYS

One alternative to statistical studies is to survey the actual actors in the economic game in order to see how they would describe their actions and the rules of the game. Recently, two economists, Piore and Doeringer, extensively interviewed plant managers and other personnel to study how labor was allocated within the firm—the internal labor market.[15] During the course of these interviews, they visited plant designers to see how these designers incorporate the relative costs of different factors of production into their designs for constructing factories.

If the plant designers were optimizers in accord with the dictates of marginal productivity, they would look at market wage differentials for different types of labor and then adjust their plant designs to minimize costs. When it came to choosing the optimum capital-labor proportions to employ, plant designers seemed to be operating in accordance with the marginal-productivity model. Knowledge of the average cost of labor and the average cost of capital was employed to find minimum cost combinations. But they did not seem to be optimizing across different types of laborers in the same manner. Typically, they did not even know, much less use, the wage differential across different types of labor.

The easiest way to respond to such results is what I shall call "Hall's Law" after an M.I.T. colleague of mine who is fond of enunciating it. "All survey questions about economic motivation elicit stupid answers." The basic argument is that economic actors operate in terms of the standard economic paradigms even though they would not explain their actions in terms of the paradigms. This may be true, but if it is true, we are thrown back to the statistical data that are hardly more comforting to the basic hypothesis under investigation. Neither descriptions of behavior nor observed actions seems to be in accordance with the basic paradigm.

Conclusions

There is a wide variety of more technical puzzles in the labor market, but the preceeding observations give the flavor of the problem.[16] All of these observations are difficult to explain from the perspective of single marginal-productivity theories. If any one of them existed by itself, it could be dismissed as a minor aberration that needed explanation, but not as a challenge to the basic theory itself. Viewed separately, there often are plausible explanations for the various deviations, but, as we have seen, these explanations are often inconsistent from one deviant observation to another. Together, the deviant observations constitute a challenge to the basic theory itself.

These observations do not indicate that marginal productivity is wrong, but they do indicate that a substantial fraction of our observations about the distribution of income are not in accordance with a simple version of it. Some other market mechanisms may exist. The problem is to see if the rules of other mechanisms can be deduced. Or, put another way: can the observations that are deviations from what would be expected from the perspective of simple marginal productivity be systematically explained from some other perspective?

4

JOB COMPETITION:

THE LABOR QUEUE

CAN THE DISTRIBUTIONS of economic resources outlined
in Chapter 1 and the deviant observations examined in Chapter
3 be explained in some systematic fashion? Is there some way
to unify micro-economics, macro-economics, and labor economics
rather than leaving them as three separate approaches to the
same problem? These are the questions that an observer would
pose. Can they be answered? The next two chapters are an
attempt to provide an answer. Their success will be left to the
reader to judge.

In the job-competition model, instead of competing against
one another based on the wages that they are willing to accept,
individuals compete against one another for job opportunities
based on their relative costs of being trained to fill whatever
job is being considered. Hence the new model will be called
"job competition" to distinguish it from the old "wage competition" forms of marginal productivity.

To make the presentation as clear as possible and to highlight
the differences between wage competition and job competition,
the job-competition model will be developed *as if* it exists in
isolation and is the sole market clearing mechanism. This is a

pedagogical device and not meant to imply that wage competition never exists. Wage competition and job competition are not mutually exclusive. Both could, and probably do, coexist as alternative mechanisms for clearing labor markets. In some labor markets wage competition may dominate; in other labor markets job competition may dominate. Over time, the mixture of one or the other may change. The author believes that there is a continuum between wage competition and job competition and that the American economy lies somewhere between these two extremes. The "as if" assumption is used to clarify the role of job competition by separating its impacts from those of wage competition.

The key ingredient in the job-competition model is the observation that most cognitive job skills are not acquired before a worker enters the labor market but after he has found employment through on-the-job training programs (see below). Thus, the labor market is not primarily a bidding market for selling existing skills but a training market where training slots must be allocated to different workers. The distribution of training slots and the allocation of individuals among these slots depend upon two sets of factors.

One set of factors determines an individual's *relative* position in the labor queue; another set of factors, not mutually exclusive of the first, determines the actual distribution of job opportunities in the economy. Wages are paid based on the characteristics of the job in question, and workers are distributed across job (training) opportunities based on their relative position in the labor queue. The most preferred workers get the best jobs. In this context a job is best thought of as a lifetime sequence of jobs rather than as a specific job with a specific employer. The labor queue is competitive, but workers compete for position based upon their background characteristics rather than on their willingness to accept low wages. As we shall see, the training function of the labor market makes the repression of direct wage competition profitable.

To some extent the job-competition model reverses the normal assumptions about short-run and long-run market clearing mechanisms. In the wage-competition model, wages fluctuate in the short run to clear markets, and these wage changes then induce shifts in the long-run supply and demand curves. In the job-competition model, supply and demand curves shift in the short run to clear markets. Markets clear by altering hiring requirements and the amount of on-the-job training they provide. Changes in relative wages occur only after a substantial period of disequilibrium in relative wages, if at all.

If you like to think in marginal-productivity terms, the marginal product resides in the job and not in the man. The individual's earnings depend upon the job he acquires and not directly upon his own personal characteristics. Since the individual is trained into the productivity of the job he holds, the job allocation procedure assumes a much greater importance than it does in wage competition, where an individual's skills automatically place him in some particular job market.

Given the factors that determine an individual's position in the labor queue and given the factors that determine the distribution of jobs or lifetime income ladders, it is possible to see how earnings are allocated across the work force or, more accurately, to see how individuals are allocated across the job or earnings opportunities that exist in the labor market. This is one of the key inversions of the job-competition model. People are allocated across earnings or job opportunities; there are no equilibrium wages that should be paid people based on their personal qualifications as workers upon entry into the labor force.

The Supply of Skills

In neoclassical theory the labor market exists to match labor demands with labor supplies. In the matching process, or in the mismatching process, various signals are given. Businesses are told to raise wages and redesign jobs in sectors with skill shortages. In surplus sectors they are told to lower wages. Individuals are told to acquire skills in high wage areas and discouraged from acquiring jobs and skills in low wage areas. In the process each skill market is cleared with increases or reductions in wages in the short run and by a combination of wage changes, skill changes, and production process changes in the long run.

The key ingredient in this view of the world is the assumption that workers acquire laboring skills exogenously in formal education and/or training and then bring these skills into the labor market. Possessing skills, they bid for the jobs that use these skills. Unfortunately, the underlying assumption does not seem to be correct for the American economy. Workers do not bring fully developed job skills into the labor market. Most cognitive job skills, general or specific, are acquired either formally or informally through on-the-job training after a worker finds an entry job and the associated promotion ladder.

The evidence for this is very clear for the American economy. In the 1960s the President's Automation Commission undertook extensive surveys on how workers learned the actual cognitive job skills they were using.[1] Their surveys found that only 40 percent of the work force reported that they were using any skill that they had acquired in formal training programs or in specialized education. Most of this 40 percent reported that some of the skills they were using had been acquired in informal, casual, on-the-job training. The remaining 60 percent acquired *all* of their job skills through informal, casual, on-the-job training. Even among college graduates, over two-thirds reported that they had acquired cognitive skills through informal, casual processes on the job.

Perhaps the most convincing evidence in this direction came when the survey asked workers to list the form of training that had been the most helpful in acquiring their current job skills. Only 12 percent of the work force listed formal training and specialized education. (Some of this was also done at their place of work and was directly dependent upon their having already being selected for the job in question.)

Although initially surprising, the results are not without an easy explanation. Most job skills are best taught in conjunction with the job in question, since training and production are complementary products. Goods and services produced in the process of training can be sold to lower training costs. Only actual production generates the degree of realism necessary to polish production skills. It is also the only way to guarantee that the worker will know everything he needs to know without having to learn lots of things he does not need to know. On-the-job training from one worker to another is simply the cheapest method of training.[2]

As a result, the labor market is not a market where fully developed skills bid for jobs. Rather, it is primarily a market where supplies of trainable labor are matched with training opportunities that are in turn directly associated with the number of job openings that exist. Training opportunities only occur when there is a job opening that creates the demand for the skills in question.

This situation has a profound effect on the labor market, since it means that the supply and demand curves for different types of workers are not independent. Because most skills are acquired on the job, skills are only created when there is a demand for labor with that skill. People are only trained when a job opening exists. This leads to a situation where the supply of trained labor depends upon the demand for trained labor. Thinking in terms of simple supply and demand curves (see Chart 2), the supply curve lies along the demand curve as long as the wage rate is above some opportunity wage and high enough to attract trainable labor to this particular job opportunity. If the actual wage for a particular job happens to be above the opportunity wage, training will not proceed down to the level dictated by the opportunity wage (q_0) but will stop at the level dictated by the actual wage (q_1).

CHART 2

*Supplies and Demands for Labor
in a Job-Competition Model*

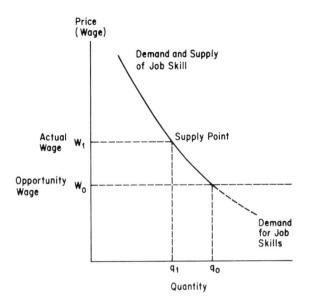

Given identical supply and demand curves, it is obviously impossible to determine an equilibrium wage rate at the intersection of the relevant supply and demand curves. They do not intersect; they coincide. Thus, there is no supply curve in the normal sense of that word. For every exogenously given wage, the demand (and supply) curve determines how many jobs openings will exist and how many workers will be trained. The demand curve cannot, however, determine a wage by itself. The wage must come from elsewhere in the economic system (see below). It is also not determined by a process of competitive bidding between potential suppliers and demanders—there are few, if any, independent potential suppliers of the desired skills.

In the process of normal job turnover or as the result of business cycles, individuals may acquire cognitive job skills and be unemployed, but, as we shall see later, even this limited supply of trained labor is restricted in its ability to bid back into their old job categories. To allow them to bid back into their old job categories at lower wages would bring on-the-job training to a halt and be counterproductive in the long run (see below).

FACILITATING TRAINING

If, as I have suggested, we live in an economy where laborers acquire many of their cognitive job skills through informal training from other workers or from their immediate supervisors, we need a differently structured labor market than we would if the only purpose of the labor market were to allocate skills and establish equilibrium wages. A labor-training market must be so structured as to maximize the willingness of existing laborers to transmit their knowledge to new workers and to minimize every worker's resistance to acquiring new skills and accepting new technology.

Eliminating direct wage competition and limiting employment competition to entry jobs is a necessary ingredient in the training process. If workers feel that they are training potential wage or employment competitors every time they show another worker how to do their job, they have every incentive to stop giving such informal training. In that case each man would seek to build his own little monopoly by hoarding skills and information to make himself indispensable. Wage and employment insecurity also means that every man has a vested interest in resisting any technical changes that might reduce his wages or employment opportunities. To encourage training, employers must repress wage competition and build employment security. If they do not, the essential training processes within their plants come to a halt.

Conversely, in a job market where no one is trained unless a job is currently available (this is what on-the-job training means), where strong seniority provisions limit employment insecurity to a clear minority (the newly hired), and where there is no danger that some competitor with the requisite skills is going to be allowed to bid down wages, employees are going to be willing to transmit information to new workers and to accept new techniques. If anyone is to be made redundant by such techniques, it will be a clearly defined minority—new workers. The teacher does not injure himself by being willing to teach.

Consider the market for construction labor in the United States. To some extent it is the paradigm wage-competition labor market. An actual job shape-up exists so that workers do not have permanent jobs. In most areas, such as Boston, substantial short-run wage fluctuations occur. If unionized labor is in short supply, premiums will be paid in excess of union scales. If unionized labor is in surplus supply, union workers will leave the unionized sector and work for nonunion wage scales on nonunion construction. In terms of wage and employment competition, the construction labor market comes closer to the wage-competition model than any other. But what does it produce?

Severe restrictions are placed upon training, and the resistance to technical innovations is legendary. Let me suggest that construction workers and their unions exhibit the same responses and motivations as the rest of the population. Their attempts to build countervailing monopoly positions and their resistance to technical change are just what the rest of us would do if faced with the reality of wage and employment competition.

To illustrate the problem at close range, imagine that M.I.T. were to start hiring economics professors in the same way that construction workers are hired. Instead of the standard academic system of employment, M.I.T. institutes a shape-up. Every morning, all of the potential teaching candidates from the most illustrious professor to the most illiterate graduate student bid (on a quality-adjusted basis, of course) for the teaching jobs of that day. First, the process could be time-consuming and costly. Outside experts would be needed to determine the quality-adjusted prices that were being offered. There would have to be periodic evaluations of the knowledge possessed by each individual. Second, at the risk of libeling myself and my colleagues, I would be willing to bet that the education process would deteriorate. Each professor would have a vested interest in teaching false information or small amounts of information so that his students could not effectively bid against him. Every bright graduate student would be viewed as a potential threat. We would act to preserve our wage and employment conditions just as construction workers act to preserve their wage and employment conditions.

It is easy to say that bids could take into account the professor's willingness to teach the right information, but this is difficult and expensive to do in practice. An equally competent inspector would need to sit in every class to determine what was being taught. Classes would need two competent people—one teacher and one inspector—rather than one. There would also be the problem of how to accept bids for the job of "economics quality control inspector." Inspectors would be needed for inspectors. In some sense the static inefficiencies of the present tenure system promote the dynamic efficiencies of the present system. They minimize the resistances to spreading information and job skills.

A lack of wage competition is not peculiar to the United States. Even more repression of wage and employment competition can be seen in Western Europe and Japan. It is typically much more difficult to fire workers in Europe than it is in the U.S. In Japan large industrial firms extend tenure to their employees in the same manner that U.S. universities extend tenure to their professors. Wages are even more heavily constrained by age and seniority as opposed to personal skills and merit. Although the absence of wage competition in the case of Japan may lead to static inefficiency, it certainly has not led to dynamic inefficiency. Japanese workers are held up as examples of a labor force being willing to accept technical change and to cooperate with each other to increase productivity. This is what we would expect from the perspective of job competition. If individuals can only raise their own incomes by raising the productivity of the entire enterprise, they have a direct incentive to increase training and to accept technical change. It cannot hurt their wage and employment positions, and it should help.

As a result, the types of wage and employment competition that are the essence of efficiency in simple, static neoclassical models may not be the essence of efficiency in a dynamic economy where the primary function of the labor market is to allocate individuals to on-the-job training ladders and where most learning occurs in work-related contexts. Here, wage and employment competition becomes counterproductive.

No one quarrels with the proposition that flexible wages are necessary for an economy to maximize its current production (reach its static efficiency frontier), but an argument is being made that efforts to maximize current production may engender a slower future rate of growth of production (its dynamic efficiency frontier). Since the potential gains from maximizing long-run growth usually dominate the potential gains from maximizing current production, employers find it *profitable* to structure the labor market in order to maximize long-run growth at the expense of short-run output. Repressing wage and employment competition becomes a tool for increasing long-run productivity.[3]

This is why rigid wages and seniority rules are just as common in nonunion as in unionized sectors of the economy. In the long run it is profitable to limit wage flexibility. The real choice is between a market structure that maximizes current production and a market structure that maximizes the rate of growth of production. From this perspective the lack of wage and employment competition that we observed in the previous chapter is not an illustration of a "market imperfection" that produces inefficiency but rather represents a functional market adjustment that produces long-run efficiency. More knowledge is transmitted with it than without it.

MARGINAL PRODUCTS, INDIVIDUALS, AND JOBS

Since a job opening is the initial ingredient in the job-competition model, marginal products are inherent in jobs and not in individuals. The individual will be trained into the marginal productivity of the job he is slated to hold, but he does not have this marginal productivity independent of the job in question. This is true even if the worker has managed to acquire the necessary job skills in some exogenous manner or if he has acquired the job skills on the job and has been laid off due to fluctuations in aggregate demand.

To keep the training process going, employers will not allow the unemployed to bid back into his old job at lower wages. For example, there is no reason why an unemployed pilot for Pan American could not bid to become a pilot for TWA or to undercut the remaining Pan American pilots. Everyone flies the same planes. Yet he is not allowed to do this because it would retard the long-run gains that are to be made by facilitating training. In other words, the short-run profits that are to be made by lowering pilots' wages are not worth the long-run costs. This example is taken from a unionized sector of the economy, but similar nonunion examples occurred in the early 1970s among unemployed aerospace engineers in New England who were not allowed to bid against those engineers who remained employed. Technically, the individuals had the necessary job skills, but they were frozen out of the market and thus did not represent an effective potential supply of labor. Their personal productivity and skills were irrelevant even though they existed. Similarly, manpower training programs report that they often have trouble placing trained workers since these workers are not allowed into the jobs for which they have been trained.[4]

The net result is the formation of a series of internal labor markets with limited ports of entry.[5] Outside of these ports of entry jobs, the supply and demand conditions of the external labor market are basically irrelevant. Because of the institutional need to facilitate informal on-the-job training, workers cannot regain employment opportunities by accepting lower wages. Technically, the individual may possess the necessary skills, but institutionally speaking he does not. His wage bid will not be accepted.

Background Characteristics

Although workers do not possess laboring skills, they do possess a variety of what I shall call "background characteristics." These background characteristics (education, innate abilities, age, sex, personal habits, psychological test scores, etc.) affect the cost of training a worker to fill any job even though they do not constitute a set of skills that would allow the worker to enter directly into the production process. Individuals do not have marginal products, but they do have an associated vector of the training costs necessary to allow them to fill different jobs in the economy.

Because individuals have different background characteristics, they will have different potential training costs for each of the job ladders they might enter. For some jobs training costs will be low; for other jobs they will be high. Because of the importance of innate abilities, they may be infinite in a few jobs. I, for example, do not possess the abilities to be a professional athlete or an opera singer regardless of the training investments in me.[6]

Because of differences in background characteristics, each person will have a different structure of associated training costs. The problem for an employer is to pick and train workers so that they can generate the desired marginal product of the job in question with the least investment in training costs.

Training costs, as the term is used here, include the costs of inculcating norms of industrial discipline, good work habits, and the uncertainty costs associated with hiring workers whose training costs are more variable or unknown.

To minimize training costs employers rank potential workers on the basis of their training costs. This leads to the labor queue. But lacking direct information on training costs for specific workers, employers rank workers in accordance with their background characteristics, which they use as indirect indicators of the costs necessary to produce the standard work performance. For new workers and entry level jobs, background characteristics form the only basis of selection. Those workers with the background characteristics that yield the lowest training costs are offered employment first. Depending upon the acceptance rate, an employer moves down his labor queue until he fills the available job openings—training slots. For old workers with job experience, existing jobs skills (including skills such as reliability and punctuality) become relevant to the selection process to the extent that they lead to lower training costs. Job or training ladders emerge when skills are complementary (knowing the first skill lowers the costs of acquiring the second skill) and when workers can receive the necessary on-the-job training with the least disruption of the production process. Usually, this means gradually learning the new skill and gradually moving from one job category to another.

Because each worker has different training costs for different jobs, workers will appear at different places in the labor queue for different jobs. Since this just complicates the analysis without altering its basic character, I shall proceed as if each worker had one and only one associated training cost. Subjective elements may also enter the labor queue. If employers discriminate against blacks, blacks will find themselves lower in the labor queue than their other background characteristics would warrant. The smaller the objective differences in training costs, the larger the role that subjective preferences can play in determining the final order. If all workers had identical training costs, blacks could be placed at the bottom of the labor queue with no loss in efficiency.

As far as the employer is concerned, the problem is to find those background characteristics that are good predictors of potential training costs differences. Given this desire, it is not surprising that educational attainment and performance become critical background characteristics. Education is a form of training. The ability to absorb one type of training probably indicates something about the ability to absorb another type of training. Education becomes an indirect measure of an individual's absorptive capacity and is relevant to the employer even when no cognitive job skill is learned in the educational process. Through education one learns how to be trained or exhibits that one is trainable.

Education also is one way for workers to show that they have "industrial discipline." Having gone through the educational process, the worker has demonstrated an ability to show up on time, take orders, do unpleasant tasks, and observe certain norms of group behavior. These characteristics are also fundamental to the work process. Often they are more important than specific job skills. Many manpower training programs report that industrial discipline is more difficult to teach than specific job skills.[7] Schools may or may not teach these economically desirable characteristics, but traditionally they have provided the employer with an opportunity to find out whether the individual does or does not have them.

THE INCIDENCE OF TRAINING COSTS

Before examining the labor queue in greater detail, it is necessary to look at the incidence of training costs. Who pays for training, the employee or the employer? The question arises because the job-competition model postulates that employers rank workers on the basis of their potential training costs, whereas the wage-competition model argues that most employers are not interested in training costs—that they are borne by the employee.[8]

In the wage-competition model, general training costs are paid by the employee and specific training costs are paid by the employer. General training costs are incurred in the process of acquiring skills that are of use to more than one firm, and specific training costs are incurred in the process of acquiring skills that are of use to one and only one firm. This incidence of training costs arises from the observation that each worker is paid his marginal product in a competitive market. If a firm does not pay in accordance with marginal productivity, the employee simply moves to a firm that does. As a consequence, a firm would never incur general training costs. To do so would be to lose money: total labor costs (wages plus training costs) would exceed labor's marginal product. Since firms will not pay employees more than their marginal products, the employee must pay for his own general training. This may, and probably does, take the form of being willing to work at lower wages than could be obtained elsewhere for a period of time rather than of a direct cash payment to the employer. Conversely, no employee would ever be willing to invest in specific training since it cannot be sold. If the employer needs specific skills, he must pay for the necessary training. Since very few skills are technically specific to one and only one firm, most training costs in wage competition must be borne by the employee rather than by the employer.

With wage differentials tailored to pay for training costs—on-the-job human capital investments—employers should not care whom they hire. On a quality-adjusted basis, each individual costs the same amount—everyone is paid his marginal product minus his training costs. To accomplish some task the employer may have to hire more low-quality workers than high-quality workers, but this is irrelevant to him since each group is going to be paid its net marginal product. There is no reason for him to prefer one worker over another, because there are no economic profits to be made by hiring one worker rather than another. The employer only has a preference when he can exploit one group—pay them less than their marginal product—and make economic profits.

Yet in fact employers seem intensely interested in whom they hire and invest large amounts of money in screening prospective employees. Typically, they report that they are looking for the best possible employees—the employees with the least training costs. Employer interest in screening the labor force is one of the pieces of evidence indicating job competition rather than wage competition. With the exception of specific skills, interest in employee quality should not exist in a wage-competition world, yet it does seem to exist.

In the job-competition model, training costs become important, since the role of wage differentials and worker-quality differentials (training-cost differentials) are reversed. In wage competition, wages fluctuate to reflect differences in worker quality. In job competition, wage differentials are fixed (they must be to maximize training), and the employer searches for workers with quality differentials that match or exceed the existing wage differentials. Ideally, he would like to find employees whose training costs are less than the existing gap between a job's marginal product and its wage. If such workers can be found, economic profits can be made. Conversely, if the employer cannot find workers of the desired quality, he may have to absorb losses. In that case wages plus training costs exceed the marginal productivity of the job for which training is occurring. Although this situation cannot occur for every job if the employer is to survive, it can occur for some jobs.

In a job-competition labor market, the employer can also be expected to pay for much more training than he would in a wage-competition market structure. Much of what appears to be general training if one looks at its potential usefulness to other employers is specific training if one looks at the institu-

90

tional possibilities for selling these skills to other employers. With internal labor markets and restricted wage and employment competition, employees are not going to be allowed to bid for existing jobs if they become unemployed. Economically, they cannot take their skills with them into the general labor market. Institutionally, the skills are firm specific even though other firms could theoretically use them. As a result, employers must pay for their acquisition.

Since employers are going to be incurring a substantial fraction of total training costs and may be able to earn economic profits on this investment, training costs are central to a firm's profit picture. The employer is interested in ranking potential employees in a labor queue on the basis of their estimated training costs, since this is essential to selecting those workers who will lead to maximum profits.

The Labor Queue

Basically, employers use background characteristics to indicate expected training costs and then attempt to rank and hire their potential labor force from those with the lowest training costs to those with the highest training costs. There is an average ranking for each background class, but this ranking is a composite of the rankings of each individual employer. Employers have a range of jobs for which they seek trainees, and desirable characteristics may differ across the range of jobs. Different employers may also place different weights on the background characteristics used as indicators of potential training costs. For any background set there may be some employers who regard these characteristics as the best possible set of characteristics and other employers who regard the same set as the worst possible set of characteristics.

The net result is that individuals with identical background characteristics will not necessarily have identical jobs, training investments, or earnings. Depending upon the supply of workers with a particular set of background characteristics and the demand for individuals with this set of background characteristics, similar individuals will be distributed across a range of job opportunities and earnings. In effect, they will participate in a lottery.

In the job-competition model, identical individuals do not necessarily earn identical incomes as they do in wage competition. They do not receive identical amounts of training even if they have identical preferences, since substantial amounts of on-the-job training are provided by employers and not purchased by employees. Thus, the job-competition model provides an explanation for the observed variance in earning among workers with identical background skills and work efforts.

The actual labor queue is multidimensional since it depends upon a number of background characteristics. But imagine that these characteristics can be collapsed into a general indicator of training costs. (This simplifies the analysis without changing the results and makes it possible to represent the labor queue on a two-dimensional graph). Within each set of background characteristics there will be a labor queue that depends upon how potential employers rank that set of background characteristics and upon the number of people in the set. The employers' rankings depend upon how the background characteristics in question affect training costs and the number of jobs for which these training costs are relevant. The supply of workers is relevant since it determines how far down the distribution of jobs the group is forced to go to be fully employed. A group might, for example, be fully employed before it reached employers that did not value its background characteristics.

Particular workers may be the best—lowest cost—workers for some employers and the worst—highest cost—workers for others, but each set of background characteristics will have some average position of desirability as well as a range of possible positions. In Chart 3 background characteristics B_1 and B_2

CHART 3
The Labor Queue
Ranking number of workers from least
preferred to most preferred

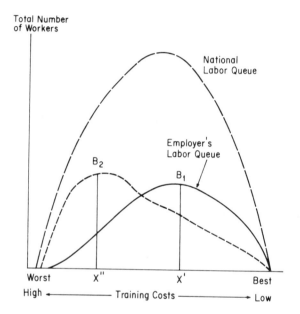

are distributed across the entire range of possibilities, but B_1 characteristics are on the average preferred to B_2 characteristics (X' exceeds X'').

The shape of the national labor queue depends upon adding up the underlying distributions for each background class. Depending upon employer preferences and upon the distribution of background characteristics, the labor queue might be highly concentrated or highly dispersed. If every worker had the same background characteristics, the labor queue would be highly concentrated regardless of employer preferences. If employers thought that background characteristics had little or no impact on training costs, the labor queue would be highly concentrated regardless of the distribution of background characteristics. Conversely, a widely dispersed labor queue would emerge if employers thought that small differences in background characteristics would lead to large differences in training costs or if background characteristics were widely dispersed and played a moderate role in determining labor costs. Equalizing the distribution of background characteristics (training costs) or reductions in employers' preferences across different types of background characteristics would lead to a more highly concentrated labor queue, whereas a more highly dispersed labor queue would be produced by the opposite changes.

Changes in the shape of the labor queue do not, however, mean that the distribution of earnings must necessarily change, for the distribution of earnings is a function not only of the labor queue but also of the distribution of job or training opportunities. An equal group of laborers (with respect to training costs) might be distributed across a relatively unequal distribution of job opportunities. After receiving the resultant on-the-job training, the initially equal workers would have unequal productivities since they would now have unequal skills. Conversely, an unequal group of workers might be distributed across relatively equal distributions of job opportunities. On-the-job training would lead to a more equal distribution of incomes and jobs than of background characteristics or training costs. As a result, the distribution of earnings is determined by the distribution of job opportunities and not by the distribution of the labor queue, which only determines the order of access—and the distribution of access—to job opportunities. The two are related, however, since changes in the distribution of training costs may induce changes in the distribution of job opportunities (see Chapter 5).

Based on such a labor queue, jobs and their corresponding training ladders are distributed in the labor market with employers working down from those at the top of the queue to those at the bottom of the queue. The best jobs will go to the best workers and the worst jobs will go to the worst workers. Given a need for untrained (raw) labor, some workers at the bottom of the labor queue will receive little or no training. In periods of labor scarcity, however, training will extend farther and farther down the labor queue as employers are forced to train more costly workers to fill job vacancies. Conversely, if there are an inadequate number of jobs, those at the bottom of the labor queue will be left unemployed.

Thus, cyclical fluctuations in the demand for labor show up not as fluctuations in wage rates but as fluctuations in demanded background characteristics. When labor is plentiful, hiring characteristics escalate; when labor is in short supply, hiring characteristics relax. When better—that is, lower training cost—workers can be hired, they are hired. Hiring characteristics rather than wages serve to equilibrate or clear labor markets. When less labor is needed, the supply curve is reduced by increasing the qualifications of eligible workers. Escalation and de-escalation of hiring characteristics over the course of the business cycle is a phenomenon that can be explained by the job-competition model but not by the wage-competition model. The escalation and de-escalation of hiring characteristics means that movements in the supply curve of potentially trainable labor serve to clear markets in the short run. When hiring characteristics escalate, the potential supply curve is lowered; when hiring characteristics relax, the potential supply curve is increased. Thus, changes in the number of people being trained rather than changes in relative wages of those already trained clear markets.

THE IMPORTANCE OF RELATIVE POSITION

Job competition differs from wage competition in that an individual's relative position with respect to background characteristics becomes more important than his absolute position. Consider the problem of deciding whether or not to acquire a college education. Assume that you have decided that you are not going to acquire a college education but then notice that your neighbors are acquiring a college education. Under the wage-competition model, this observation will confirm your original decision not to acquire a college education. A substantial increase in the supply of college-educated workers will cause their wages to fall, whereas the wages of the remaining noncollege-educated workers will rise because of the reduction in the supply of noncollege workers. Thus, your wage will rise above what you previously expected and theirs will fall below what you previously expected. If the rate of return on a college education was previously below your rate of time preference, or the rate of interest at which you can borrow, it is now even farther below this cutoff.

In the job-competition model, your observation about your neighbors' actions would lead to different conclusions. Remember that an individual's background characteristics are used to place him in a labor queue. Based upon his *relative* position in this queue, he will be selected for different job or training opportunities. The best, highest income jobs go to the best workers. Consequently, the job distribution open to each set of background characteristics depends upon the supply of people who possess superior background characteristics. Increases in the numbers of individuals with more preferred background characteristics can lead to a deterioration in the expected earnings of less preferred groups. Every additional college worker, for example, may mean a deterioration in the position of the remaining high-school workers.

In the job-competition model, education may therefore become a defensive necessity. As the supply of more highly educated labor increases, individuals find that they must improve their own educational qualifications simply to defend their current income position. If they do not go to college, others will, and they will not find their current job open to them. Education becomes a good investment, not because it would raise an individual's income above what it would have been if no others had increased their education but because it raises his income above what it will be if others acquire an education and he does not. In effect, education becomes a defensive expenditure necessary to protect one's "market share." [9]

The larger the class of more highly educated labor and the more rapid its growth, the more imperative do such defensive expenditures become. In the job-competition model, educational investments may become good investments (the rate of return rises to exceed the rate of time preference or the rate of interest) if you notice many other individuals making the investment that you initially rejected. The private rationality of such defensive expenditures, however, can easily lead to too much expenditure on education from the point of view of society as a whole, just as it can lead to too much advertising from the point of view of an industry as a whole.

Conclusions

The labor queue is a key item in the job-competition model of income distribution, but it is only a part of the necessary apparatus. To it must be added the distribution of job or income opportunities for which individuals will be trained. As we shall see in the next chapter, the labor queue and job distribution are interconnected—they do not move completely independently of each other—but they also are not mirror images of each other. Changes in the shape of the labor queue do not necessarily induce the same changes in the shape of the job distribution.

5

JOB COMPETITION:
THE JOB DISTRIBUTION

THE DISTRIBUTION of job opportunities—that is, the distribution of jobs over which the labor force will be distributed and for which it will be trained—is the other essential ingredient in the job-competition model (see Diagram 1). Like the labor

DIAGRAM 1
The Distribution of Job Opportunities

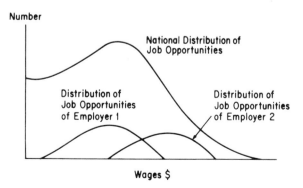

queue, the national distribution of job opportunities is determined by adding up the distributions of job opportunities for each potential employer. The only overall constraint on the job distributions is that the total number of filled jobs cannot exceed the total number of workers available in the labor queue. There can, of course, be unfilled job openings.

Although changes in the shape of the labor queue may have an impact on the distribution of job opportunities (see below), the distribution of jobs is not simply a mirror image of the distribution of background characteristics. The two are related, since some of the same factors affect both, but they are not identical. As we shall see, equalizing the distribution of background characteristics (training costs) does not, for example, automatically lead to an equalization in the distribution of earnings. Under some circumstances, it may in fact lead to a more unequal distribution of earnings. In contrast, under the wage-competition model the distribution of earnings and the distribution of skills or human capital are always identical.

The major analytical problem is to isolate the factors that determine the shape of the distribution of job opportunities. Basically, there are three sets of factors that influence the distribution of job opportunities: the distribution of knowledge, the sociology of wage determination, and the distribution of training costs (the shape of the labor queue). Although much of the discussion in this chapter will focus on the latter factor, since this is the economic part of the problem, this is not meant to imply that the first two are less important in determining the ultimate shape of the distribution of job opportunities.

The Distribution of Knowledge

To some extent the distribution of job opportunities reflects the underlying distribution of technical knowledge. Knowledge governs not only the growth in average incomes but also the distribution of incomes around this average. Different products, machines, skills, and production techniques generate jobs with different marginal products. This occurs in both the wage- and job-competition models. Although employers will search for minimum-cost techniques of production in both models, this search is limited or constrained by technical knowledge. It is not possible to use unknown techniques.

If, for example, there were one and only one production technique (an input-output world) for producing output, technology would completely determine the distribution of job opportunities. There would be one and only one technique for doing everything, with no room for choosing alternative technologies based upon relative factor prices or availabilities. There would be a fixed distribution of jobs necessary to produce any Gross National Product. As the number of alternative techniques rises from one to infinity, the job distribution is less and less dominated by technology and more and more influenced by economic substitutions within the spectrum of existing knowledge. But technical knowledge always plays a role since it determines how easy it is to shift among techniques and the boundaries beyond which it is impossible to make substitutions.[1]

Thus, to be able to explain fully why a particular distribution of job opportunities arises, it would be necessary to explain why a particular distribution of technical knowledge arises. Although there has been some work in this area, this is a task that is, as yet, beyond the competence of economists. Such ignorance does not, however, diminish the importance of the distribution of knowledge in determining the distribution of job opportunities.

Although economists can neither predict nor explain the distributional characteristics of knowledge, they have investigated the possibilities of induced technical progress. Induced technical progress exists if increases in the relative supplies of some factor of production cause technology to develop in such a direction as to use more of the relatively abundant factor. Induced technical progress is potentially important in the job-competition model since it could serve as a link between the distributions of background characteristics and job opportunities. If induced technical progress exists, increasing the supply of some particular background characteristic would lead to more jobs that use individuals with such characteristics. Changes in the job distribution would reflect changes in the labor queue due to induced technical progress.

Extensive economic analysis has concluded, however, that there is no reason for induced technical progress to occur under standard neoclassical economic assumptions. The frontiers of technology will not necessarily change in the directions necessary to absorb more of a relatively abundant factor of production. This result can be shown mathematically, but the economic reasoning is fairly simple.[2]

Induced technical progress would occur if there were some economic rationale for focusing research and development expenditures on the use of factors of production that were becoming relatively more abundant. But the rationale of profit maximization does not lead to such a focus. The purpose of research and development is to develop profitable new products or to lower production costs for old products. In neither case does profit maximization call for the use of relatively abundant factors of production. Rather it calls for selection based upon potential profitability. The use or avoidance of a factor of production has nothing to do with a product's or process's potential profitability. In selecting products and processes, the common distinction between cheap and expensive has no economic meaning. Each factor is paid its marginal product and on a productivity basis is equally expensive or cheap.

Cheap and expensive have an economic meaning only if they are used to describe the difference between a factor's marginal productivity and its marginal cost. A factor is cheap when its marginal productivity is greater than its market price; it is expensive when its marginal productivity is less than its market price. In a perfectly functioning competitive economy, factors are always paid their marginal products. No factor is cheap or expensive and there is no economic incentive to direct research and development expenditures toward (or away from) the use of any factor of production. A dollar saved on using less sand and gravel in a production process is just as valuable as a dollar saved using less diamonds. A new product's profitability is not determined by whether it is made out of tin or gold.

There is therefore nothing inherent in the nature of technical progress that would lead it to adjust the demand for factors to the available supplies. Just because a particular type of labor is relatively abundant or earns a low wage does not cause technical progress to change in such a manner as to use more of that factor. Technical progress may call for the substitution of a low-wage, low-skill worker for a high-wage, high-skill worker, but it is just as apt to call for the reverse. Unskilled workers may be replaced by skilled workers.[3]

Whereas the analysis of induced technical progress took place in the normal neoclassical framework of wage and price flexibility, exactly the same conclusions hold in the job-competition model if you think of each worker as being paid in accordance with the marginal productivity of the job he holds. Since every job is paid its marginal product, no job is cheap or expensive, and there is no reason to direct research and development expenditures toward using or avoiding different types of jobs. No technical pressures exist to alter the distribution of job opportunities so as to reflect shifts in the labor queue.

Induced technical progress may occur, however, if jobs are not paid in accordance with their marginal productivity (a subject that we shall investigate in the next section of this chapter). In that case there is an incentive to direct research expenditures toward using those jobs for which wages are less than marginal products and away from those jobs for which payments exceed marginal products. The relevant question then is whether there is any *systematic* element to the distribution of exploitation across the distribution of job opportunities. For induced technical progress to occur there must be some systematic element that leads groups that are becoming relatively more abundant to be exploited (i.e., paid less than their marginal products).

Such a systematic element would exist if the wages associated with each job were fixed *and the employer paid for training costs*. An increase in the supply of workers with lower training costs would induce some employers to find jobs for which the combination of wages and training costs are less than the marginal productivity of the job. Employers would then have an incentive to direct their research expenditures to expanding the use of a particular skill within their productive processes. The net result in this particular case is a linkage between the labor queue and the distribution of background characteristics. In all other cases exploitation may also occur, but it would not systematically lead to the absorption of factors becoming relatively more abundant. In other words, the induced shifts in the job distribution would not necessarily mirror the initial changes in the labor queue.

In both wage and job competition, factor proportions can change via substitutions in the product market. In wage competition supply increases lead to wage reductions. Goods that make use of the cheaper labor in greater than average amounts become relatively cheaper. Being less expensive, more units are sold and the derived demand for the factor in question rises.[4] A similar process exists within job competition, except that the substitutions depend upon training costs rather than wages. As the supply of workers with some particular training characteristic expands, employers who have been using labor of this type or employers who have been using inferior grades of labor find that they can hire more relatively low-training-cost workers. To the extent that the employer pays for training costs, profits rise and costs fall. With lower costs profit maximization calls for price reductions and a resultant expansion in production and in the use of the new labor supply. The distribution of job opportunities changes not because the distribution of job opportunities has changed for any employer but because the relative size of some employers has increased. (This type of substitution will be examined in greater detail later in this chapter.)

The importance and effects of technical progress are similar in both the wage- and job-competition models. In either case technology is an important ingredient in the distribution of earnings opportunities. In either case changes in relative factor supplies will lead to shifts in factor use through the product market. The major difference occurs in the area of induced technical progress. Induced technical progress does not occur in the wage-competition model, but it can occur in some limited circumstances in the job-competition model. When it does occur, it provides a linkage between the shape of the labor queue and the shape of the job distribution (see below).

The Sociology of Wage Determination

Within the wage-competition framework there are three cases in which the marginal-productivity distribution cannot hold: (1) If there are economies of scale in production, paying each factor its marginal product more than exhausts total output. In that case the output to pay marginal products does not exist. (2) If there are diseconomies of scale in production, paying each factor its marginal product leaves some extra output. Who is to get it? (3) If goods or services are produced in a joint production process in which each factor is absolutely essential to production, marginal productivities cannot be determined. Output drops to zero when any one factor is removed. In none of these cases is there an economic theory of distribution. Some principle other than marginal productivity must determine factor returns. Since there is no economic principle of distribution, bargaining and sociology must operate in the vacuum left by economics.

Although these three cases are important exceptions to marginal productivity, there is an even more fundamental problem, one that affects the possibility of paying people their marginal products in the wage-competition model and paying jobs their marginal products in the job-competition model. Marginal-productivity payments implicitly assume that individuals look only to their own wages and productivity to determine whether or not they are fairly paid. Yet they often look at their neighbor's wages. Preferences are interdependent rather than independent. Utility depends upon relative income rather than absolute income.

As we have seen, a wide variety of more recent evidence points to the existence of interdependent preferences. Over the past three decades, the Gallup poll has asked, "What is the smallest amount of money a family of four needs to get along in this community?" The seventeen answers to this question have all fallen between 53 percent and 59 percent of the average income of the year in which the question was asked.[5] The responses are consistent with respect to the average income in the year in which the question was asked but grow in absolute terms as average incomes grow. Lee Rainwater has shown that when people are asked to categorize others as "poor, getting along, comfortable, prosperous, or rich," they do so rather consistently relative to average incomes.[6] A University of Pennsylvania economist, Richard Esterlin, has reviewed the evidence as to how happiness is related to income in different countries of the world.[7] He finds that happiness (utility?) is almost completely dependent upon one's relative income position within one's own country and almost not at all dependent upon whether one is located in a high-income country or a low-income country.

Actually, utility functions seem to be heavily, if not completely, determined by relative incomes and interdependent preferences rather than absolute incomes and independent preferences. Sociologists call interdependent preferences "relative deprivation," labor economists refer to wage contours, psychologists talk about envy. But whatever the name, interdependent preferences seem to be a widespread phenomenon.

To say that utility functions are highly interdependent, however, is not to say that men are going to be able to implement their interdependent preferences in the labor market. What allows individuals to exercise their interdependent preferences in the labor market? My utility may depend upon the income of my neighbor, but this would not influence my own wages or productivity in the standard wage-competition model. Like it or not, each individual would be paid his marginal product.

The lack of interest in interdependent preferences flows from two factually incorrect assumptions implicit in the wage-competition model. First, individuals are wrongly assumed to have fixed marginal products—skills—that they sell in the labor market. In fact, depending upon their motivations, individuals have a variety of possible marginal products. An unhappy worker can lower his productivity, often in such a manner that it is difficult and expensive to determine whether or not he has in fact done so. Although a worker's happiness or utility is irrelevant if he has a fixed marginal product, it is highly relevant if he has a variable marginal product. Employers need to set a wage structure that elicits voluntary cooperation and motivates their work force. The net result is an avenue whereby interdependent preferences can influence the wage structure.

Second, individuals are wrongly assumed to be interchangeable parts in the production process. In fact, most production processes require a degree of teamwork that can only be acquired through on-the-job experience and a high degree of internal harmony. A production team that has a revolving membership and is unhappy with its wage structure has a lower productivity than a team that is satisfied with its wage structure and has a stable membership. There is a high degree of truth in the old aphorism, "There is no institution that cannot be brought to its knees by working to rule." Efficient economic production is not possible if everyone does just what is required or what is compelled. The net result is an avenue whereby group preferences about a "just" wage structure can have a major impact on production. Because it can have an impact on productivity, it must be taken into account by the employer.

Economists have ignored the problem of getting individuals and groups to produce, but industrial psychologists have made this their key problem.[8] They ask how wages and other incentive systems can be used to promote maximum productivity. Economists see the work decision as a go-no go decision according to which the individual either does or does not sell his time and a fixed productivity for the offered bribe. Industrial psychologists see the work decision as a more continuous decision. A person decides to work, but he also decides how much effort and cooperation to provide. Economists might respond that workers can always be fired if they are not producing at the agreed upon level, but this ignores the costs of hiring and firing, the costs of determining whose productivity is below the norm, and the costs of disrupting the production team. Although there is a limited role for inspection and punishment, productivity in the final analysis depends upon voluntary cooperation, and this requires a wage structure that is in harmony with the interdependent preferences of the work force.

The variability of individual and team production functions creates problems for the marginal-productivity theory of distribution since there is not *a* distribution of marginal products but *many* potential distributions of marginal products. If an employer attempts to pay a group its marginal products and these run counter to the interdependent preferences of the group, the employer may find a completely different set of marginal products from what he originally found. What is worse, an employer who attempts to impose a marginal-productivity distribution of earnings on a contrary set of interdependent preferences may find that productivity substantially decreases in the process. Interdependent preferences lead to a situation in which group and individual performances depend upon having a set of relative wages that the group itself regards as fair and equitable.

Employers are anxious to establish wage structures that their employees regard as equitable since their profits depend upon it. There is a profit-maximizing wage structure, but it need not be a marginal-productivity wage structure. Individual marginal products may have little to do with the structure of wages, for the structure of wages is dependent upon the structure of interdependent preferences rather than upon the structure of marginal products. Employer and employee interests in establishing an equitable distribution are easy to find in the economy. Bargaining about relative wages is at least as pervasive as bargaining about absolute wages. Perhaps the best recent example occurred in Sweden, where college workers struck to increase their pay *relative* to noncollege workers. Their demand was not for more income but for wider wage differentials.

Interdependent preferences combined with self-controlled individual and team production functions reinforce the employer's and employee's interest in reducing or eliminating wage and employment competition above the entry level. Direct wage and employment competition becomes counterproductive in the production environment since wage increases for one worker show up as real wage (utility) reductions for other workers. This loss in utility causes them to lower their own productivity and to disrupt team activities. Given the need for production teamwork and the existence of interdependent preferences, wages are negotiated and set on a team rather than an individual basis. Unions formalize and perhaps strengthen this process, but they do not cause it. Nonunion profit-maximizing employers have the same interest, and nonunion wage structures do not differ noticeably from union wage structures.

Team wage structures lead to different wages for the same skill (one of the major deviant puzzles). Some workers with a particular occupational skill work on high-productivity teams, whereas others work on low-productivity teams. Raw unskilled labor makes a very different wage, depending upon whether it works for General Motors or for a Mississippi plantation. The two workers have exactly the same skill, but they are effectively segregated from each other. The low-wage Mississippi farm worker is not allowed to make a bid for the job of the unskilled auto worker. One's employer becomes an important element in determining one's wages in a way that could not occur under simple wage competition. The net result is a structure of wages that is often more homogeneous within firms or industries than it is within occupations.

Although the wages for particular jobs may be heavily conditioned by the structure of interdependent preferences, this does not prevent each job from being paid in accordance with its marginal product. Within each job category employers hire workers until the marginal productivity of that job is driven down to the level given by the exogenous wage. Each job is paid in accordance with its marginal product, but the distribution of earnings is not determined in a process by which wages are used to clear markets or in which wages are necessarily equal for different employers. Marginal productivity still exists, but it has become a theory of employment rather than a theory of wages. It tells you how many people will be hired, but it does not tell you the wage rate for each skill.

Analytically, the problem is to know what factors produce and alter interdependent preferences and group norms of industrial justice. Sociologists have extensively studied this process under the title of "relative deprivation." [9] Their studies indicate that individuals feel strongly that economic benefits should be proportional to costs (i.e., effort, hardships, talents, and the like) but that equals should be treated equally. Since there are various "costs" and rewards (income, esteem, status, power, etc.) in any situation, the problem immediately arises as to how equals are defined and how proportionality is to be determined. This leads to the difficult problem of "reference group" determination. To what group do you belong and to what groups do you compare yourself when trying to determine whether or not you are being treated equally and proportionally? In any historical situation it is relatively easy to describe the different reference groups that exist, but it has proven difficult, or impossible, to find general principles that govern reference group formation.

Reference groups seem to be both stable and restricted. People look at groups that are economically close to themselves and require great social shocks, such as wars and economic depressions, to change their specifications of relative deprivation. Conceptions of what constitutes proportionality and equality tend to be heavily determined by history and culture. The distributions of the past are considered fair until proven unfair.

This explains why inequalities in the distribution of economic rewards that are much larger than inequalities in the distribution of personal characteristics seem to cause little dissatisfaction, and why people tend to ask for rather modest amounts when asked how much additional income they would like to be making. The happiest people seem to be those who do relatively well within their own reference group rather than those who do relatively well across the entire economy.

The importance of social shocks can be seen in the income changes caused by the Great Depression and World War II. In the Great Depression an economic collapse provided the mechanism for change. Large incomes simply had farther to fall than small incomes. In World War II there was a consensus that the economic burdens of the war should be relatively equally ("equal sacrifice") shared, so the federal government used its economic controls over wages to achieve more equality. Wage policies during World War II were a manifestation of a change in the sociology of what constitutes "fair" wage differentials or relative deprivation. As a consequence of the widespread consensus that wage differentials should be reduced, it was possible to reduce wage differentials deliberately. After the wage differentials of the Great Depression and World War II had become embedded in the labor market for a number of years, they became the new standard of relative deprivation and were regarded as "just" even after the egalitarian pressures of World War II had disappeared. Basically, the same differentials exist to this day, thirty years later.

It is important to note, however, that the new standards were not imposed by government on a reluctant population but were imposed on the labor market by popular beliefs as to what constituted equity in wartime. No one knows how to engineer such changes in less extreme situations. Indeed, some sociologists have concluded that only wars can cause changes in norms of relative deprivation.

The labor economics literature discusses the concept of relative deprivation under a different name—wage contours.[10] As in relative deprivation, workers see themselves as belonging to a particular wage contour that has some fixed wage relative to workers in other contours. Over time, relative wages are very stable across contours.

From the perspective of the wage-contour hypothesis, wage and price controls can play an important role in controlling inflation. One of the major elements leading to wage inflation is the leapfrogging that occurs when wage structures accidentally get out of line with historical wage contours. One group gets ahead of its historical position and other groups attempt to reestablish their historical position, or even to get ahead so as to "get even" for the initial violation of "equity." As with relative deprivation, the wage-contour theory runs into problems. Thus, it seems to be impossible to find general principles that explain why specific wage contours exist. This makes it difficult to know how to alter reference groups or wage contours, but it in no way diminishes their importance to the structure of wages.

If utility functions are interdependent and conditioned by experience and history, relative wages may be rigid regardless of changes in the underlying supply and demand conditions. The historical wage differentials have the sanction of time and are assumed to be just until proven unjust. Moreover, the longer they exist, the more they condition workers' beliefs about what constitutes justice and injustice.[11] The high degree of stability in the post–World War II wage structure is probably more an indicator of stable interdependent preferences than it is an indication of stability in the underlying distribution of technology.

To say that relative earnings are conditioned by interdependent preferences is not to say that relative earnings are immutable. Slow changes in relative earnings might be accepted since they never seem to challenge the accepted norms. Relative deprivation does, however, stop short-run wage changes from being used as a market-clearing mechanism. The static benefits to be gained by clearing markets with wage changes simply are not large enough to offset the losses from the labor disruptions that would follow.

Relative deprivation reinforces the employer's interest in reducing wage and employment competition. The desire to promote training and the acceptance of technical change is the carrot leading to reduced wage and employment competition; the consequences of violating the norms of relative deprivation are the stick preventing competitive wage and employment policies. The net result is a rigid structure of wages that provides little opportunity to bid into a job by being willing to accept lower wages.

Thus, if we are to understand the structure of earnings and the factors that produce changes in it, we shall need a sociology or psychology of interdependent preferences. Lacking a consistent theory of reference group determination, the sociology of wage determination is in a rudimentary form, but this does not diminish its importance. Workers' views about what constitutes an "equitable" wage structure have an important role to play in the determination of wages. Relative deprivation, wage contours, interdependent preferences, and envy all mean that economic stratification is man-made but that it is, to a large extent, self-perpetuating and autonomous.

The Distribution of Training Costs

The distribution of training costs—the shape of the labor queue—is the third factor affecting the distribution of job opportunities. When the distribution of training costs is altered, changes are induced in the distribution of job opportunities. The changes that occur are dependent upon the answer to the following four questions:

1. Who bears training costs—the employee or the employer?
2. What set of background characteristics did the individual have prior to improving his characteristics and what set of background characteristics does the individual possess after improvements in his characteristics?
3. What is the elasticity of training costs with respect to improvements in background characteristics across the distribution of job opportunities? Do changes in background characteristics have a large or a small effect on training costs?
4. What is the distribution of training costs across the distribution of job opportunities? Are training costs large or small at each earnings level?

The importance of each of the four questions can be seen in relation to Diagram 2.

Who bears training costs is important because it determines who pays for training and who will have such payments subtracted from his income. Suppose all training costs are paid by employees. In that case subtractions would be made from an employee's earnings to compensate the employer for training costs. The employee's net earnings (net of training costs) or his

DIAGRAM 2
Gross and Net Marginal Products of Employees

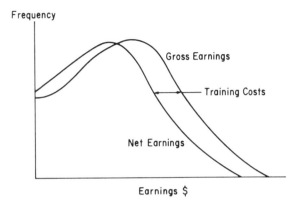

reported earnings would be less than his gross earnings. (If no training cost payments were required, the employee would have had higher earnings than those he actually enjoyed and reported.) Thus, we could think of plotting two earnings figures for each worker—his gross earnings and his net earnings. The difference between the two would be his costs of training. If training costs had been completely borne by employers, then no subtractions would be made from an employee's earnings and his net and gross earnings would be identical. Training costs would, however, lower income of employers and would have to be subtracted from their gross income along with other expenses to yield a net income or profit figure.

The precise shift in background characteristics is important because it determines where training costs will be reduced on the distribution of job opportunities. If training costs for high-earnings workers are reduced, then the net earnings curve will move closer to the gross earnings curve for high-earnings workers. Conversely, if training costs are reduced for low-earnings workers, then the net earnings curve will move closer to the gross earnings curve at the lower end of the job distribution. Depending upon the precise shift in background characteristics or training costs, the distribution of reported earnings could become more or less equal even though there were no changes in the distribution of gross earnings.[12]

The elasticity of training costs with respect to background characteristics and the distribution of training costs are important because together they determine the size of the training-costs reductions and the extent of net-earnings increases that will emerge from any change in the distribution of background characteristics. If elasticities are high, background characteristics have a large effect on training costs. They fall rapidly in percentage terms when characteristics are improved. The absolute size of training costs at each net-earnings level is important since the percentage reductions in training costs determined by the elasticities are multiplied by the absolute size of training costs to determine the increase in net dollar earnings. If elasticities are large but training costs are small, the net effect will still be a small dollar increase in reported earnings.

For the sake of a simple illustration, assume that education is the only background characteristic and that there are three classes of education: grade-school workers, high-school workers, and college workers. To simplify the analysis even further, assume a deterministic world in which all college workers are preferred to all high-school workers, who in turn are preferred to all grade-school workers. Employees pay for training costs. As Diagram 3 indicates, this yields a distribution of job opportunities and earnings for each group even though the members of each group have homogeneous background characteristics.

Within each educational group, workers are given different amounts of on-the-job training so that *ex post* they have different productivities even though they were exactly equal *ex ante* and held identical positions in the labor queue. Although they were all initially equal, they were randomly selected to receive different amounts of training and earnings.

As an initial example of how changes in the distribution of

DIAGRAM 3
Distribution of Gross and Net Earnings

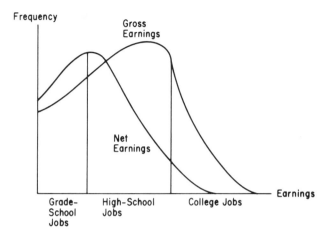

training costs influence the distribution of job opportunities, assume that employees bear training costs. In this case improvements in background characteristics can have no impact upon gross earnings, but lower training costs will shift the distribution of net earnings (measured earnings). Employees with lower training costs will find that they need to pay their employers less of the gross earnings as a payment for training. As mentioned, the size of the reduction depends upon answers to questions three and four (see Diagram 3).

Now assume that the supply of college workers has been increased by educating high-school workers (reducing the supply of high-school workers). Employers would substitute college workers for high-school laborers in what had been the best (highest earnings) high-school jobs, since there is now a larger supply of low-training-cost, college-educated workers. The new college workers would receive the same jobs that had previously gone to high-school laborers, but the observed wages (net earnings) would rise above the level paid high-school employees in

116

DIAGRAM 4
*Possible Changes in Distribution of Earnings
from Transforming High-School Workers
into College Workers*

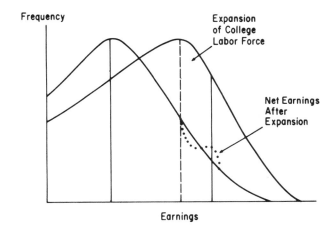

these jobs since training costs have been reduced. The number of jobs with high net earnings increases even though the distribution of gross earnings remains unchanged. A possible shift in net earnings is indicated by the dotted line in Diagram 4.

The precise shift in the distribution of background characteristics is important since an individual's job opportunities are affected by his *relative* position in the labor queue. For example, the position of high-school laborers differs depending upon whether an increase in the supply of college employees arises from transforming existing high-school laborers into college laborers or whether it arises from transforming existing grade-school laborers into college laborers by providing the latter with both a high-school and a college education.

In the first case, high-school workers must compete against a larger supply of college workers, but there are also fewer high-school workers to provide intragroup competition. The average earnings of high-school workers fall since they are deprived of what were their best earnings possibilities (they are in a less advantageous lottery), but not as much as earnings do in the second case, when grade-school workers are transformed into college workers. In this case high-school workers must compete against more college workers and against the same number of high-school workers. This means that the average earnings of high-school workers fall even more than they do in the first case. In the new lottery for high-school workers, they are deprived of what had been their highest earnings opportunities and are forced to add some low-earnings jobs that had previously been reserved for grade-school workers (see Diagram 5).

Because high-school workers have lower training costs in these

DIAGRAM 5

Possible Changes in the Distribution of Earnings
from Transforming Grade-School Workers into
College Workers

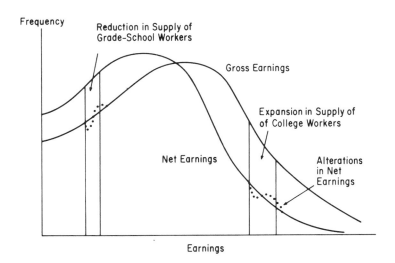

new low-earnings jobs, the jobs will have higher net earnings than when they were reserved for grade-school workers, but there will still be below-average earnings opportunities for high-school workers. The possible changes that might arise from transforming grade-school workers into college workers are shown in Diagram 5. There are induced alterations in net earnings at two margins—the margin between college and high-school jobs and the margin between high-school and grade-school jobs—and the high-school work force is forced farther down the distribution of job opportunities.

The differences between the wage-competition hypothesis and the job-competition hypothesis can be clearly seen in their different predictions as to what would happen as a result of an exogenous increase in the supply of college-educated labor. Under the wage-competition hypothesis, an exogenous increase in the supply of college workers and an exogenous reduction in the supply of grade-school workers would lead to a lower equilibrium wage for college workers, a higher equilibrium wage for grade-school workers, and an unchanged equilibrium wage for high-school workers. Grade-school wages would rise relative to high-school and college wages, and college wages would fall relative to high-school wages. Overall, a more equal distribution of earnings would emerge. Within each educational classification workers would be paid the same wage.

Under the job-competition hypothesis, the same supply changes would result in a very different set of predictions. Average earnings would fall for each of the three educational groups. A larger supply of college workers would extend the college work force farther down the distribution of job opportunities. In the process the average college wage would fall. With more college workers, high-school workers and grade-school workers would be forced farther down the distribution of job opportunities and their average wages would also fall. Changes in relative earnings would depend upon the shape of the earnings distribution and the changes in net earnings due to lower training costs. Assuming that there is a greater density of workers at the grade school–high school margin than at the high school–college margin, average college wages would fall faster than average high-school wages. An extra million college workers might, for example, cause the marginal college wage to fall by $1,000, whereas an extra million high-school (or better) workers might cause the marginal high-school wage to fall by only $500. The results would be an increase in high-school earnings relative to college earnings.

Depending upon the observed net wage increases at the two margins, the entire distribution of earnings might become more or less equal. If the reduction in training costs is larger at the high school–college margin than at the grade school–high school margin, then the entire distribution of earnings would become more unequal. More of total earnings are now concentrated in the upper tail of the earnings distribution. If training cost reductions were large at the grade school–high school margin, the entire distribution of earnings would become more equal.

Within each group there would be a distribution of earnings rather than an equilibrium wage. Depending upon the overall shape of the earnings distribution, predictions could be made as to what would happen to the intragroup inequalities. As Diagram 5 indicates, college earnings would become more equal since a more equal (dense) than average group of workers has been added to the labor force.[13] Similarly, grade-school workers would end up with a more equal distribution of earnings since they lose a group of high-earnings workers and are squeezed back into the relatively flat lower tail of the earnings distribution. The distribution of earnings among high-school workers would once again depend upon the density of workers at the two margins. Since the high school–college margin is less dense than the grade school–high school margin, high-school workers are being squeezed into a more concentrated part of the overall earnings distribution and their intragroup distribution of earnings also becomes more equal. As a consequence, wages could equalize within each group even though they were at the same time becoming less equal across the entire distribution of earnings.

Since the wage-competition and job-competition models differ substantially in their predictions as to what would happen as the result of an exogenous shift in the supplies of different types of labor, it is clearly possible, at least in principle, to test which of the two theories is operative in particular circumstances. As we shall see later, different policy recommendations also follow.

Up to this point we have been assuming that employees bear training costs. A different set of predictions would occur if we were to assume that employers pay training costs. When employers pay for training costs, there is no difference between gross and net earnings. Instead, reductions in training costs show up as extra profits for the employer. His costs have been reduced. In this case the elasticity of training costs with respect to background characteristics and the absolute size of training costs are important since together they determine the profit increases (training costs reductions) that will result from any shift in background characteristics.

Assuming competitive product markets, the industries with the high profits will lower prices and expand. As these industries and employers expand, their relative weight as employers will grow. Since the national distribution of job opportunities is the summation of underlying firm distributions of job opportunities, increasing the relative size of particular employers will alter the shape of the national job distribution. The relative weight of the expanding firms will increase, and other firms will find that they cannot hire labor because of the shift in background characteristics and their relative importance will fall.

For example, assume that the shift in background characteristics leads to a doubling of the size of a firm with job distribution "A" and to the elimination of a firm with job distribution "B" (see Diagram 6). This might lead to a shift in the national job distribution such as that shown in Diagram 6. To determine the precise shift in the distribution of job opportunities it would be necessary to know the job distribution characteristics of both the expanding and contracting firm. Here again a more equal distribution of background characteristics could lead to a more unequal distribution of earnings. If the expanding job opportunities are farther above the median income than the contracting job opportunities are below it, earnings become more unequal.

As these examples indicate, changes in the shape of the labor queue do not automatically generate similar changes in the

DIAGRAM 6
*Induced Changes in the Distribution of Job Opportunities
When Employers Bear Training Costs*

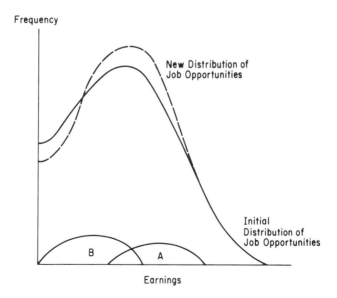

shape of the job distribution. A more equal labor queue may or may not lead to a more equal distribution of earnings. Even the basic shapes of the two distributions may differ substantially. Imagine, for example, that a homogeneous (equal training costs) group of workers was distributed across a dispersed job distribution. In this case workers would be picked at random and given different amounts of on-the-job training. After being trained, they would be different workers earning different wages even though they were initially identical and even though they were equally willing to make human capital investments. Since the employer's demand for labor determines the number of training slots, there simply may not be enough training slots to go around. As a consequence, someone gets left out and has lower earnings. The result might be an egalitarian labor queue and an inegalitarian distribution of earnings (jobs). Conversely, a widely dispersed group of workers (with respect to training costs) might be allocated across a rather narrow distribution of job opportunities. In this case on-the-job training would be allocated to make the distribution of earnings or jobs much more egalitarian than the distribution of the labor queue.

A Gedanken Experiment

Imagine the following mental experiment: In 1949 you were told that by 1969 the adult white male labor force was going to change its characteristics from 47 percent grade-school workers, 38 percent high-school workers, and 15 percent college workers to 20 percent grade-school workers, 51 percent high-school workers, and 28 percent college workers.[14] What would you have predicted about the 1969 distribution of earnings given these actual changes in the distribution of education?

To make the mental (gedanken) experiment realistic, each reader should make his own predictions. But just as a foil to start the thinking process, what would have been predicted by the believer in simple wage competition who treated the problem as one of shifting relative supplies of labor? The supply curve of grade-school labor is predicted to shift rapidly to the left, whereas the supply curve of both college and high-school labor is predicted to shift to the right but with a much larger relative shift for college labor than for high-school labor. Rising productivity would have been expected to lead to higher absolute wages for each group, but with these predicted shifts in supply curves, the wages of grade-school workers would rise relative to both high-school and college workers. And since the college labor force is predicted to grow much more rapidly than the high-school labor force, college wages would fall relative to high-school wages. Such changes in relative wages would have led to a more equal overall distribution of earnings. Nothing would have been predicted about intragroup distributions of earnings since the wage-competition model has nothing to say about this phenomenon.

What would have been predicted by an application of the job-competition model? Knowing nothing else about the future, the user of the job-competition model would also treat the problem as if it were one of shifting relative supplies of labor. As in the wage-competition model, rising productivity would have led to absolute income increases for each group, but the predictions about relative wages would have differed substantially.

Additional supplies of college and high-school laborers would force both these two groups and grade-school workers farther down the job distribution. As a result, the earnings of all three groups would fall relative to the national average. Being squeezed into the lower tail of the earnings distribution, grade-school earnings would fall relative to both high-school and college earnings. Given a large absolute expansion in the high-school labor force and the push-down effect of more college labor, high-school earnings would fall relative to college earnings.

Assuming that training costs are larger for high-income jobs than for low-income jobs, the entire distribution of earnings would become more unequal. The expansion of earnings at the high school–college margin in the upper part of the earnings distribution is larger than the expansion of earnings at the grade school–high school margin in the lower part of the earnings distribution.

Within each group the job-competition model would predict earnings equalization. The college labor force is extending into denser and denser portions of the earnings distribution. As a consequence, its earnings become more equally distributed. High-school incomes also become more equally distributed since they are also forced back into a denser region of the entire earnings distribution. Grade-school earnings become more equal since they lose some of the relative high-earnings opportunities.

Given these two sets of predictions, what actually happened between 1949 and 1969? As has been already noted in Chapter 4, the distribution of earnings became slightly more unequal over these two decades. The coefficient of determination (variance divided by the mean) increased by 1 percent. As the data in Table 16 indicate, the increasing college work force spread down the earnings distribution and forced high-school workers to take lower paying jobs. The effects were compounded for grade-school workers since they faced competition from more college workers and more high-school workers. Between 1949 and 1969 the percentage of grade-school workers holding jobs in the top decile of jobs fell from 4.3 percent to 1.7 percent. Similar declines can be seen for both high-school and college workers. The proportions of workers holding jobs in the top decile fell from 10.5 percent to 6.5 percent for high-school workers and from 28.9 percent to 25.6 percent for college workers. Throughout Table 16 push-down effects are evident.

An examination of average incomes reveals that all three groups fell relative to the national average. The average earnings of college workers fell from 148 percent to 144 percent of the national average, that of high-school workers fell from 119

TABLE 16
Distribution of Jobs over Each Education Class
(Adult White Males)

Figures for:
1950—Money Income in 1949, Population in 1950
1970—Money Income in 1969, Population in 1970

QUALITY OF JOBS (DETERMINED BY INCOME OF TOTAL MALES WITH INCOME, 25 YEARS AND OLDER)	ELEMENTARY (1950)	ELEMENTARY (1970)	HIGH SCHOOL (1950)	HIGH SCHOOL (1970)	COLLEGE (1950)	COLL (197
10% best jobs Provide income of: 1950: $5,239.3 and up 1970: $15,000 and up	4.3	1.7	10.5	6.5	28.9	25
Second best 10% 1950: $4,028.84–$5,239.2 1970: $12,506.26–$14,999	6.0	3.5	13.2	11.3	16.3	14
Third best 10% 1950: $4,028.84–$5,239.2 1970: $12,506.26–$14,999	7.6	3.5	13.4	11.3	10.0	14
Fourth 10% 1950: $3,025.2–$3,519.6 1970: $7,573.9–$8,751	7.7	6.2	13.4	12.5	9.9	9
Fifth 10% 1950: $2,101–$2,553.5 1970: $6,449.6–$7,573.8	9.4	6.9	12.1	12.5	6.9	8
Sixth 10% 1950: $2,101–$2,553.5 1970: $6,449.6–$7,573.8	10.7	8.7	10.6	12.4	6.1	7
Seventh 10% 1950: $1,530–$2,553.5 1970: $5,148.3–$6,449.5	11.8	11.3	9.0	11.5	6.0	5
Eighth 10% 1950: $706–$1,529 1970: $3,576.6–$5,148.2	13.1	15.6	7.0	9.3	6.2	5
Ninth 10% 1950: $270.6–$705 1970: $2,008.2–$3,576.5	14.8	19.6	5.2	7.1	4.6	4
10% Worst Jobs 1950: $0–$270.5 1970: $0–$2,008.1	14.4	23.0	5.6	5.5	5.1	3
	100	100	100	100	100	10

Source: Compiled from data in U.S. Bureau of the Census, *Current Population Reports: Consumer Income 1969* (Washington, I Government Printing Office, 1970), p. 101; and U.S. Bureau of the Census, *U.S. Census of the Population: 1950* (Washington I Government Printing Office, 1953), pp. 5B–108.

percent to 105 percent of the national average, and that of grade-school workers fell from 75 percent to 57 percent of the national average. College earnings rose relative to both other groups—from 124 percent to 137 percent of high-school workers' earnings and from 198 percent to 254 percent of grade-school workers' earnings. Conversely, grade-school workers fell relative to both other groups—from 50 percent to 39 percent of college workers' earnings and from 63 percent to 54 percent of high-school workers' earnings. This leaves high-school earnings falling relative to college earnings and rising relative to grade-school earnings.

Within each of the three groups, wages equalized. The earnings of the top quartile of the college work force fell from 53.9 percent to 46.0 percent of the total earnings of the college group, whereas the earnings of the bottom quartile rose from 6.3 percent to 9.0 percent of the total. Similarly, the earnings of the top quartile of high-school workers fell from 46.0 percent to 41.6 percent of total high-school earnings, whereas the earnings of the bottom quartile rose from 8.2 percent to 10.2 percent of the total. Among grade-school workers the top quartile fell from 53.5 percent to 49.4 percent of total grade-school earnings and the bottom quartile rose from 2.9 percent to 6.6 percent.

As this gedanken experiment indicates, the actual changes in the distribution of earnings are in accordance with what would have been predicted on the basis of job competition. Although the results are suggestive, they do not prove that the job-competition model is right and that other models are wrong. The job-competition model was constructed in light of the actual changes in the distribution of earnings. The basic argument for the job-competition model must be that it provides a simpler and more consistent explanation of the facts. In the end each reader must perform his or her own gedanken experiment and decide which model, or which combination of models, provides the best explanation of what has occurred.

Conclusions

Although the illustrations of the job-competition model have used education as the background characteristic that affects training costs, education is obviously not the only relevant factor. It has been used in the illustrations because it is a major factor and because it is one of the few background characteristics that is regularly measured and incorporated in basic statistical data. The statistical data exist to examine the impacts of education but they do not exist to examine the impacts of other factors such as personality.

The whole question of what particular personal characteristics contribute to economic ability—lower training costs—is one of the key questions in the applications of a job-competition model, but it is also a relevant question in most other distributional theories. Because of the ease of measurement, education and IQ probably have been overemphasized as sources of economic ability. Physical dexterity, personality, or a host of other characteristics may eventually prove to be more important personal background variables than those we typically consider.

6

THE DISTRIBUTION
OF PHYSICAL WEALTH

IN ADDITION to the great concentration in ownership (see Chapter 1), our observer of the economic game would notice two other factors when he looked at the distribution of physical wealth. Large fortunes are passed from generation to generation and great fortunes occur suddenly.

Table 17 indicates the importance of inheritances for the

TABLE 17
Inherited Assets

1962 INCOME	MEAN WEALTH	NONE	SOME	SMALL	SUBSTANTIAL
$0–4,999	$9,731	84%	16%	16%	6%
5,000–9,999	17,626	84	16	12	4
10,000–14,999	30,389	84	16	11	5
15,000–24,999	74,329	73	27	21	6
25,000–49,999	267,996	58	42	34	8
50,000–99,995 *	789,582	71	26	12	14
100,000 and over *	1,554,152	31	66	9	57

* 3 percent not ascertained
Source: Dorothy Projector and Gertrude Weiss, *Survey of Financial Characteristics of Consumers,* Federal Reserve Technical Paper (Washington, D.C.: Government Printing Office, 1966), p. 148.

population as a whole. For most income classes inherited wealth affects a small and roughly constant proportion of the population, but for the highest income group—a group with a mean wealth of $1,554,152—it rises dramatically to become the dominant factor. Among these families 57 percent reported inheriting a substantial proportion of their assets, and 66 percent reported some inheritance. For many of this latter group, inheritances were important even though they did not account for the bulk of their assets. A small relative amount can be a large absolute amount and provide the initial capital without which more cannot be acquired.

As you move up the scale to great fortunes, inheritance increases its importance. *Fortune* magazine provides the best window on large fortunes since it periodically examines the very wealthy by name (see Appendix B). In 1957 it found seventy-six individuals with wealth in excess of $75 million,[1] forty-one of whom were recipients of substantial inheritances. In 1968 it listed sixty-six individuals with fortunes in excess of $150 million.[2] Since 1957, the *Fortune* list has not specifically identified who inherited substantial wealth, but an examination of the lists indicates no significant shift in the proportion of the very wealthy who inherit wealth. Roughly speaking, about 50 percent of the great fortunes are inherited fortunes.

In addition to inheritance the distribution of wealth is marked by the rapid accumulation of great wealth—an accumulation so rapid that it cannot come about by a patient process of savings and investment. In the Federal Reserve Board study, 43 percent of the wealthiest group did not inherit a substantial amount and 31 percent inherited nothing. Whereas forty-one out of the seventy-six wealthiest individuals in the United States in 1957 inherited great wealth according to *Fortune*, thirty-five individuals did not. Even more to the point, in 1973 *Fortune* listed thirty-nine individuals who had made from $50 to $700 million in the previous *five* years without inheriting wealth or having previously been on *Fortune*'s list of the wealthiest, and one individual whose wealth had gone from $50 million to over $500 million in the same *five* years.[3]

The prevalence of instant wealth is also visible if one looks at the names of the richest Americans (see Appendix B, pp. 231–239). True, the current generation of Rockefellers, Mellons, Fords, Duponts, Whitneys, and Posts may have inherited their wealth, but their fortunes were made very quickly at some point in the past. Their families did not become rich over a long period of time but made their fortunes in a matter of a few years.

After looking at these facts about the distribution of wealth, our observer would have three basic questions. First, why is the distribution of wealth so much more unequal than the distribution of earnings or the presumed normal distribution of abilities? Second, why are large inheritances passed from generation to generation? Third, how can you explain the quick, almost instantaneous, generation of very large fortunes?

A Patient, Self-Limiting Process of Accumulation

If our observer were to retreat to the library and look at the economics of wealth accumulation, what would he find?

He would find that neoclassical economics treats wealth as stored future consumption. Each individual starts off his life with some initial inheritance of wealth provided by his parents and some earnings potential from his raw labor.[4] Inheritances plus raw earnings place a limit on his potential consumption in the current period of time. The individual can, however, devote some of his potential current consumption to savings and investment so as to enhance his future consumption potential. This trade-off between present and future consumption is at the heart of the standard economic rules for wealth accumulation.

The amount of wealth that any individual will accumulate depends upon three empirical factors. First, what is the individual's initial budget constraint? How much wealth does he or she inherit and what is his or her raw earnings potential? Second, what opportunities for investment (exchanging present consumption for future consumption) are presented by the economy? What is the rate of return on savings and investment? Third, what is the individual's rate of time preference? At what exchange rate is the individual willing to give up consumption today to have consumption tomorrow? If an individual, for example, is willing to trade $1 worth of consumption this year for $1.10 worth of consumption next year, this means that he has a 10 percent rate of time preference. He will undertake any investment projects that earn more than a 10 percent rate of return and will reject any investment projects that earn less than a 10 percent rate of return.

Although time preferences are partly a matter of taste, there is also a systematic interaction between time preferences and budget constraints. The lower the initial budget constraint, the higher the rate of time preference for any given pattern of tastes. This can be most clearly seen by imagining a man on the edge of starvation. If he does not receive food today, he will die. Such a man rationally has an infinite rate of time preference. There is no rate at which he would be willing to trade consumption today for more consumption tomorrow. He will be dead tomorrow if he does not consume today. As a result, the rate of time preference will fall as the individual's budget constraint rises.

Other individuals affect his investment decisions since their decisions to invest, or not to invest, determine the market's competitive rate of return on being willing to give up current consumption privileges. If other individuals choose to save, market interest rates will be lower than if they do not choose to save and there is a greater scarcity of capital funds. Competitive capital markets lead to a situation in which every individual borrows or lends at the same rate and as a consequence has the same marginal rate of time preference. Suppose, for example, that the market rate of return is 10 percent per year. Imagine an individual not in equilibrium with a rate of time preference in excess of 10 percent (i.e., he is not willing to trade $1 worth of consumption today for $1.10 worth of consumption next year). Such an individual would reduce his future consumption and increase his present consumption until he was just indifferent between $1 this year and $1.10 next year. Doing this would raise his lifetime utility since he would be substituting a more valued good (today's consumption) for a less valued good (tomorrow's consumption). Conversely, an individual with a rate of time preference below 10 percent would find that he could raise his lifetime utility by consuming less today and consuming more tomorrow. He also would rearrange his lifetime pattern of consumption until his rate of time preference was brought back into equilibrium with the market rate of return.

As a result, each individual will save and invest some fraction of his initial consumption potential and devote it to providing future consumption benefits. His wealth would be given by the current price of the legal title to his future consumption benefits. This price is easily determined by discounting these future consumption benefits to yield a net present value. The market rate of return is the appropriate discount rate since it is equal to everyone's marginal rate of time preference.

This process of wealth accumulation leads to several empirical propositions about the distribution of wealth. First, any initial inequalities in the distribution of wealth (or any random shocks that produce inequalities) are apt to be magnified in the process of accumulation. Those with higher budget constraints will (on the average) have lower rates of time preference, be willing to accept lower-yielding investment opportunities, and therefore will devote a larger fraction of their potential current consumption to providing future consumption. Thus, any differences in wealth will tend to cumulate over time. Those with higher incomes will devote larger fractions of their incomes to providing higher incomes in the future. This occurs even if every individual has an identical pattern of time preferences or if time preference patterns are randomly distributed across the population. A rational economic investment calculus expands inequalities; it does not contract them.

Second, wealth accumulation is a patient process of savings and investment. To accumulate great fortunes requires substantial periods of time. For example, an individual who started with $10,000 in initial investment funds and who reinvested all of the interest would require thirty years to accumulate $100,000 with an 8 percent market rate of return (sixty years would be necessary to accumulate $1 million), and, given taxes, much longer periods of time would be necessary to accumulate even modest fortunes. Thus, with a 50 percent tax rate approximately sixty years would be necessary to build $10,000 into $100,000, and even relatively small fortunes would require several lifetimes of patient self-denial and accumulation.

Third, although inequalities in wealth cumulate, the inequalities are inherently self-limiting. There is a limit beyond which it does not pay to accumulate more wealth. Every individual has a finite lifetime and must allocate his time optimally across investment, production, and consumption activities. The time constraint is particularly severe in the case of human wealth. Since extensive amounts of time are necessary both to acquire and to use human capital, there is a very low limit to the amount of human capital that any individual can profitably acquire and use. As an individual accumulates human capital, the opportunity cost of his time rises and eventually leads to a situation in which it no longer pays him to acquire more human capital. With physical capital, time constraints are not as severe. Large financial investments can be made quickly, and the individual does not need to use his own time to employ physical capital.

In addition to investment and production time constraints, however, time constraints also emerge from the technology of consumption. Since time is necessary to consume and since wealth is stored future consumption, a finite life-span implies a maximum amount of wealth (future consumption) that any individual can use. Because of time budget constraints, economic man would also start to de-accumulate at some point in his lifetime. As an individual grows older, the probability of dying grows larger. The value of future consumption falls since the individual is less and less likely to be alive to enjoy it. Analytically, this means that the individual's rate of time preferences grows.[5] Consumption next year has less and less value relative to consumption this year. Every economic man should want to have zero assets on the day of death since at that point future consumption would have no value.

Time budget constraints lead to a rapidly diminishing marginal utility of future consumption expenditures (wealth). The problem is easily seen by performing the mental experiment of imagining the maximum amount of money that you could use to promote your own consumption welfare. Remember that many of the things you might purchase—houses, paintings, etc. —are not pure consumption expenditures but partly investments. Consumption expenditures on housing, for example, are the costs of operating a home or homes minus any market appreciation in the value of those homes or rents earned while the home was not being personally used. Many of the expenditures associated with the high living standards of the very rich are not pure consumption expenditures but partly investment expenditures. Personal expenditures can be much higher than personal consumption. In any period of time there is clearly a finite amount of consumption expenditures that can be used. Corresponding to this limit should be a limit on the amount of wealth that any individual would wish to accumulate.

Puzzles

How would our observer of the economic game compare what he sees with what he finds inscribed in the neoclassical economic rule book? The first proposition seems in basic accordance with what is observed. Savings rates rise as income and wealth rise.[6] This automatically leads to a process whereby initial differences in wealth are expanded. Since the acquisition and use of physical capital is less subject to personal time constraints than the acquisition and use of human capital, individuals will shift more and more toward physical investments as they grow wealthier. As a result, we would expect the distribution of physical wealth to be much more unequal than the distribution of earnings (human capital). And so it is.

The empirical problems arise with propositions two and three. Wealth does not seem to arise from a patient process of savings and reinvestment. It arises too quickly. The pattern of inheritances also does not seem to be in accordance with what would be expected of economic man. Large fortunes are passed from generation to generation; too much wealth is accumulated over a lifetime, and it does not seem to be possible to find the turning points where individuals start to de-accumulate.

If you think of the time necessary to consume all of the wealth possessed by *Fortune*'s wealthiest Americans, their fortunes are too large. Potential consumption expenditures exceed the time available for consumption. This is especially true since the average age of the sixty-six individuals with fortunes over $150 million was sixty-five. Economic man does not accumulate a fortune he cannot use, yet these individuals have fortunes they cannot possibly consume.

Similarly, it seems impossible to find the predicted turning

TABLE 18

Savings Rates by Age *

AGE OF FAMILY HEAD	SAVINGS RATE
Under 25	25.7%
25–34	31.9
35–44	29.8
45–54	30.0
55–64	28.0
65–74	28.2
75 and over	30.7
Total	29.8

* Measures net change in liabilities and assets rather than more conventional savings rates.
Source: U.S. Department of Labor, *Survey of Consumer Expenditures,* BLS Report 237 (Washington, D.C.: Government Printing Office, 1965), p. 11.

point where individuals start to de-accumulate in expectation of death. It simply does not exist. At every age (see Table 18) savings rates are positive. Individuals typically save—storing up future consumption—right up to their day of death. By contrast, economic man starts de-accumulating to reach zero wealth on his day of death, and the richer he is the earlier he must start de-accumulating if he is to have time to make use of all of his potential consumption privileges.

Although there does not seem to be any way to bring the rapid generation of large fortunes into the general-equilibrium neoclassical model of wealth accumulation, there is a conventional technique for rescuing the neoclassical model of wealth accumulation from the shoals of the empirical facts about inheritances. The simple model must be expanded to allow individuals to gain utility from their children's consumption as well as from their own. No one quarrels with this modification of the basic model, but the implications of the modifications need to be examined. Under examination they fail to explain what must be explained.

Desires to raise the consumption of one's children still exist within the budget constraints imposed by time and wealth. The only difference is that the individuals now make trade-offs not only between their own present and future consumption but between their own present and future consumption and their children's present and future consumption. Some of the motivations in this expanded calculus of trade-offs lead to more accumulation, but many lead to less. To the extent that the individual thinks the present consumption of his children is more valuable than his own future consumption, accumulation will be retarded. Only in the case where the individual decides that the future consumption of his children is more important than his present and future consumption and their present consumption will wealth accumulation be accentuated.

But even in this latter case there will still be a rather limited maximum amount of wealth that an individual would wish to accumulate. At any moment economic man has a rate of time preference given by the market rate of interest. He saves or dissaves to bring his time preferences into equilibrium with the market rate of interest. This rate of time preference also serves as his discount rate and tells him how far to look into the future. Regardless of his interests in future generations, he is not going to make provision for them into the infinite future. With an 8 percent market rate of interest, he knows that $1 worth of consumption benefits thirty years from now has a present value of only 10 cents regardless of whether he or someone else is going to enjoy them. The provision of future consumption benefits quickly approaches zero with any reasonable market rate of interest, and this leads to a finite desire for accumulation. Basically, the amount that can be consumed over the next thirty to forty years limits the total amount that would be accumulated. If children want or are expected to earn some of their own income, the maximum amount of parental accumulation would be even smaller.

The desire to aid one's children in the future also does not necessarily lead to any modification in the expected lifetime pattern of wealth accumulation. If an individual simply wishes to aid his children, he will transfer assets to them before death. This lowers the estate tax that the children will pay (see below) and provides them extra economic freedom. They can then decide whether present or future consumption is more valuable to them. If wealth is given away before death, there still will be a turning point toward de-accumulation and the individual will still be progressing toward zero assets at death even if he is not personally consuming his wealth. To change the lifetime pattern of wealth accumulation, one must assume that a parent is interested in his children's future consumption but not in their current consumption, and that he does not trust them to limit their current consumption.

To determine the net effects of inheritances on the distribution of wealth, it is also necessary to think about the rational actions of sons or daughters who know that they will be receiving inheritances. They are making their own trade-offs between present and future consumption benefits. To the extent that parents provide for future consumption benefits, economic man's children will cut back on their own provision of future consumption benefits. Basically, what is saved by one generation will be dissaved by another. Net saving only rises in accordance with the second generation's pattern of time preferences and budget constraint. Offsetting actions always occur unless the second generation is ignorant of the provisions by the first generation or is assumed to be irrational.

The mystery of large fortunes at time of death is further compounded by the U.S. tax law. Under our laws a substantial amount of money can be given to the next generation tax-free if it is given before death, and all of it can be given at much lower tax rates than if wealth is transferred at death and subject to estate taxation. If a person were really interested in the future consumption of his children, the tax laws provide a strong incentive to transfer the desired wealth before death. Yet very little use is made of this loophole.[7] Parents do not give their money away before death even though their children would have much more wealth if they did so. Such actions hardly square with the view of parents sacrificing themselves and accumulating wealth to raise the consumption standards of their children. When given a tax-free or low-tax method to take care of their children, they do not use it. As a result, some other motivation must be found to explain large fortunes at death and the absence of de-accumulation.

Sometimes uncertainties about the precise time of death are used to explain the pattern of wealth accumulation. Consider an individual who may be well-off if he were to live to a normal life expectancy but who is uncertain about when he will die. He is age sixty-five with a life expectancy of fourteen years. Assume that he has $35,000 in net assets and can earn a 6 percent interest rate. If he were certain of death at age seventy-nine, he could consume $3,767 per year. If he were to live to be one hundred (a very unlikely event), he could consume only $2,414 per year. If he is lucky enough to live a very long time, he may be poor. To prevent this lucky-unlucky problem, he must be risk-averse and act as if he were going to live a long time even though he will in all probability not live a long time. According to this argument, being uncertain as to when he will die he must accumulate more than he otherwise would have to accumulate and is unable to program his expenditures so that he reaches zero assets at death.

Although this explanation focuses on a valid problem, it once again does not explain what needs to be explained. The great fortunes exceed anything that would be needed as insurance against the uncertainties of death, and as long as an individual can trust his own children it still pays to give away all of his wealth before death. It also ignores the existence of annuities. Annuities allow an individual to insure himself some desired level of consumption for the rest of his life regardless of the uncertainties about future longevity.[8]

The Motivation of Economic Power

The motive that has been left out of neoclassical economics is that of economic power—within either the family or the community. Whereas consumption possibilities are finite, subject to diminishing marginal utility and severely limited by time budget constraints, economic power is not subject to the same limitations. Appetites for power are larger and may be subject to increasing marginal returns. Great economic power takes no longer to wield than small economic power. If one likes economic power, then one wants to maintain it until death. To de-accumulate assets or to give them away is to give up economic power.[9] The individuals on the *Fortune* list may be sixty-five years of age and may have no possibilities of consuming their own wealth before death, but they have and enjoy economic power. They will leave a fortune at death simply because there is no way to enjoy economic power until death without leaving a fortune at death.

The role of economic power helps us understand why more individuals do not use the tax loophole of transferring their assets before death. The problem is that to do so is to give up economic power. Parents typically fear that their children will not give the assets back if they need them (unexpected medical bills, etc.), or they fear that they will not have "respect" or "filial" devotion if the family assets are transferred before death. To give up economic power within the family is to give up one's status and station. Few individuals are willing to give up their economic power even vis-à-vis their own children.

For a similar reason individuals do not buy annuities even though they would guarantee consumption expenditures over an uncertain future. To buy an annuity is to give up exactly what the individual wants—economic power. Your assets are given to some institution in exchange for a guaranteed lifetime stream of income. You lose control.

The desire for economic power does not fit into neoclassical models for a number of reasons, the most basic being the assumption of perfect competition. In a perfectly competitive economy, economic power does not exist and therefore economic power cannot be a goal. It is as unattainable as the pot of gold at the end of the rainbow. If you refuse to invest in some project in an attempt to exercise economic power, some other investor will simply replace you. If the project earns a market rate of return, it will always be done with or without your capital. Similarly, you also cannot increase economic investments above the level dictated by the market. If you seek to do so, some other investors will withdraw from the area, leaving the total volume of economic activity just what it was.

In the real world there are, however, opportunities to exercise economic power within the family, the economy, and the political process. The holder of wealth has some leverage to redesign his family, private charities, the economy, and the political structure in his own image. What does not exist in perfect competition may lie at the heart of wealth accumulation in our less than perfectly competitive world. The net result of a desire for economic power is an accumulation of wealth and a transmittal of wealth that is irrational from the point of view of simple consumption economics.

The Random Walk

Although the desire for economic power explains why individuals wish to hold large fortunes, it does not explain their generation and initial distribution. The real conundrum is to explain the instant wealth of this generation and of previous generations. To do so we must search in a different direction. The answer will be found in a phenomenon called the "random walk" and in the existence of disequilibrium rather than equilibrium.

In the standard economic model, capital markets are in equilibrium and each investment yields some common rate of return. To understand the real world, on the other hand, it is necessary to think of at least two different capital markets. The first capital market is the market for real investments. In this market firms and individuals make real investments in plant and machinery. The second capital market is the financial market where individuals buy financial instruments without directly managing real plant and equipment. Stocks, bonds, real estate trusts, etc., are examples of the latter; factories, stamping presses, lathes, etc., are examples of the former.

The basic characteristic of the real capital market is disequilibrium. Both over time and at any one point in time there is a wide variance in rates of return. This variance exists both among and within industries. Table 19 indicates the after-tax annual rate of return on stockholder equity by industry for 1960 and 1972. In 1960 the after-tax returns varied from 3.6 percent for lumber and wood products to 16.8 percent for drugs, with an average rate of return of 9.2 percent. In 1972 the range was from 5.9 percent in primary nonferrous metals to 18.6 percent in drugs. The large differences in rates of return in any one year extend over considerable periods of time. Thus, industries with high rank orders in 1960 tend to have high rank orders in 1972. The same stability in position and dispersion in results can be seen in *Fortune*'s list of the 500 largest industrial firms. In 1973 returns ranged from a 37 percent rate of return for Cook Industries to minus 75 percent for Mattel, with a median rate of return on stockholders' equity of 12.4 percent.[10]

Within a single industry the dispersion is just as large. Table 20 shows the rates of return for the four major American automobile manufacturers. Although there is some year-to-year variance, there are large consistent differences that have existed over almost twenty years. General Motors earned 17.9 percent, Ford earned 12.0 percent, Chrysler earned 8.4 percent, and American Motors earned 14.7 percent. American Motors is also

TABLE 19

Annual Rates of Profit on Stockholders' Equity, by Industry
(percent)

	INDUSTRY	1960	1972
1.	All manufacturing corporations, except newspapers	9.20	10.60
2.	Durable goods	8.55	10.70
3.	Transportation equipment	11.68	12.33
4.	Motor vehicles and equipment	13.48	14.45
5.	Aircraft and parts	7.35	7.35
6.	Electrical machinery, equipment and supplies	9.53	10.83
7.	Other machinery	7.58	10.73
8.	Metalworking machinery and equipment	5.28	6.53
9.	Other fabricated metal products	5.60	11.03
10.	Primary metal industries	7.18	6.00
11.	Primary iron and steel	7.18	6.05
12.	Primary nonferrous metals	7.13	5.93
13.	Stone, clay, and glass products	9.88	10.10
14.	Furniture and fixtures	6.50	12.93
15.	Lumber and wood products, except furniture	3.60	15.88
16.	Instruments and related products	11.60	14.33
17.	Miscellaneous manufacturing and ordnance	9.18	10.85
18.	Nondurable goods	9.85	10.48
19.	Food and kindred products	8.73	11.18
20.	Alcoholic beverages	7.18	10.60
21.	Tobacco manufactures	13.38	15.43
22.	Textile mill products	5.85	7.50
23.	Apparel and other finished products	7.70	11.93
24.	Paper and allied products	10.18	9.03
25.	Printing and publishing, except newspapers	10.58	12.03
26.	Chemicals and allied products	12.20	12.85
27.	Basic chemicals	11.13	12.00
28.	Drugs	16.83	18.55
29.	Petroleum refining and related industries	10.13	10.00
30.	Petroleum refining	10.10	8.63
31.	Rubber and miscellaneous plastic products	9.10	8.63
32.	Leather and leather products	6.30	9.08

Source: Federal Trade Commission, Securities and Exchange Commission, *Quarterly Financial Reports for Manufacture Corporations* (Washington, D.C.: Government Printing Office), *First Quarter 1961*, p. 10, and *First Quarter 1973*, p. 10.

TABLE 20
Automobile Rates of Return
(percent)

	1956	'57	'58	'59	'60	'61	'62	'63	'64	'65	'66	'67	'68	'69	'70	'71	'72 STOCK-HOLDERS EQUITY %
General Motors	18.5	17.2	12.6	16.3	16.5	14.8	21.9	22.4	22.8	25.8	20.6	17.6	17.8	16.7	6.2	17.9	18.5
Ford	11.9	13.2	4.5	17.3	14.9	13.1	14.1	13.1	12.6	15.6	12.9	1.8	12.7	10.5	9.4	11.8	14.6
Chrysler	3.1	16.4	4.9	.8	3.3	1.6	8.5	17.5	19.1	14.7	11.1	10.9	14.1	4.2	.4	3.7	8.9
American	15.9	10.6	19.8	31.6	21.6	10.4	13.7	13.8	9.4	1.9	4.9	42.4	6.2	2.4	27.6	4.8	12.3

Source: Table compiled from data appearing in the "Fortune 500" issues of *Fortune* magazine, published every May.

consistent in its inconsistency, earning large returns in some years and small returns in other years.

Data on real capital markets indicate little, if any, tendency for real capital markets to approach equilibrium. Substantial differences exist in real rates of return, and these differences are often perpetuated over long periods of time. The reasons for this fundamental disequilibrium are many and varied, but most of them spring from a fundamental imperfection in the real capital market. Investment resources simply do not flow across firms and industries so as to equalize real rates of return.

In 1973, 71 percent of all U.S. savings took the form of re-tained earnings and depreciation allowances. If you subtract those funds that go into residential housing, then over 99 per-cent of all industrial and commercial investment funds were internally generated.[11] If one thinks of a real capital market as a place where the savings of the household sector are allo-cated to the business sector, then the United States does not have a real capital market. The household sector's savings are basically used to finance the direct investments of the house-hold sector (housing), and the business sector is self-financing.

But the real capital market is even more atrophied than the lack of net household saving would suggest. There is also very little transfer of saving from one firm to another within the business sector. Firms almost always reinvest their own internal funds and seldom make long-term loans or investments in other firms.[12]

To explain why internal funds are frozen into the firms gen-erating them, it is only necessary to think about the basic characteristics of U.S. capitalism. It is managerial capitalism. Large firms are controlled by individual managers who usually do not own any substantial fraction of the firm that they man-age. Although a stockholder might like to see his funds invested in the highest rate of return industries, regardless of who man-ages these industries, the existing manager clearly has other incentives. He wants to use internally generated savings for investments under his management, since this is the pattern of investments that brings him increasing returns in the form of income, power, and prestige. As a result, those who direct real investments are simply not the profit-maximizing investors imagined in simple neoclassical economics. They are interested in maximizing profits, but only profits from operations that they themselves manage. If a stockholder thinks that one firm is going to be more profitable than another, his only recourse is to alter his own financial portfolio (a subject to which we shall return).

If we ask why managers with large internal savings do not start subsidiaries in high-profit industries rather than reinvesting in their own low-profit industries, we come face to face with the entire structure of restricted competition in the U.S. economy. Barriers to entry are often high, and managers often do not have the specialized knowledge necessary to make profits in another industry. The existence of high profits in the cosmetics industry, for example, does not mean that iron and steel executives could earn high profits there. True, the firm might be able to earn high profits, but it would have to fire its existing managers and hire new managers. The existing managers are not about to fire themselves, and they are wise enough to know that they could not run a successful cosmetics firm. As a result, they stay in the steel industry and reinvest their internal funds in steel regardless of the relative rates of return.

The existence of internal savings also tends to distort the flows of those few investment funds that do flow through real capital markets. In the real world, lenders face risk and uncertainties about actual returns. If they lend to firms with large flows of internal savings, they can have great confidence that borrowers are going to repay their loans regardless of the success or failure of the actual project for which the funds were lent. Because of the low risk of default, funds are attracted to those firms with large internal savings regardless of whether or not they are earning above-average rates of return on their capital investments.

The net result is a flow of market investments that does not serve to equalize real rates of return across the economy. Thus, if we look at Table 19, we find that drugs provided a rate of return 50 percent above average in both 1960 and 1972. Over a twelve-year period, the real capital market did not drive the rate of return in drugs down to the market average, as it should in a perfect capital market. Real capital markets are thus marked by substantial differences in long-run rate of return. What is more, in a dynamic economy investment, opportunities offering new high rates of return will appear periodically.

This dispersion in rates of return in the real capital market provides the role for financial markets. It serves not to generate and direct real capital to high rates of return investment opportunities but to capitalize away the differences in real rates of return. Consider a new real investment opportunity costing $10 million and earning a 30 percent rate of return, or $3 million. With a market rate of return of 10 percent, this investment would be valued at $30 million ($3,000,000 ÷ 0.10). With a rate of return of 5 percent, it would be valued at $60 million ($3,000,000 ÷ 0.05). If the investment is in something that can be expanded (according to the 1973 *Fortune* article, the largest new fortunes were made by men in McDonald's hamburgers and in Hartz Mountain pet food and accessories) so that additional real capital can be invested and also earn 30 percent rates of return, the market may capitalize current investments at very high multiples because of the prospect of future real investments at above-average rates of return.[13] In that case current investments are not the appropriate base for capitalization, since prospects exist for earning 30 percent rates of return on a much larger base.

Based on current and future earnings, shareholders shift their financial portfolios from low real rate of return firms to high real rate of return firms. In the process their actions lower the market value of the first firm and raise the market value of the second firm. When enough shareholders have shifted their investments, the financial rates of return will be equal regardless of the differences in underlying real rates of return on capital investments.

Large instantaneous fortunes are created when the financial markets capitalize new above-average rate of return investments to yield average rate of return financial investments. It is this process of capitalizing disequilibrium returns that generates rapid fortunes. Patient savings and reinvestment has little or nothing to do with them. To become very rich one must generate or select a situation in which an above-average rate of return is about to be capitalized.

If real capital markets reach equilibrium quickly, large fortunes could not be made in this way. In that case once a new investment opportunity was discovered, real investment funds would quickly flow into the area and bring the real rate of return down to the market rate of return. Thus, above-average profits could not be expected to last very long and there would be no possibility of obtaining a monopoly on future above-average investment opportunities. Other people would move into the area and future investments would only earn the market rate of return.

Although the process of capitalizing disequilibrium rates of return explains instantaneous fortunes, we still have to investigate the process whereby these fortunes are allocated to individuals. This brings us to the "random walk." Although the random walk has been extensively tested and is widely accepted among professors of finance in business schools, it has not percolated into either the public arena or into basic courses in economics.[14]

The random-walk literature attempts to prove several hypotheses. First, the expected rate of return on any financial investment is equal to the expected rate of return on any other financial investment in the same risk class.[15] Financial markets are like the economist's vision of perfect capital markets in that they equalize rates of return but only *expected ex ante* rates of return are equalized. *Actual ex post* returns will differ since returns are generated in a probabilistic process.[16]

Second, once the appropriate adjustment is made for the risk class of an investment, the expected rate of return on any investment will be equal to the average rate of return on all investments (the market average).[17] Once again, the financial market is like a perfect market in that every investment earns the same rate of return but only on an expectational basis.

Third, the expected rate of return on a financial investment, given no information about that investment (except its risk class), is equal to the expected rate of return on an investment, given all of the legally available public information.[18] Since all information is quickly capitalized into the price of an asset, information has a zero value. It is from this principle that the name "random walk" springs. If information is already capitalized into the price of an asset, knowing it does nothing to make you a good investor. Throwing darts at the financial pages of the *New York Times* is just as good an investment strategy as trying to accumulate all of the relevant information about a stock. Dart throwing is in fact a better investment strategy since it costs nothing whereas attempts to collect information are expensive.

Fourth, within each risk class there is a random lottery in which individuals place bets on individual investments with equal expected values (an equal chance of winning) but in which investments yield very different returns *ex post*. As in any lottery, there is an expected average rate of return for any invested dollar, but also, as in any lottery, someone will win and someone will lose. Even more specifically the lottery within each risk class is a nonnormal random lottery.[19] There is a long upper tail. This tail says that there is a very small prob-

DIAGRAM 7
A Nonnormal Random Lottery

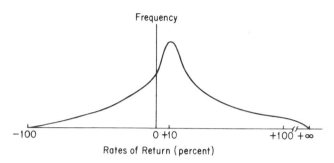

Rates of Return (percent)

ability of making a very large return on an investment. As we have seen, an investment may be capitalized at a very high multiple. At the same time losses are limited, since it is not possible to lose more than you invest (see Diagram 7).

For example, in the early 1950s you might have invested in a risk class of firms that included Xerox. In 1950 all of these firms would have looked alike and all would have had an equal expected rate of return. *Ex post,* some would have gone broke and disappeared, most would have earned the market rate of return, some would have earned more than the market rate of return, and a few, perhaps one, would have been an investment such as Xerox. Those who owned shares in it became wealthy. They won the lottery.

The random walk is a process that will generate a highly skewed distribution of wealth regardless of the normal distribution of personal abilities and regardless of whether the economy does or does not start from an initial state of equality. Once great wealth has been created, the holder diversifies his portfolio and after that is subject to diversification and to earning the market rate of return. Because most holders of wealth eventually diversify their portfolios, great fortunes remain even after the underlying disequilibrium in the real capital markets disappears. It should be emphasized that there is no equalizing principle in the random walk. Those who have had good luck are not then more apt to be subject to bad luck than the random individual. There is no tail of large negative losses to balance the tail of large positive gains. You cannot lose more than you have, but you can make many times what you have.

What is the evidence for the random-walk hypothesis? First, an examination of large financial firms (such as mutual funds) indicates that none of them is able to outperform the market averages.[20] Professional financial managers able to make large investments in obtaining market information are not able to outperform the market average or a random drawing of stocks. Second, no one has been able to design a set of decision rules (when to buy and sell) that yields a greater than average rate of return.[21] Third, tests indicate that stock prices quickly adjust to changes in information (announcements of stock splits, dividend increases, etc.). Fourth, there is no serial correlation among stock prices over time. The price at any moment in time or its history cannot be used to predict future prices. When put together, all of these findings form an impressive body of evidence as to the existence of the random walk.

The net result is a process that generates a highly skewed distribution of wealth from a normal distribution of abilities. Fortunes are created instantaneously or in very short periods of time. Personal savings behavior has little or nothing to do with the process. Once created, large fortunes maintain themselves through being able to diversify and through inheritance.

Many of the great fortunes represented in Appendix B represent a combination of entrepreneurial activities and financial investments. Although entrepreneurial activities cannot be investigated in the same manner as financial investments (the unsuccessful entrepreneur is not visible in the same manner as the unsuccessful stock), they may also be subject to the same random-walk principle. Within a group of individuals with equal entrepreneurial talents, there may be a nonnormal random lottery. There is an expected rate of return for the group as a whole but a wide dispersion in individual results around this average. Entrepreneurial talent is a necessary condition to entering the lottery, but it is not a sufficient condition for making instantaneous wealth.

If you read the *Fortune* biographies that accompany its lists of the most wealthy, the winners will be described as brighter than bright, smarter than smart, quicker than quick. But look beyond the description to see if they were simply lucky or possess some unique abilities. Remember that the unsuccessful entrepreneur of equal ability will not be featured in *Fortune*. To what extent were they like many other people but in the right place at the right time? The real test of unique abilities is to ask how many have repeated their performance. How many have made a great fortune on one activity or investment and then managed to go on to earn another great fortune on another activity or investment? If the *Fortune* list is examined, it is impossible to identify anyone whose personal fortune was subject to two or more upward leaps.[22] The typical pattern is for a man to make a great fortune and then to settle down and earn the market rate of return on his existing portfolio.

In any case the nonnormal random walk found in recent research on financial markets seems to lie at the center of the process generating wealth. Within risk and entrepreneurial-ability classes, a random lottery is conducted. As with all lotteries, someone wins even though the probability of winning is very small. Chances of winning the lottery twice are almost nonexistent, but once a great fortune is made it earns the market rate of return.[23] Diversification of portfolios means that even if the initial disequilibrium in real investments is eventually eliminated, the personal fortune is apt to be maintained. Because of diversification, the losses associated with eliminating above-average real rates of return are shared across the population.

153

There is no feedback principle in the random walk that tends to equalize the distribution of wealth once it has become unequal.

Conclusions

At any moment in time, the highly skewed distribution of wealth is the product of two approximately equal factors—instant fortunes and inherited wealth. Inherited fortunes, however, were themselves created in a process of instant wealth in an earlier generation. These instant fortunes occur because new long-term disequilibriums in the real capital market are capitalized in the financial markets. In this capitalizing process the average expected rate of return is equal to the actual average rate of return, but the average is itself a product of a nonnormal widely dispersed distribution of actual *ex post* returns. Those who are lucky and end up owning the stocks that are capitalized at high multiples win large fortunes in the random walk. Once fortunes are created, they are husbanded, augmented, and passed on, not because of "homo economicus" desires to store up future consumption but because of desires for power within the family, economy, or society.

7

DISCRIMINATION AND

THEORIES

OF INCOME DETERMINATION

AS THE DATA provided in Chapter 1 indicated, our observer would notice differences in earnings by race or sex even after corrections had been made for occupation, hours of work, and other variables that could legitimately be expected to have an impact on productivity. Any theory of distribution must be able to explain these earnings and wealth differentials. What causes them and what allows them to persist?

The nature of the problem can be seen in Table 21, which gives the distributions of earnings for white males, white females, black males, and black females who are year-round full-time workers. As these data indicate, the distributions differ substantially. In terms of relative earnings, black males make 66 percent as much as white males, white females earn 55 percent as much, and black females earn 48 percent as much. Whereas 21.4 percent of the white males earn over $15,000 per year, the corresponding percentages are 4.2 percent, 1.6 percent, and 1.3 percent for black males, white females, and black females, respec-

TABLE 21

*Distributions of Earnings For Year-round Full-time
Workers by Race And Sex in 1972*

INCOME	WHITE MALES	WHITE FEMALES	BLACK MALES	BLACK FEMALES
$0–$999	1.7%	1.9%	1.4%	1.8%
$1,000–$1,999	1.2	1.5	2.7	5.3
$2,000–$2,999	1.4	4.1	1.7	7.5
$3,000–$3,999	2.3	10.0	7.2	15.3
$4,000–$4,999	3.4	15.2	10.9	17.1
$5,000–$5,999	5.2	16.2	11.0	14.1
$6,000–$6,999	6.6	13.8	10.6	10.5
$7,000–$7,999	7.8	11.9	12.0	9.1
$8,000–$9,999	16.6	12.7	18.0	9.9
$10,000–$14,999	32.4	9.9	19.4	7.2
$15,000–$24,999	16.2	1.4	3.5	1.0
$25,000 and up	5.2	0.2	0.7	0.3
Median	$10,593	$5,998	$7,301	$5,147
Mean	$11,640	$6,368	$7,674	$5,578

Source: U.S. Bureau of the Census, *Current Population Reports: Consumer Income, 1972* (Washington, D.C.: Government Printing Office, 1973), p. 144.

tively. Although the data are not collected as regularly, earnings gaps would also emerge for Spanish-speaking Americans and American Indians. The problem is to explain the mechanism whereby the economy produces these earnings gaps.

A Competitive Theory of Price or Wage Discrimination

The competitive theory of discrimination treats discrimination as if it were a restrictive practice that interrupts free trade between two independent societies: white and black, male and female, etc.[1] With free trade (no discrimination) each society would export that factor in which it was relatively abundant and import that factor of which it was relatively short until the marginal products of all factors were equal in both societies. A black society might, for example, export labor (its relatively abundant factor of production), and a white society might export capital (its relatively abundant factor). Exports come about because they are necessary for each society and each individual to maximize their incomes. Without them marginal products cannot be equalized.

When there is discrimination, individuals in the white society (the discriminators) maximize a utility function that depends upon both income and physical distance from blacks. The greater the physical distance between whites and blacks, the higher the utility of whites, so whites are willing to pay a premium not to associate with blacks. They have a taste for not associating with blacks just as they might have a taste for French wines.

Analytically, each white has a personal "discrimination coefficient," d_i, that corresponds to a tariff in international trade. If an employer were faced with a money wage rate "W" for a particular factor, he is assumed to act as if $W (1 + d_i)$ were the real wage rate for blacks, where d_i is his personal discrimination coefficient against employing blacks. Similar personal discrimination coefficients would exist for all economic interactions. If the monetary price of some good were "P," a white buyer would act as if the price were $P (1 + d_i^*)$, if the purchase were made from a black salesperson. The d_i^* is the individual's discrimination coefficient against associating with black sales personnel. If a white worker were offered a money wage of W, he would act as if the real wage were $W (1 - d_i^{**})$, where d_i^{**} is his personal discrimination coefficient against having to work with black workers. Potentially, every demand or supply curve of the white community could be altered by the extent of its discrimination coefficients. These discrimination coefficients could also differ for different types of interactions. Individuals may have

DIAGRAM 8
White Gains and Losses from Discrimination

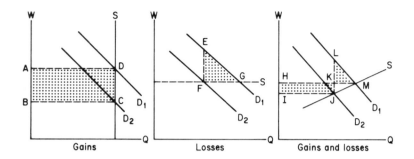

Gains   Losses   Gains and losses

large discrimination coefficients against working with blacks but only small discrimination coefficients against being served by blacks.

The implications of these shifts can be seen by looking at the changes induced by an employer's discrimination coefficient. As the result of his discrimination coefficient, there is a downward shift in the white employer's demand for black labor (see Diagram 8). The effect depends upon the size of the discrimination coefficient (the downward shift), but it also depends upon the supply elasticity of black labor and the white demand elasticity for black labor.

If the supply elasticity (S) is zero (the first panel), black wages (W) decline with a downward shift in demand from D_1 to D_2, but the quantity of black labor (Q) is constant. The income of the white community rises since black wages are now less than their marginal products.[2] Black wages and incomes fall. In this panel white gains are equal to the rectangle ABCD. If the elasticity of supply is infinite (the second panel), wages are constant and all of the adjustment occurs in the quantity of labor supplied. The white community loses the intermarginal product (the producer's surplus) EFG; no gains are possible since blacks cannot be paid less than their marginal product. Black wages do not fall, but black incomes are reduced because fewer blacks are employed. If the elasticity of supply is greater than zero but less than infinite (the third panel), both gains and losses occur. The net white gain or loss depends upon the relative size of HIJK and LKM. The technical conditions for white economic gains or losses from discrimination are easily worked out.[3] In this case the reduction in black incomes is composed partly of a reduction in black wages and partly of a reduction in employment opportunities.

In most cases whites will gain from practicing employment discrimination. Discrimination is being practiced in a country where whites predominate numerically and are possessed of much larger stocks of both physical and human capital on a per capita basis. Given these circumstances, blacks have no option but to trade with (i.e., work in and borrow from) the white community. Of necessity, blacks must offer a relatively inelastic supply curve.[4] Whites might, however, continue to practice discrimination even if they suffer monetary losses. Up to some point they are compensated for these losses by the psychic income gains of not having to associate with blacks.

Not only can whites gain from discrimination but economic research has shown how to calculate the discrimination coefficient that will maximize white income gains from discrimination.[5] This research indicates the conditions under which whites can raise their incomes by discriminating against blacks, the conditions under which whites can raise their incomes in spite of retaliation by blacks, and the conditions under which blacks can raise their incomes vis-à-vis whites if they practice discrimination against whites.[6]

At the same time, total output (black plus white) falls since trade is being held below its optimum levels because of discrimination. Just as marginal products are not equalized across countries when tariffs exist, so they are not equalized across races when discrimination exists. Eliminating discrimination would produce more output for blacks and whites together, but it might very well lower the total output available to whites.

By adding or subtracting the appropriate discrimination coefficients to the relevant supply or demand curves, it is possible to generate the distribution of factor earnings that would be produced in an economy where individuals had tastes for discrimination. These can then be compared with the distribution of factor payments that would emerge if discrimination coefficients did not exist. The difference is the economic impact of discrimination.

There are several problems with this theory, but the major problem has to do with the persistence of earnings gaps between whites and blacks. The amount of discrimination in the economic system is not determined by the average discrimination coefficient of whites but by the marginal discrimination coefficient—the man with the smallest discrimination coefficient. If there were any employers with zero or low discrimination coefficients against black employees or any capitalists willing to lend money to black entrepreneurs, it would be possible to set up a business that only employed black labor at their lower wage rates. Since the firm would be paying lower wage rates, it would be making profits and could afford to sell its output for less than firms practicing discrimination and hiring high-cost white labor. The firm with only black employees would drive white firms out of business or force them to quit practicing discrimination. Since there clearly are individuals who do not have discrimination coefficients or who would be willing to lend money to black entrepreneurs in exchange for large profits, the question arises as to how discrimination has been able to last for decades. The economic pressures of a competitive market should have eliminated it long ago.

There are two explanations for the persistence of discrimination, but neither of them is completely acceptable from the point of view of competitive micro-economic theory. One explanation maintains that discrimination is held in place by white laborers and not by white employers. White employees have certain skills that they refuse to teach to blacks. Since these skills are necessary to the white employers, they are forced to accept and enforce the discrimination coefficients of their white employees regardless of their own personal discrimination coefficients.

This subsidiary theory runs into the same problem as the basic theory itself. Labor's ability to impose discrimination also depends upon labor's marginal discrimination coefficient and not upon its average discrimination coefficient. As long as there is one employee of every type of skill with a zero or low discrimination coefficient, the necessary skills can be taught to a mostly black labor force. Here again, there clearly are individual employees with zero or low-discrimination coefficients. Moreover, a monopoly (that of white laborers over skills) had to be introduced to explain discrimination in what started out to be a competitive theory. Only the existence of this monopoly allows discrimination to continue.

The other explanation for persistent discrimination revolves around the distinction between a local and a global optimum.[7] Here again, the discrimination coefficients of labor play a key role. According to this explanation, it is true that an employer could raise profits by shifting from an all-white labor force to an all-black labor force, but the employer does not perceive this truth because he only makes marginal changes. When the white employer starts adding black employees to his labor force, he finds that the hostility generated among whites is so intense that his profits go down. True, if he continued to add blacks despite falling profits he would find that his profits would go up eventually, but to get from the local optimum to the global optimum he must go through a period of low profits. Not knowing that there is such a global optimum and receiving marginal signals that are the reverse, he never shifts from a white labor force to a black labor force.

The basic problem with this explanation is that it relies on ignorance. Employers do not do what is good for them because they are too stupid to know what is good for them. They look only at empirical marginal changes and ignore all analysis—both the kind they could do for themselves and that which already exists in the economics literature. They are not so stupid in other areas; why are they so stupid here?

The persistence of discrimination despite economic theories that would seem to call for its rapid elimination is one of the major problems in the analysis of discrimination, but there are also two other major analytical gaps. Although physical-distance theories of discrimination can explain certain types of segregation, they clearly do not explain the more virulent types of discrimination practiced in South Africa, the Deep South, and elsewhere. The discriminator wants to work with, buy from, live near, be served by, and hire blacks, but he insists on specifying the relationships under which the two parties will meet and how the black individual will respond. Perhaps it is more accurate to say that whites insist on maintaining social, rather than physical, distance between themselves and blacks. A desire for social distance can lead to a very different set of actions from a desire for physical distance. The discriminator may prefer to hire black maids, black garbage collectors, or to work with blacks if he can be in a position of authority. He may also prefer to hire black laborers if he can pay them a lower wage than white laborers.

When discrimination by sex is examined, physical-distance theories make no sense at all. Men are not trying to achieve physical distance from women. Part of the problem with constructing a theory of sex discrimination is that micro-economics specifies the ultimate goals of economic man—homo economicus—too narrowly. Consumption privileges are supposed to be the ultimate goals of economic persons, but discrimination against women does not have to do with consumption privileges. In most families there is little difference in the real consumption privileges of husband and wife: they share their economic goods and services equally. Here discrimination refers to production, and not consumption, opportunities.

But why should men practice production discrimination against their own wives or other men's wives? Raising the real earnings of wives will lead to higher consumption privileges for husbands. If consumption privileges were the sole economic goal, most men—certainly every married man or man who plans to get married—would have an enormous vested interest in eliminating discrimination against wives. It would be a way to raise their real consumption standards with no effort on their part. Thus, it is not possible to explain sex discrimination either as a desire for physical distance or as a technique for raising male consumption standards. The first is not sought and the second is not achieved. In fact, precisely the opposite is achieved. Male consumption standards fall below what they could be. Thus, existing competitive theories of price or wage discrimination cannot explain sex discrimination. This is a problem to which we shall return after other theories of discrimination have been examined.

Price and wage theories are also inadequate in that they cover a limited range of all of the possible dimensions upon which discrimination can occur. Discrimination can exist even when equal wages can be paid for equal work if individuals are not allowed to perform (or acquire the characteristics necessary to perform) equal work. These other types of discrimination stand outside of the standard competitive model of wage or price discrimination.

Monopoly Models of Discrimination [8]

Some types of discrimination seem to fit the physical-distance model, but many do not. The competitive theory is more a theory of segregation than of discrimination. Discrimination cannot be adequately represented by a model of two independent societies freely trading with each other over the barriers created by economic discrimination, since it occurs in one society, not two. The dominant group controls much more than its willingness to trade or not trade with the minority group. Physical, social, or economic pressures may enable the dominant group to trade with the subservient group as if they were discriminating monopolists or monopsonists. The minority group may have few options and certainly not the option of refusing to trade. Subsistence (social or physical) may force them to. In the United States blacks live in a white supremacist society, not just a segregated society.

But although white money incomes probably rise in the process of generating physical distance in the competitive model, this is, as far as the whites are concerned, just a fortunate byproduct. The overt goal is physical distance, not higher incomes. And sometimes whites were confronted with a choice between more physical distance or greater incomes. By contrast, in a social-distance model whites wish to raise white incomes. Higher white incomes contribute to greater social distance. As a consequence, whites can deliberately and systematically set out to raise their income through discriminatory practices, knowing that these practices will contribute to more social distance. By practicing discrimination, they can raise both their money incomes and their psychic incomes from greater social distance.

Since monopolistic firms always earn at least as many profits as competitive firms, whites wish to establish monopolies vis-à-vis blacks wherever possible. If the relevant supply or demand curves are less than perfectly elastic, whites can raise their incomes with monopolistic practices. Not only is monopolization a technique for raising white incomes, but it also eliminates the problem created by the man with no prejudices in the competitive model. If a monopoly can be established, society's average desire for social distance can be put in place without being competed away by the man who does not have a taste for social distance.

In the monopoly model of discrimination, there are various types of discrimination which the monopolist attempts to adjust so as to increase his income and social distance. Since the monopolist is interested in social distance and not physical distance, he is willing to associate with those being discriminated against whenever it is profitable to do so.[9] There are a variety of dimensions upon which the monopolist could act to raise his income, but there are also clashes between these dimensions. Actions that maximize the gains from one type of discrimination may clash with maximizing the gains from other types. Indeed, conflicts between different discriminators constitute one of the major problems they face as a group. To solve these conflicts, anomalies often seem to appear in the observed pattern of discrimination.

Employment discrimination exists when blacks (or some other group) are so distributed in the work force that they suffer more than their proportional share of unemployment, resulting in more employed whites and higher white incomes than there would be if discrimination did not exist. Conversely, more blacks are unemployed and black incomes are reduced.

Wage discrimination exists when whites are able to pay blacks less than their marginal products. The whites who are able to appropriate part of the black marginal product find that their incomes rise while black incomes fall. Possible clashes between these two types of discrimination immediately become evident, for jobs with high levels of cyclical unemployment are not necessarily jobs with which it is possible to practice wage discrimination. Compromises must be made because the distribution of black employment that would be optimum from the perspective of employment discrimination need not be optimum as far as wage discrimination is concerned.

Occupational discrimination exists when blacks are not allowed into some preferred occupations and as a consequence are more than proportionally represented in the less preferred occupations. White incomes are higher than they otherwise would be since whites do not have to share high-income jobs equally with blacks. Here again occupational discrimination might conflict with wage discrimination. It might, for example, be easiest to practice wage discrimination against blacks in relatively high-income jobs.

Human capital discrimination exists when fewer state or corporate funds are invested in the human capital of blacks than of whites or when blacks are not allowed equal opportunities to purchase human capital. Whites make gains from limiting black human capital since the price of white human capital rises above what it would be if more black human capital were available. Obvious potential conflicts arise with each of the three previous types of discrimination.

Monopoly power discrimination exists when there are monopoly profits in the economy and minorities are not allowed equal access to those areas in which monopolies raise returns above the competitive rate. If whites possess most of the economy's monopolies, their incomes will rise to the extent that the monopolies extract more than competitive profits from the black community. Individual whites will, however, make much larger gains since they are able to extract monopoly profits from both blacks and those whites who do not participate in the monopoly.

Capital market discrimination exists when blacks cannot borrow or invest equal amounts of funds at equal rates. Quantitative controls in this area can be extremely important since they prevent minorities from participating in the acquisition of wealth.

Price discrimination exists when the prices of equal goods and services differ for blacks and whites. In this case income differences do not show up in money incomes but in real incomes. Blacks and whites with equal money incomes cannot purchase equal amounts of real goods and services.

In all of these seven modes of discrimination, different results will emerge depending upon whether whites think that social distance is achieved by larger absolute white incomes or by greater relative income gaps. In the first case whites take actions to raise their own incomes and will distribute blacks across the work force in such a manner as to bring this about. Maximizing relative incomes, however, leads to much harsher actions since whites are now willing to lower their own incomes if this results in even larger declines in black incomes.

The major problem with the monopoly model has to do with the enforcement mechanism. Since some whites suffer losses from discrimination—the suburban resident who could sell his home to a black for a higher price, the employer who could hire cheaper black labor—what mechanism is used to enforce losses on them?

When governments play an active role in discrimination, as in South Africa and in many American communities, the powers of government provide the enforcing mechanism. Such powers are the chief means for building and enforcing white monopsony and monopoly powers and preventing countervailing powers from emerging in the black community. When a government wishes to practice discrimination, it is the major vehicle for restricting investment in black education; it enforces the community desire for discrimination on individual whites who might prefer less of it; it encourages the export of black capital by refusing the essential governmental cooperation necessary to run a black business; its housing codes prevent whites from selling to blacks in the wrong locations; and its police powers can be used to discourage black retaliation. Moreover, with central control over the practice of discrimination, compensation can be arranged for whites who lose by it. Thus, in South Africa the occupational distribution of blacks is a subject for negotiation when the wages of white miners are being determined. White wages go up if blacks are allowed into more skilled occupations.

When government does not actively practice discrimination and does not permit explicit legal practices which facilitate it, such as restrictive housing codes or union-management agreements to practice discrimination, enforcement is more difficult. Community or social pressure is one means of forcing whites to accept the concomitant losses.

The main enforcement mechanism, however, comes from the interlocking nature of the different types of discrimination. If the various types of discrimination are viewed separately, there seem to be powerful economic pressures leading to their elimination. Suburban homeowners could gain by selling to blacks. White employers could increase profits by hiring blacks. But when the several types of discrimination are viewed together, the economic pressures are either not present or present in a much more attenuated form.

In the abstract, the white suburban homeowner should be willing to sell to blacks. Physical-distance theories cannot explain his actions. Since he is moving anyhow, proximity to blacks should not bother him and the social opinions of his ex-neighbors should be irrelevant. Perhaps his utility function includes the opinions of *former* neighbors, and social pressures prevent him from selling to blacks. Or perhaps the desire for social distance is the explanation. If blacks move into neighborhoods and homes where whites formerly lived, the social distance between blacks and whites has been reduced. Blacks are only one jump behind.

More likely, other types of discrimination prevent all but a very few white homeowners from ever having to face this situation. Other types of economic discrimination result in low black incomes so that blacks are seldom in an economic position to bid for the housing of whites. Even if an individual black has sufficient income, he still may be prevented from bidding for a white home if there is discrimination by lending institutions. Equal incomes do not lead to the same control over economic resources; a white can buy a more expensive house than a black who has a similar income.

Banks, like individuals, may have very little to lose by discrimination. Since most blacks have low incomes, the profits from lending them money are small and may be outweighed by the losses from white retaliation. If many whites were confronted by black buyers willing and able to pay high prices for housing, or if banks were faced by the loss of large profits if they did not lend to blacks, the strength of residential segregation patterns would be much less than it actually is.

A similar situation is visible in the lack of job opportunities for blacks. Employers should be willing to hire them at lower wages than are now being paid: profits would be larger and the employer need not personally work with them. Social pressures and the individual retaliatory power of white laborers may partly explain why employers don't hire blacks, but more likely, employers are simply seldom confronted by such a situation. In most instances blacks cannot be hired at lower wages. Human capital discrimination, in both school and on-the-job training, controls entry into skilled jobs. Thus, the employer may seldom see an objectively qualified black. Historical practices may have persuaded blacks not to apply. The blacks who do apply simply lack the skills he needs. Monopoly powers of white labor as a group may effectively prevent him from paying lower wages to blacks or from hiring them. In any case if he seldom or never sees a qualified black, his losses from not hiring them are obviously minimal. Since potential losses are small, less monopoly power is necessary to prevent the employment of the few blacks who are qualified.

In most cases plants and firms are willing to hire blacks for some jobs and not for others: they are not lily-white. Blacks may be hired as sweepers, janitors, and garbage men. There is a social gap between these jobs, which are not within the traditional lines of promotion, and the rest of the jobs in the organization. Blacks are not hired for other jobs since such hiring would reduce social distance between whites and blacks.

Each type of discrimination makes it easier to enforce other types. Less schooling leads to fewer job skills, easing the problems of occupational, employment, and monopoly power discrimination. Together, all of these forms of discrimination lead to low incomes, which make price and human capital discrimination easier. Together, they reduce black political power and make schooling discrimination possible. No matter what type of discrimination is examined, it is reinforced by other types. They exist in a system of mutual support. When all are viewed together, no white perceives great economic losses from discrimination. Consequently, there are only minor economic pressures to put an end to it.

But whatever the persuasiveness of the monopoly model as a set of interlinking and mutually reinforcing monopolies that raise white incomes vis-à-vis minorities, it is as unsatisfactory as the competitive model in explaining discrimination against women. White men do not raise their family (real) standard of living by discriminating against their wives. What they gain in terms of higher earnings is lost by their wives' lower earnings. Neither is it possible to explain sex discrimination in terms of social distance. Husbands and wives belong to the same social class.

Statistical Discrimination

Both competitive and monopolistic theories of discrimination have been built up in conjunction with the standard microeconomic market clearing mechanisms. Prices are used to clear markets in both models. The only difference is that in the one, prices are competitively determined and in the other, they are monopolistically determined. Since this book has been arguing for alternative explanations of how majority earnings and wealth are distributed, how would these alternative theories affect the distributional mechanisms for minorities?

The implications of the random-walk theories are most easily seen. If physical wealth is created in the types of random process that we have been discussing, then it is not possible to lower minority group probabilities of winning the lottery. Each dollar has an equal chance of winning. To prevent minorities from accumulating physical wealth, it is necessary to stop them from participating in the lottery. This can be done by keeping their earnings so low that they do not have many dollars to devote to the random walk of wealth accumulation, or by denying them the human capital or experiences necessary to establish their entrepreneurial ability and to participate in those lotteries that require such ability as one of the conditions of entrance.

Since observed differences in wealth spring from not having the entry qualifications necessary to play the wealth accumulation game, analysis of discrimination must focus on the labor market and the job-competition model. How does the labor market work to lower minority incomes or prevent minorities from acquiring entrepreneurial skills?

Market clearing through escalation or de-escalation of required background characteristics (rather than wage changes) leads to the widely observed phenomenon of statistical discrimination. Rational cost minimizing employers choose to hire workers with the most preferred set of background characteristics. Hiring standards only fall when enough labor of the desired types is not available. The result is discontinuous "zero-one" hiring rules. If a prospective employee's background characteristics are above some level, he is eligible to be hired; if they are below some level, he is not eligible to be hired regardless of his willingness to work at a lower wage than that of the more preferred groups. Conversely, when there is a need to hire more workers than can be hired from the groups above the cut-off line, the employer will discontinuously change his hiring standard to make a new group eligible. A group that before was completely unacceptable for the job in question now becomes completely acceptable. As a result, small continuous changes in qualifications lead to a large discontinuous change in job opportunities.

Consider two individuals, one who belongs to a preferred

group and another who does not. The first one belongs to a group in which the expected probability of being fired for unsatisfactory job performance is only 5 percent, whereas the second belongs to a group with a 15 percent probability of being unsatisfactory. Although 85 percent of the second group will prove to be satisfactory, the employer refuses to hire individuals from this group because he can avoid the costs of hiring and firing an additional 10 percent of his labor force. As a result, the acceptable 85 percent of the individuals in group two suffer from statistical discrimination. They are not hired because of the objective characteristics of the group to which they belong, although they, themselves, are satisfactory.

Although most types of discrimination (racial, sexual, religious, etc.) affect specific groups, statistical discrimination is a phenomenon that affects everyone. It occurs whenever an individual is judged on the basis of the average characteristics of the group, or groups, to which he or she belongs rather than upon his or her own personal characteristics. The judgments are correct, factual, and objective in the sense that the group actually has the characteristics that are ascribed to it, but the judgments are incorrect with respect to many individuals within the group.

Statistical discrimination can exist in either the wage- or job-competition model, but it is apt to be larger, more extensive, and more persistent in the job-competition model. In the simplest version of the wage-competition model, individuals are judged upon their own characteristics and not upon the average characteristics of other individuals. Even in the case where wage competition exists among groups rather than among individuals, zero-one hiring rules would not exist as they do in job competition. The wages of a less preferred group would be lower than those of a more preferred group to compensate the employer for the additional costs that he must incur to hire the least preferred group and weed out the individuals with the undesirable characteristics. But after these costs had been paid and the employer had learned which 85 percent of the group were acceptable, these workers' wages would rise to the norm for that type of labor under wage competition. The acceptable workers buy their way out of the group to which they belong.

Individuals know whether they do or do not have the desired characteristic. If they do, they can overcome their group's characteristics by offering to work for a short period of time for a wage lower than others who are believed to have the right set of personal characteristics. Then once on the job, where they can demonstrate that they have the right characteristics, their wages will rise to the level of others with the right characteristics regardless of the groups to which they belong. Conversely, the individual who is wrongly believed to have the right characteristics will quickly be fired or reduced to a lower wage.

Nor will individuals be penalized under wage competition any more than the productivity cost of the undesired characteristic in question. Suppose the undesired characteristic is consistent tardiness. If consistent tardiness is believed to lower marginal productivity from $3.00 per hour to $2.75 per hour, then the wage differential between those groups with and those without the characteristic can only be $0.25 per hour. (If there is just a probabilistic difference between two groups, then the wage differential will be even smaller. If, for example, high-school dropouts have a 15 percent probability of being consistently tardy and high-school graduates have a 5 percent probability of being consistently tardy, the dropout will be paid $2.96 [$2.75 + (.85) (.25)] and the high-school graduate will be paid $2.99 [$2.75 + (.95) (.25)].) Consistent tardiness will not lead to zero-one hiring rules according to which one group is hired and the other is not.

In the job-competition model, statistical discrimination is apt to be much larger and more enduring. Since competitive wage bidding is counterproductive, employees pay uniform wages for a job and establish an employment queue with zero-one hiring rules. An individual who belongs to a group that has a lower probability of having a desired characteristic, or a higher probability of having an undesired characteristic, is not paid less; he is completely excluded from the job in question. Being excluded, there is no way that he can demonstrate that he himself has the desired characteristic even though his group has a lower probability of having the desired characteristic.

Zero-one hiring rules and the escalation and de-escalation of hiring requirements over the course of the business cycle produce statistical discrimination, but they are also one of the pieces of evidence pointing toward job competition and away from wage competition. They are what would be expected in a job-competition world but not what would be expected in a wage-competition world.

Whenever statistical discrimination occurs, the linkage between individual characteristics and individual earnings is broken. The individual has the desired characteristics, but he cannot sell these characteristics since he has no way of demonstrating that he has the desired characteristics. His earnings are conditioned by the characteristics of his peers rather than by his own characteristics. Groups are objectively treated; individuals are not objectively treated. If groups with known work characteristics are large and heterogeneous, statistical discrimination can lead to substantial amounts of variance in the distribution of earnings. There is a deterministic linkage between group characteristics and group earnings but not between individual characteristics and individual earnings.

Although groups are treated objectively when statistical discrimination occurs, statistical discrimination can still have an "unfair" impact on the average earnings of a group. Remember our example in which 15 percent of all high-school dropouts and 5 percent of all high-school graduates were consistently tardy and tardiness was worth $0.25 per hour. In a wage-competition world, every tardy worker would be docked $10 per week for his tardiness ($0.25 × 40 hours). Given the 10 percent probability difference, the average high-school graduate would make $1 more than the average high-school dropout, since 5 percent of all high-school workers would be docked $10 per week and 15 percent of all high-school dropouts would be docked $10 per week. Under statistical discrimination the high-school dropout would not be hired for the job under consideration and would be forced to take the next best jobs in the economy. These might well pay much less than the hypothetical $1 per week difference in the preferred job. If they do, statistical discrimination has produced a distribution of earnings that is more disperse than the distribution of characteristics. Each group is treated objectively, but the net result is a greater reduction in earnings than would be warranted from an examination of the objective characteristics of the group. Thus, statistical discrimination not only produces unwarranted (relative to intrinsic productivity or training costs) differences in individual earnings but also unwarranted differences in group earnings.

In addition to its direct effects, statistical discrimination also serves as one of the main, if not the main, underpinnings for the monopoly model of discrimination. As I have already mentioned, in a job-competition world it is economically rational for an unprejudiced employer to practice statistical discrimination. His profits go up if he hires workers from groups with higher average probabilities of having the desired background characteristics. If those who are prejudiced (the discriminators) can lower the average background characteristics of a minority by lowering the characteristics of even a few workers, the unprejudiced statistical discriminator will not hire members of the minority even though the prejudiced discriminators were not able to lower the background characteristics for every member of the minority. As a consequence, it is not possible for individual members of a minority to escape from the impacts of discrimination even though their own characteristics have not been adversely affected. Because they are to some extent going to be judged on their group's characteristics, their individual escape depends upon their group's escape as a whole. To prevent this, those who wish to establish social distance need only affect a relatively small proportion of the group against which they wish to discriminate. They need not have monopoly powers over an entire minority.

If on-the-job training is the major mechanism for producing cognitive job skills, as it is in the job-competition model, statistical discrimination will also have a much greater effect than if job skills were acquired exogenously. When the unprejudiced employer practices statistical discrimination, he produces the human-capital discrimination desired by those who are prejudiced. He rationally distributes human capital only to those who are in the preferred group. Minority-group members who want these skills cannot get them because they are not for sale, and they are not for sale because it is rational not to sell them. To do so would be to bring the training process to a halt. The skills are unsellable.

The on-the-job production of human capital in the job-competition model also lowers both the perceived economic losses and efficiency costs resulting from practicing discrimination. Since cognitive job skills do not exist in the external labor market, employers do not confront equal quality labor willing to work for lower wage rates. They must train workers in the desired skills, and to keep this training process going they must pay equal wage rates.

Because of on-the-job training, the economy also does not suffer the efficiency losses that would otherwise be implicit in not using the existing skills of minorities. The only losses are the extra training costs incurred when whites are trained for a job rather than blacks. These extra training costs could easily be small or nonexistent. Imagine a labor queue in which everyone had equal training costs and was identical. In the absence of discrimination, a random lottery would occur and the work force would be distributed across the economy's jobs. In this world blacks could, however, be systematically relegated to the bottom of the job distribution with no loss in efficiency—extra training costs. Discrimination would simply mean the establishment of a two-stage lottery. First, the best jobs would be randomly distributed among the white labor force and then the remaining jobs would be randomly distributed among the black labor force. Blacks and whites would have very different earnings, but there would be no efficiency losses for the economy as a whole.

Sexual Discrimination

Neither the physical-distance competitive model nor the social-distance monopoly model seem particularly applicable when discussing discrimination against women. Men want neither physical nor social distance from women, assuming that these phrases are used with their normal linguistic connotations. Although the discriminator often raises his real income by practicing discrimination in the competitive model and always raises his real income by practicing it in the monopolistic model, he cannot make economic gains from male-female discrimination because of the process of sharing income with the family. As I have already noted, single males might gain from sex discrimination, but married men—the vast majority—would lose.

Sex discrimination can be explained, however, from the perspective of the job-competition model. As we have seen, statistical discrimination plays a much larger and more enduring role in the job-competition model than it does in the wage-competition model. Statistical discrimination also serves as a powerful conservative force in the distribution of earnings. If the distribution of earnings starts off with differences between men and women, statistical discrimination will serve to preserve and perhaps enlarge these initial differences.

Suppose a group has certain undesired characteristics. Statistical discrimination prevents or retards the gradual elimination of these characteristics on an individual by individual basis. As long as any members of the group have the undesired characteristics, the entire group will be treated as if every member of the group had the undesired characteristics. Individual members of the group will not be upgraded in the labor queue even though they have eliminated their own undesired characteristics and are, on an individual basis, just as good potential workers as members of the preferred groups.

Consider the phenomenon of lifetime labor force participation. For a wide variety of historical and cultural reasons, women have had lower participation rates in the paid labor force than men. Even as late as 1973, participation rates for women averaged 52.3 percent compared to 95.1 percent for men in the prime working years of twenty-five to fifty-four. In addition, 22 percent of the women but only 2 percent of the men in this age group voluntarily held part-time jobs.[12]

Any employer faced with these differences in work probabilities will practice statistical discrimination even though there are millions of women who will be in the full-time paid labor force for their entire lifetimes. *Ex ante,* he cannot tell which women will be lifetime year-round full-time employees and which women will leave the labor force or become part-time employees. Because the employer provides on-the-job training, he will want to invest in those who are more likely to stay in the full-time labor force. If he provides training to women, he is less likely to be able to recoup his investment. As far as the employer is concerned, the higher probability of women leaving the full-time labor force is not counterbalanced by the higher probability of job switching among males. Even though the average period of employment by any one employer is not much different between males and females, employers are still interested in lifetime labor force participation. If a skilled male employee threatens to leave one employer for a better job opportunity elsewhere, the employer at least has the option of bribing the employee to stay. Such countervailing bribes will be much less effective in stopping women from having children, for here the trade-off is not between two basically similar economic opportunities where economic rewards can make a big difference. Nonmarginal and noneconomic decisions are being made.

Whereas statistical discrimination may be rational for employers, it still has discriminatory impacts in the job-competition model. The woman who will participate in the paid labor force for her entire lifetime is being treated unfairly. She is being assigned a background characteristic that she does not have, but there is no way for her to demonstrate that she does not have the characteristic. Given the job-competition model, she also cannot buy her way out of the situation by being willing to work for lower wages until the employer determines that she is in fact a lifetime worker.

Women as a group may also be unfairly treated. They are confronted with zero-one hiring rules even though there is not a zero-one difference in labor force participation rates. With zero-one hiring rules, they are not eligible for certain jobs at all. As a consequence, they are pushed down the job distribution and may receive jobs that are far lower in wages than would be objectively warranted by the extra costs of lower lifetime labor force participation rates. They are in exactly the same circumstances as the tardy worker examined above. Job competition acts to expand the earnings differentials beyond those that would be warranted by the extra training costs that would be incurred by hiring a group with lower expected lifetime participation rates.

The job-competition model also increases the importance of the handicap suffered by women who leave the full-time labor force to care for small children and then return at some later date. If skills were created in formal education or training programs, female re-entrants could simply invest in the skills necessary for them to catch up with their male compatriots. They could then sell these skills on an equal competitive basis with men. If skills are created through an on-the-job training process as they are in the job-competition model, then it is not possible to invest more heavily in skill acquisition and catch up with men who have been in the labor force for their entire working lifetimes. Once a worker falls behind, he or she stays behind.

There is some maximum rate of skill acquisition that depends upon the willingness of other workers to train and upon the possibilities of promotion. Time is probably more important in skill acquisition than a willingness to invest monetary resources. If the years twenty-five to forty are the years when most skills are acquired, the skill deficit can be very large since these are the years when women are most likely to be spending part of their time caring for small children.

Statistical discrimination and the job-competition model can thus produce large differences in male and female earnings in a world where there is neither a desire for physical or social distance. Objective group characteristics are magnified to produce earnings differences larger than the characteristics would warrant; individual women are assigned adverse work characteristics that they do not have, and once an individual falls behind economically it is impossible to catch up. The net impact is discrimination against women as a group and as individuals even though there is not a basic taste for discrimination against women.

Conclusions

The basic problem with the wage-competition theories of discrimination—whether competitive or monopolistic—is that they cannot provide a persuasive explanation of how discrimination manages to perpetuate itself. All of the economic incentives and pressures are on the side of eliminating discrimination. Yet discrimination does not fall under its own economic weight. The question is why. Similarly, they have difficulty handling the problem of sex discrimination. The motivations that lead to racial or religious discrimination just do not make sense when applied to sex discrimination.

From the perspective of the job-competition model, both sex discrimination and the persistence of other types of discrimination are easier to explain. The job-competition model leads to the widespread existence of statistical discrimination, but it also magnifies the effects of statistical discrimination beyond what it would be in a wage-competition model. Statistical discrimination serves as a powerful conservative force. If a group starts with inferior background characteristics (for whatever reason), statistical discrimination will retard the group's acquisition of better background characteristics and will prevent individuals from escaping from discrimination on an individual basis. To cause statistical discrimination those interested in monopolistic discrimination need only adversely affect part of the group that they wish to discriminate against. If they can affect some of the group, average background characteristics will fall and statistical discrimination will spread the effects across the entire group. Statistical discrimination will then interact back upon individual decisions to acquire background characteristics (they will appear as less profitable investments) and lead to less acquisitions of background characteristics than that of the preferred group for those who do not directly suffer from monopolistic discrimination. Statistical discrimination is thereby reinforced.

In the end a robust framework of discrimination can exist even though those who are not prejudiced might be in a large numerical majority. Discrimination exists regardless of personal tastes for discrimination.

8

POLICY IMPLICATIONS

DISTRIBUTIONAL THEORIES are judged by their ability to explain and predict what has occurred, what is, and what will be. But it is also important to know their implications for how the economic game should be played. If alternative specifications do not have different policy implications, the choice between any two alternatives is ultimately not very important. In that case no matter which theory is correct, the same actions and policies will be optimal.

Our observer would therefore want to know the policy implications of the random-walk and job-competition models. If these models of distribution are correct, what should be done differently? Which of our current policies are based upon incorrect distributional assumptions and need to be replaced? How should individual economic actors change their actions if they believe in alternative theories of distribution?

Calculating Rates of Return on Investments in Background Characteristics

Although mistakes can occur under any distributional mechanism, in a world dominated by conventional marginal productivity there is no set of incentives leading to systematic short-run mistakes. Every investment is carried to the point at which its marginal rate of return is equal to the economy's interest rate. Of course, if the underlying structure of the economy is changing over time, investments undertaken in accordance with the investment calculus or marginal productivity can prove to be *ex post* mistakes, but at any moment of time they are *ex ante* correct. In addition, under marginal productivity what is optimum from the point of view of the individual investor is also apt to be optimum from the point of view of the society as a whole. Only externalities and market imperfections can lead to a difference between private rates of return and social rates of return.

In the job-competition model, on the other hand, there are large systematic differences between private and social rates of return on investments in formal education and training. Any individual's total investment is composed of a sequence of investments. Some are under the direct control of the individual; some are not. Since individuals are not allowed to make direct wage bids to acquire their desired jobs, they are forced to bid indirectly in the form of better background characteristics. In effect, the individual buys into a more favorable lottery by acquiring background characteristics that yield a lower training cost in his desired job. Most often this means acquiring more education, since this is one of the few types of background characteristics that is controlled by the individual.

When an investor buys background characteristics, he is indirectly buying training by lowering his costs of on-the-job training. If the individual were the only investor, he would invest indirectly in background characteristics only as long as this was cheaper than the direct purchase of training. The problem springs from the fact that he cannot make direct training investments since he is not the sole investor in himself. Whereas the individual buys background characteristics, the firm allocates direct training investments.

Investments undertaken in a queueing framework with lottery outcomes can lead to a situation similar to the well-known prisoner's dilemma. Each individual faces incentives to undertake activities that will help him, if he and he alone responds to the incentives, but that will hurt him and his fellows if everyone responds to them. Consider a set of individuals wishing to bid for some desired job and the associated training. Initially, they all have identical background characteristics and they all have an equal *ex ante* probability of being selected for the desired job. *Ex post*, however, some will not be selected. If any one individual improves his background characteristics and others do not, he significantly increases his probability of getting the desired job. The private rate of return on making such an investment may be very high if only one individual makes it.

Other individuals face the same investment calculus, however. If everyone purchases additional background characteristics, no one increases his or her probability of getting the desired job, but everyone has incurred the extra costs of acquiring more background characteristics. In this kind of a competitive process, the acquisition of background characteristics can easily go beyond the point at which there is a positive social (group) rate of return. If the costs of acquiring background characteristics exceed the associated reduction in training costs, the social rate of return is negative. *Ex ante* there is a positive private rate of return to each individual, but *ex post* the private rate of return can be negative to all individuals.

The same result occurs even if individuals do not make simultaneous investment decisions. As more and more individuals improve their background characteristics, they increase their probability of getting the desired job but they also lower the probability for those who have not improved their background characteristics. These latter individuals started off with an equal chance to get the desired job, but they now have a less than equal chance. Indeed, if there are enough people with the new background characteristics, the employer may upgrade the necessary characteristics for obtaining this job, leaving those without these new characteristics with no chance of getting the desired job. As a result, the second group is now forced to invest in the extra characteristics to protect their economic position. If they do not invest, they will find themselves with a lower income. In other words, there may be a high private rate of return on making the necessary background investments, not because it will raise their income above what it would have been if no one made any investments but because it will raise their income above what it will be if others make investments and they do not. Defensive necessity forces them to make the investment. Thus, the social rate of return may be negative and the *ex post* private rate of return for each individual may be negative, but the *ex ante* private rate of return is positive for each individual. By reacting to this *ex ante* return, they all make investments that are inappropriate as far as the economy is concerned.

To determine whether or not there is a positive social rate of return in making some background investment, it is necessary to determine the reduction in on-the-job training costs associated with any background characteristic. If reductions in training costs are larger than the costs of acquiring background characteristics, there is a positive social rate of return and a positive *ex post* private return.[1] If the reductions in training costs are smaller than the costs of acquiring the background characteristic, however, there is a negative social rate of return and a negative *ex post* private rate of return, although individuals may perceive positive *ex ante* rates of return.

Such perverse investment incentives may in fact be occurring in higher education. Although going to college may look like a good investment for each individual, it may not be a good social investment to have every individual go to college. *Ex post,* everyone may just be playing a zero-sum game in which he has exactly the same income that he would have had if he and everyone else had not acquired extra education. To determine whether the game is a zero-sum game or a game in which the costs exceed the benefits, it would be necessary to determine the extent to which college education lowers training costs.

If social returns from a college education are negative, the market will cause systematic misallocations of resources, creating a difficult problem for social planning. In that case governments must act to bring *ex ante* private rates of return calculations into balance with social rates of return. In the wage-competition model, this would not be necessary since increasing supplies of college workers would lower the college wage and raise the high school wage until there was no longer a positive *ex ante* private rate of return from acquiring a college education. With a queueing model like the job-competition model, the expanding college labor force pushes high-school labor farther down the job distribution and preserves a positive wage differential between the average college worker and the average high-school worker. As a result, any calculation based on these average earnings differences (i.e., the standard human-capital calculation) will be misleading. To determine whether there is or is not a positive return to more education, it is necessary to know the marginal effect of more education on training costs. Mathematically, average wage differentials exist, but they have no economic significance.[2] As a result, our standard techniques for calculating whether education is or is not a good investment need to be recast. The current calculations are simply irrelevant if the real world is a job-competition world rather than a wage-competition world.

Prevailing distributional theories have led government data collection to focus on differences in earnings across educational levels rather than finding out the extent to which education does or does not lead to reductions in training costs. But without such training cost data, it is impossible to say whether higher education does or does not have a positive social rate of return as an economic investment.

There is another systematic difference between the wage-

and job-competition models: the element of risk. Standard human-capital calculations have ignored the problem of risk or variance in returns. Risk, on the other hand, is a central element in the job-competition model. No investment in background characteristics yields a certain rate of return. Better background characteristics simply place one in a more favorable lottery.

Although it is all right for social decisions to ignore the distribution of lottery outcomes and focus on the lottery's expected value, private decisions must include an allowance for risk. There simply is no way for an individual to diversify his portfolio of human capital in the way that even a relatively small investor can diversify his portfolio of physical investments. As a result, individuals need to be told of the variance in returns to any investment, such as education, as well as the expected gain.

But private allowances for risk create a gap between private and social rates of return. Since societies hold a balanced portfolio of human capital, social returns are quite properly calculated on the basis of expected (average) values. Individual members of any society, however, should be risk-averse since they cannot have a balanced portfolio.[3] Depending upon the individual's degree of risk aversion, something will be subtracted from the expected rate of return on any investment. As a consequence, a summation of all of society's individual decisions will also be risk-averse. This will lead to too little investment from the social point of view, since individuals in aggregate will act as if rates of return are less than they actually are.

As a result, societies need to intervene in the markets for background characteristics in at least two ways. First, calculations need to be made as to whether an investment has a positive social rate of return and a positive *ex post* private rate of return, or whether it is an investment with positive *ex ante* private rates of return but negative social and *ex post* private rates of return. If the latter proves to be true, then some technique must be found to stop individuals from collectively overinvesting in their own background characteristics. Second, to prevent private risk premiums from biasing aggregate investments, it is necessary to bring private benefit-cost calculations into balance with social benefit-cost calculations. The easiest way to do this would be to provide positive subsidies equal to the negative private risk premiums. If this were done, the positive investment effects of the subsidies would counteract the negative investment effects of risk. Risk thus provides an economic argument for subsidizing education to a limited extent.

Policies to Alter the Distribution of Earnings

From the standard marginal-productivity perspective, altering the distribution of earnings is straightforward in principle, although it may be difficult in practice. To alter the distribution of earnings, it is necessary to alter the underlying distribution of personal productivities, which in turn depends upon the distribution of human-capital investments. Thus, if the distribution of earnings is to be made more equal, then the distribution of human-capital investments must also be made more equal.

Equalizing human-capital investments, especially educational investments, is at the heart of many of the economic and social policies that have been adopted over the past fifteen years. However much they may differ on other matters, the left, the center, and the right all affirm the central importance of education (human investment) as a means of solving our social problems, especially poverty. To be sure, they see the education system in starkly contrasting terms. The left argues that the inferior education of the poor and of minorities reflects discriminatory efforts to keep them from competing with better-educated groups and to force them into menial, low-income jobs. The right argues that the poor are poor because they have failed to work hard and get the education that is open to them. Moderates usually subscribe to some mixture of these arguments: the poor are poor because they have gotten bad educations, partly as a result of inadequately funded and therefore inferior school systems, but partly also as a result of sociological factors (e.g., disrupted families) that prevent poor children from absorbing the education that is available. Yet, despite these differences, people at all points of the political spectrum agree that, if they were running the country, educational policy would be the cornerstone of their efforts to improve the condition of the poor and of minorities on the assumption that if the poor or the minorities were better educated, they could get better jobs and higher income.

In the marginal-productivity theory, it is assumed that people come into the labor market with a definite, pre-existing set of skills (or lack of skills) and that they then compete against one another on the basis of productivity. Education is crucial in this competition since it creates the skills that people bring into the labor market. This implies that any increase in the educational level of low-income workers or minorities will have three powerful—and beneficial—effects. First, an educational program that transforms a low-skill person into a high-skill person raises his productivity and therefore his earnings. Second, it reduces that total supply of low-skill workers, which in turn leads to an increase in their wages. Third, it increases the supply of high-skill workers, and thus lowers their wages. The net result is that total output rises (because of the increase in productivity among formerly undereducated workers), the distribution of earnings becomes more equal, and each individual is still rewarded according to merit. What could be more ideal?

But if this standard prescription is imposed upon a job-competition world, the outcome may be very different. As has been outlined in detail in Chapters 5 and 6, educational investments that equalize the distribution of human investments can produce a more unequal distribution of earnings. Making grade-school workers into high-school workers can lead to a situation in which high-school earnings expand relative to grade-school earnings. The extra high-school workers take what had been the best jobs available for grade-school workers. With this shift in job openings, the average wage for grade-school workers falls. This is the exact opposite of what happens in a marginal-productivity world. Depending upon the importance of training costs and their relationship to background characteristics, the average wage for high-school graduates would also fall relative to the national average, but the decrease would not be as large. The net result is an expanding wage differential rather than a contracting differential between high-school and grade-school workers. The distribution of earnings may become more unequal even though the distribution of human-capital investments has become more equal.

Thus, it is not possible to proceed on the simple theoretical assumption that any changes that equalize the distribution of human investments will equalize the distribution of earnings. Not only does the evidence indicate that this procedure has not worked in the past (see Chapter 3), but there is also no reason to believe that it should work in a job-competition model. In each case it is necessary to do some hard empirical analysis to determine the answers to the questions posed in Chapter 6. Who bears training costs, the employee or his employer? What is the precise shift in background characteristics that is contemplated? What is the elasticity of training costs with respect to improvements in background characteristics? How important are training costs? Only when answers to these questions have been determined will it be possible to predict the changes in the distribution of earnings that will flow from changes in the distribution of background characteristics.

Instead of focusing attention on the supply side of the labor market, the job-competition model concentrates on the demand side of the labor market. The supply curve of laboring skills becomes a function of the demand curve for laboring skills since cognitive job skills are learned on the job and are not generated unless a job opening is generated. It follows that efforts to alter the distribution of earnings must focus much more attention on employer demands and on how employers allocate on-the-job training investments. To significantly alter the distribution of earnings, it is necessary to significantly alter the distribution of on-the-job training. This is equally true regardless of whether employers or employees pay for training, for jobs are allocated by the employer even if he does not ultimately pay training costs.

Public policy makers, in their efforts to equalize the distribution of earnings, probably have most to learn from the World War II experience. At that time, there was an overwhelming social and political consensus that the economic burdens of the war should be more equally shared. This type of a consensus is a necessary ingredient since it allows changes in the distribution of earnings to occur without running counter to the existing structure of interdependent preferences. If wage contours are to be changed, most of the people in the existing contours must support the changes. If they do not, they are in a position to veto the resulting changes by refusing to cooperate in the team-work necessary for production. Strikes, working to rule, refusals to train, etc., are all devices for insuring that changes in wages cannot be imposed on the wage structure by outside fiat.

The basic problem with existing programs to equalize the distribution of earnings is that they have been elitist and to some extent secretive. A more equal structure of wages is to be imposed on the labor force by constructing a more equal distribution of human investments and productivities. Although efforts to improve educational qualifications and to initiate formal manpower training programs obviously had to be public, little has been said about their impact on the distribution of earnings. The normal practice, moreover, has been to maintain that minorities and the poor could be upgraded without any adverse impacts on the rest of the population.

But in both the wage- and job-competition models, this is factually incorrect. If some group is economically upgraded, someone else's wages are below what they otherwise would be. In the wage-competition model, equilibrium wages fall for those skill groups whose supplies have been augmented. In the job-competition model, wages fall for all groups with background characteristics equal or inferior to those of the upgraded group. But in the wage-competition model, it is possible to force a more equal distribution of earnings on the labor force by pumping a more equal distribution of human capital into the economy. As we have seen, this need not occur in the job-competition model. Here, a more equal distribution of background characteristics need not lead to a more equal distribution of earnings.

Even more important, it is not possible to force major changes in the distribution of earnings upon an unwilling labor force. Major changes in the distribution of earnings require alterations in the existing structure of interdependent preferences. Thus, if wage structures are to be changed, interdependent preferences and norms of industrial justice must also be changed. Without such changes it is impossible to eliminate earnings variances within skill groups—variances that explain much if not most of the variance in the entire distribution of earnings. Individuals can be moved across categories (occupations, etc.), but unless variances within these categories are reduced, the total variance cannot be reduced by more than 20 to 40 percent—the amount of the total variance that can be explained by group differences.

Although the need to convince the labor force that the structure of wages should be changed presents an obstacle, it also presents an opportunity. If the public does in fact want a more equal distribution of earnings, the public can quickly have it at a very low cost. Wages can be equalized without massive long-run investments in education and manpower programs. The wage structure can be quickly altered the way it was during World War II to reflect a new pattern of interdependent preferences. To some extent the wage policies of World War II were a deliberate—and successful—attempt to change the sociology of what constitutes "fair" wage differentials. Or it would perhaps be more accurate to say that the war changed our judgments as to what constitutes fair differentials and that this change was reflected in wartime wage policies, which deliberately sought to reduce wage differentials. After the new differentials had been embedded in the labor market for a number of years, these new differentials came to be regarded as the "just" differentials and stuck after the egalitarian pressures of World War II disappeared.

It is necessary to be realistic and perhaps a little cynical. The literature on relative deprivation maintains that only wars and other great social upheavals lead to changes in the structure of relative deprivation. If that is true, the pattern of interdependent preferences may not be subject to deliberate change. There is probably some room to alter the distribution of earnings within the existing structure of interdependent preferences and norms of relative deprivation, but major changes will depend upon changes in these norms.

Generalizing from this experience, it would seem that any time a consensus emerges on the need for more equality, it can be made at least partly by making a frontal attack on wage differentials. Educational programs, training programs, efforts to alter the skill-mix generated by technical progress, government jobs, fiscal and monetary policies to create labor shortages, public wage scales designed to pressure low-wage employers, and incentives to encourage private employers to compress their wage differentials all have a role to play. But a necessary condition for the success of these programs is a change in the norms of relative deprivation or economic justice. Without this essential ingredient, all of these programs are apt to have a limited effect on the distribution of earnings.

Increasing the Rate of Growth of Productivity

Productivity is one of those items, like God and Motherhood, that seem to be an unmitigated good. If the rate of growth of productivity were raised, a lot of economic problems (such as the balance of payments, lack of resources, inflation, low living standards, etc.) would be solved or attenuated. As a consequence, government officials periodically decide that extra efforts should be made to raise productivity. The most recent effort along this line is former President Nixon's now seemingly moribund President's Commission on Productivity.

Recommendations from such groups tend to be based on the virtues that economists claim for their model of perfect competition. "Remove market imperfections" is the general answer to any and all questions. Usually the only analysis revolves around isolating the areas where the economy does not seem to fit the model of perfect competition. Once these areas are found, recommendations are made as to how the area could be made more competitive. In such cases the model of perfect competition is employed in its normative sense. Actual institutional arrangements are to be hammered into conformity with the model.

Yet from the perspective of the job-competition model, many of the market imperfections that are to be removed are in fact central to the conditions necessary for an economy to be dynamically efficient. Thus, in order to promote training and the acceptance of technical change, the labor market is so structured as to reward those giving training and accepting change by minimizing their chance of potential loss. Wages are inflexible and seniority provisions abound. No one denies that wage competition is an essential ingredient of static efficiency. Without flexible wages, labor cannot be allocated in accordance with the principles of static efficiency. But in a job-competition model, there is a question about the virtues of flexible wages in the context of dynamic efficiency.

The basic argument revolves around a trade-off between static and dynamic efficiency. Many of the changes that would cause improvements in static efficiency would cause deteriorations in dynamic efficiency. The problem is to balance the gains and losses that come from both sources of efficiency. In general, the gains from increasing knowledge and skills will be much larger than the gains from increasing the utilization of existing skills and knowledge. The latter is a once and for all gain, whereas increases in skills and knowledge can go on forever. Thus, the trade-off should be heavily weighted in favor of dynamic efficiency over static efficiency. To improve productivity the job-competition model might, for example, suggest moving to a more highly structured labor market, like that of the Japanese, rather than trying to introduce more wage competition into the existing structure. Under such policies, dynamic efficiency would improve, although there might be a price to be paid in terms of a slightly lower level of static efficiency.

In practice, attempts to impose the theoretical conditions necessary for static efficiency may also cause deterioration in static efficiency. If individual production functions (motivation) and team production functions are sensitive to the structure of wages, attempts to impose wage competition on a highly structured set of interdependent preferences might result in substantial short-run reductions in output as well as a slowdown in long-run growth. Theoretically, the economy would move to its potential production possibilities curve, but the actual production possibilities curve might decrease. Even the potential static gains may not be realized in practice.

When it comes to improving productivity, the job-competition model calls for a lot more empirical analysis and caution than is required under wage competition. The higher rates of productivity growth in Continental Europe and Japan provide at least some evidence that perhaps we should be reducing wage competition and not increasing it. Japan is the extreme example, but all of these countries have substantially less wage competition than is to be found in the United States. Most of them also have higher rates of productivity growth.

In these countries it is much harder to dismiss workers during cyclical downturns. The dismissals that do occur tend to be concentrated among foreign workers rather than among the local work force. Whatever you may think about the cause and effect, or lack of cause and effect, among these factors, the experience of Europe and Japan at least indicates that it is not axiomatic that more wage competition automatically leads to more productivity or efficiency.

Now that some European countries have a higher per capita GNP than the United States, it is not even possible to argue that U.S. labor market practices, even if they have not demonstrated their superiority in the post–World War II period, have demonstrated their superiority in the long run. Nor is it possible to explain higher rates of productivity growth as a natural process of catching up with the higher absolute level of productivity in the United States, for the United States no longer has the highest absolute level of productivity. Similarly, within the United States the sectors that are marked by wage competition and job insecurity (construction, etc.) are not those sectors that have performed well in terms of productivity. This does not prove that more wage competition would lead to less productivity, but it does suggest extreme caution in advocating the establishment of more wage competition based on theoretical models of how the economy operates.

Altering the Distribution of Physical Wealth

From the point of view of neoclassical economics, the distribution of wealth can only be changed by changing savings behavior or by taxing wealth and income from wealth. Whereas changing savings behavior has almost no role to play from the point of view of the random-walk theory of wealth generation, wealth taxes do have a role to play. They could stop the passage of wealth from generation to generation even if they did not stop the initial creation of wealth.

It is interesting that actual efforts to control the distribution of wealth have also focused on wealth taxes rather than on changing savings behavior. Since the time of the Declaration of Independence, inheritance taxes have been advocated as a means of preventing fortunes from being passed on from generation to generation. Financially, everyone was to start the economic race roughly equal. Individual winners could keep their winnings, but they could not pass them on to the next generation. Although the random-walk model does not change the usefulness of inheritance taxes (approximately half of all great wealth is inherited), it does undercut the idea of limiting wealth taxes to inheritance taxes. From the point of view of marginal productivity, a person is only wealthy if he contributed a lot of productivity to the economy. The contributor, therefore, should be allowed to keep the fruits of his contributions. Under the random-walk model, however, the wealthy are not wealthy because their productive contribution is higher than others, but because they are luckier than others. For most people luck does not command the same respect as productive merit when it comes to determining whether or not individuals should be allowed to retain control over large aggregations of wealth.

Under the meritocratic visions of marginal productivity, stiff inheritance and gift tax laws have been built into the U.S. tax code, but there are no provisions for annual wealth taxes such as those that exist elsewhere.[4] In theory, inheritance and gift taxes could reduce the concentration of wealth substantially. In practice, loopholes have become so large that inheritance taxes have virtually ceased to exist: collections amount to an annual wealth tax of less than 0.2 percent. For all practical purposes, gift and inheritance taxes do not exist in the United States. They do not stop wealth from being transferred from generation to generation. The list of names in Appendix B is the most obvious demonstration of the ineffectiveness of American inheritance taxes.

The technical problems of preventing large inheritances from passing from one generation to another are not large or unknown.[5] Rather, the basic problem is one of political power. Are effective inheritance taxes zero because a democratic society decides that they should be zero? Or are zero inheritance taxes merely the best example of the political power that wealth can buy?

Proponents of the first argument can maintain that the popular will is best revealed in low effective tax rates rather than in high nominal tax rates. The public may verbally subscribe to an equal start, but they do not really believe their own rhetoric. Although this is not a completely preposterous argument, it is hard to understand why the public should want to go through the fiction of legislating high nominal rates and then nullifying them with generous loopholes unless someone is to be fooled. The most obvious purpose of high nominal rates and low effective rates is to use the high nominal rates as a smoke screen to hire the transfer of wealth from generation to generation. The public is led to believe that stiff inheritance taxes exist when in fact they do not exist.

If inheritances were to be prevented or reduced, the most effective technique would be to substitute a cumulative lifetime accessions tax for the current inheritance tax.[6] The inheritance tax is not a good instrument for preventing the transfer of assets across generations, since it is levied on the giver rather than the recipient so that a person who will inherit wealth from more than one source can become wealthy regardless of the tax on each individual giver. In a cumulative lifetime accessions tax, the tax is levied on the recipient. What is more, the rate structure is based on total lifetime accumulations of inheritances and gifts. One of the principal techniques for avoiding inheritance taxes is to split inheritances into several inheritances through trusts, etc.[7] Under an accessions tax the person pays the same tax on a series of small inheritances as he would on one large inheritance.

The problems in this area are not economic ones. Rather, the problem is ascertaining public preferences and then translating those preferences into political power. First, what degree of restriction on the transfer of wealth from generation to generation is in accordance with the public's equity judgments? Second, given these preferences, is it in fact possible to pass the laws necessary to embody these preferences? Or has economic power and the ability to translate economic power into political power reached the point where it is politically impossible to limit economic wealth and power? Efforts to close tax loopholes are hardly reassuring on this point. Individual loopholes are occasionally closed, but new ones are also opened up. The net result is little or no progress toward reducing the gap between nominal and effective rates.

Discussion of taxation often sounds as if the ideal tax system would consist solely of a personal income tax. It is important to understand that this implicit assumption is not warranted when discussing possible taxes on wealth. Economic reasoning does not rule out wealth taxes. At the beginning of each year, an individual or a family starts with some initial stock of wealth (W_0). At the end of the year, the individual has some stock of wealth (W_1) and has consumed some quantity of goods and services (C_1). The individual's income during the year is simply the summation of his consumption activities and his net change in wealth $(Y_1 = W_1 - W_0 + C_1)$. Savings are defined as changes in net wealth $(S_1 = W_1 - W_0)$, and income can be alternatively defined as consumption plus savings $(Y_1 = C_1 + S_1)$.

Within this economic accounting framework, there are a variety of items that might be taxed—wealth, consumption, and savings (additions to wealth). At no place in the framework, however, is there any basis for the distinction between realized and unrealized capital gains or between capital gains and income. Whether or not a person trades a real asset for cash during the course of the year (realizes his gain) has no impact on wealth, consumption, or savings. Realization may affect the ease with which an individual can raise the necessary cash to pay his tax bills and the ease with which the tax collector can measure his economic position, but it in no way affects his basic economic position. Wealth is wealth regardless of whether it is generated out of earnings or from owning appreciating assets.

The ideal tax base depends upon one's analysis of the social-welfare function of the society. Some have argued that the ideal tax system would consist solely of a consumption tax.[8] They say that only consumption can generate utility and only it should be taxed. People should therefore be taxed on what they take out of the economy (consumption) and not on what they put into the economy (earnings and wealth). Since wealth is just stored future consumption, it should be taxed when consumed. The advocates of income taxes respond to this proposition with a wider analysis of individual utility. Individuals presumably save until the marginal utility of savings is equal to the marginal utility of consumption. Since savings generate equal utility per dollar, savings should be taxed at the same rate as consumption expenditures. Hence, the optimal tax is a comprehensive income tax. The same utility argument can be extended even farther, however. Savings represent additions to wealth. Hence, each individual is equalizing the marginal utility of wealth and consumption in his savings-consumption decisions. Since wealth yields utility, the appropriate tax base is not savings plus consumption but consumption plus wealth. Only if you tax consumption plus wealth can you effectively tax the individual's total utility.

All of these positions ultimately rest upon the existence of an individualistic social-welfare function. Everything springs from private-personal utility. None of these positions considers the problem of economic power. By contrast, an individual-societal social-welfare function might contain limits on the accumulation of power as one of its arguments. Our individual-societal preferences may call for an economic game with limits to differences in power. In this case wealth and consumption might be taxed with quite different tax systems. Consumption taxes exist to control the distribution of consumption expenditures, and wealth taxes (the inheritance tax is simply a once in a lifetime wealth tax) exist to control the distribution of economic power. Nothing says that society has to have the same distributional goals in these two areas.[9] Society may well wish one to be more unequal than the other.

Our previous analysis has indicated, however, that inheritances explain only half of the current concentration of wealth. Instantaneous fortunes and the random walk explain the other half of current fortunes and the historical genesis of inherited fortunes. If inheritance taxes do not provide an adequate vehicle for controlling the distribution of wealth, it becomes necessary to alter the conditions of the random walk. In the random walk instantaneous fortunes are created in the process of capitalizing disequilibrium in the real capital markets into equilibrium in the financial capital markets. Although the capitalization cannot be prevented as long as capitalism exists, it is possible to eliminate or reduce the disequilibriums in the real capital markets.

To eliminate or reduce disequilibrium in the real capital markets, it is necessary to improve the flow of real capital funds across the real capital markets. Essentially, this means that more of the country's total savings must be forced into the real capital markets so that they can be allocated to the highest bidder. And that means reversing the current corporate tax policies that encourage internal savings. Instead of allowing generous depreciation allowances and taxing corporate earnings at a lower rate than the maximum rate paid by individuals,[10] taxes should be so adjusted as to force corporations to pay out all of their depreciation allowances and earnings. If the funds were paid to stockholders, they could flow back into the real capital markets and be allocated to those areas with the highest rates of return. The simplest procedure would be to abolish the current corporate income tax, but to require that all firms distribute all of their earnings and de-preciation allowances to their stockholders. The earnings would then be taxed at normal personal income tax rates, and firms would be forced to sell equities or bonds if they had good in-vestment projects. If the real capital markets were restruc-tured in such a fashion, disequilibrium in the real capital mar-kets might be smaller and less lengthy. With less disequilibrium there would be fewer and smaller capitalized fortunes.

Second, instantaneous fortunes would be reduced if unreal-ized capital gains and realized capital gains were taxed as normal income. At present, unrealized capital gains are un-taxed and realized capital gains are taxed at less than the normal rate for income.[11] If both were taxed at normal income tax rates, instantaneous wealth would still be large but not as large as it is today.

From an equity perspective it would also put the instan-taneous wealth on a par with the wealth that is created by patient savings out of earnings. Those who generate wealth out of their earnings must pay taxes on those earnings before they can save and invest. Those whose wealth comes from capi-talization do not have taxes reducing their wealth generating potential. If their wealth is saved (unrealized), they pay no taxes. An examination of the tax forms of those individuals who became enormously wealthy in the last five years would find that most of them paid little or no taxes. They did not realize their gains.

As a result, improvements in real capital markets and full taxation of realized and unrealized capital gains would sub-stantially reduce the concentration of wealth. As with inheri-tance, the problem is not designing technical measure for con-trolling instantaneous wealth but making the political decisions as to how severely they should be applied, if at all.

Eliminating Discrimination

From the point of view of competitive physical-distance theories of discrimination, only changes in tastes can eliminate or reduce discrimination against minorities, and there is little that governments can do. Governments are also unlikely to adopt programs to change tastes even if such programs are available. If discrimination is to exist at all, all whites must have tastes for discrimination against blacks, since the system is dominated by the discriminatory tastes of the person with the least taste for discrimination. If whites are in the majority and all whites have a taste for discrimination against blacks, democratic governments are unlikely to undertake actions to change the tastes of not just the majority, but all whites.

From the point of view of monopolistic social distance theories of discrimination, there is a larger role for governments. They can seek to break overt monopolistic practices wherever they exist. Since the monopolies could be perpetuated by minorities of the white population, there also is at least the logical possibility that governments might be interested in stopping monopolistic discrimination.

As we have seen, neither of these two theories of discrimination can tell us what should be done about sex discrimination since neither of them provides a convincing explanation of sex discrimination. Without knowing how and why sex discrimination is perpetuated, it is impossible to design programs for eliminating it.

From the job-competition point of view, statistical discrimination becomes a key ingredient in any system of discrimination. Statistical discrimination occurs when employers judge the potential training costs of prospective employees based upon the objective characteristics of the groups to which they belong. Statistical discrimination is practiced because it is efficient and employers can cut their training costs by practicing it. But as we have seen, it is inequitable in the job-competition model because it leads to treating both individuals and groups unfairly relative to their productive characteristics.

The same problem exists in formal educational programs and the acquisition of other skills and background characteristics. Imagine a medical-school admissions committee. Suppose it checks its alumni records and finds that 95 percent of all the men they have admitted have finished medical school and that 95 percent of these graduates went on to be lifetime practitioners. But the committee finds that only 90 percent of all the women they have admitted finished medical school and that only 90 percent of these graduates went on to be lifetime practitioners. Based on expected values, the admissions committee would then know that there was a 90 percent probability (0.95×0.95) that every man admitted would practice medicine and a 81 percent probability (0.9×0.9) that every woman who was admitted would practice medicine. If the admissions committee was simply being efficient, it would notice that it could generate more doctors per unit of resources by admitting men rather than women. Efficiency considerations would lead them to admit all men and no women.

But this decision would be inequitable to both the 81 percent of the women who would go on to become lifetime doctors and to the group relative to its average characteristics. Although there is only a 9 percent difference in the male-female probabilities of practicing medicine, this is translated into a 100 percent difference in their chances of becoming doctors.

For each employer or admissions committee, statistical discrimination is efficient (it maximizes their output per unit of resources), but from the point of view of the economy as a whole it is inefficient. Statistical discrimination stops the economy from making use of the talents and working desires that are available to it. As in human capital investments, there is a systematic difference between what is privately rational and what is socially rational.

As always when there is a systematic difference between private and social rates of return, government needs to act to bring private rates of return into line with social rates of return. But it should be recognized that to achieve both equity and social efficiency, individuals must pay a price in terms of less private efficiency. Employers and other screening agencies must give up the use of some perfectly good statistical indicators of future performance and replace them with more expensive tests that relate to expected individual performances and not to expected group performances.

Eliminating statistical discrimination is also important because such discrimination is the major technique for enforcing and spreading monopolistic social-distance discrimination against minorities. Under statistical discrimination, prejudiced individuals can create and enforce discrimination if they can lower the characteristics of even a few members of the group being discriminated against. If they can affect even a few members of the group, the group's average characteristics will fall and statistical discriminators will act as if all members of the group had the lower characteristics. Not only will this practice be unfair to individual minority-group members who have the desired characteristics, but it will lead to larger income gaps between the discriminator's group and the discriminatee's group than their average characteristics would warrant.

Eliminating statistical discrimination is difficult, for it requires that employers and other screening agencies refrain from using objective and efficient information. It can only be done by some type of affirmative action that requires institutions to hire or admit women and members of minorities, and thus forces them to search among these groups for individuals who have the characteristics they desire. Unless they are under affirmative action pressures, all of their incentives will lie in the direction of practicing statistical discrimination. Affirmative action is simply a device by which private and social returns are brought into line in the area of statistical discrimination. It creates "equal opportunity" at the level of the individual rather than at the level of the group to which the individual belongs.

Eliminating statistical discrimination is important to minorities and women, but it is also important to adult white males as individuals. Although they might belong to the age-sex-race group with the best statistical background characteristics, statistical discrimination is also practiced within background subgroups such as educational classes. Adult white males who happen to fall into less preferred subgroups but who have the desired characteristics will find that they also suffer from discrimination. Adult white males may find that they benefit from statistical discrimination as a group (i.e., their average incomes are higher with it than without it), but millions of individual adult white males will find that their own incomes are lower than their own individual performance characteristics would warrant.

The zero-one hiring rules of the job-competition model lead to greater discontinuities in individual economic positions than data on training costs would warrant. A continuous distribution of individuals is broken into discontinuous groups. Individuals whose characteristics are only slightly different find that they participate in radically different lotteries. The discontinuities may also exist over the working lifetime of one individual. When a worker loses his job in the job-competition model, he may not be able to re-employ the skills that he has learned on his old job and loses the benefits of whatever senority he has accumulated. He is not working along a continuum where the willingness to accept a small reduction in wages will guarantee re-employment at his old skills. This may be one of the reasons why job security typically heads the list of desirable job characteristics.[12] If a willingness to accept marginal reductions in wages would guarantee re-employment, job security would not dominate wages as a desirable job characteristic. Job security could be cheaply purchased by anyone who wished to have it.

Individual Versus System Determinism

From the point of view of simple marginal-productivity theories, there is a direct linkage between any individual's inputs (hours of work, skills, savings, etc.) into the productive process and his outputs (earnings and increases in physical wealth). An individual gets what he or she produces. To get more output one must simply contribute more inputs. Marginal productivity is deterministic at the level of the individual economic actor. Each individual is justly treated in the sense that he has a position in the distributions of earnings and wealth that is in accordance with his own contribution. If he wants another position, he need only change his contribution.[13]

Analytically, stochastic disturbance terms can easily be added to simple marginal-productivity models, but this is not normally done because it substantially alters the characteristics of the model and the policy conclusions that can be drawn from it. From a stochastic point of view, for example, it is not axiomatic that raising an individual's skills will raise his or her earnings.[14] Individual economic justice does not automatically occur.

In both the job-competition model and the random-walk models, conditional random lotteries are at the heart of the distributional process. In the random-walk model the lotteries are conditional upon the degree of risk desired, and in the job-competition model the lotteries are conditional on the background characteristics that the individual has acquired. But in both cases there will be a distribution of economic outcomes for those who are willing to accept equal risks and for those who have acquired equal background characteristics. Individual positions in the distributions of earnings and wealth are to a great extent determined by the characteristics of economic lotteries rather than by their own individual characteristics. The economic system is deterministic in the sense that it will generate some known and predictable distribution of outcomes, but the position of any one individual is not deterministic. In this sense, job-competition and the random walk are similar to quantum mechanics. The overall distribution of atoms is known, but the place of any one individual atom is stochastic. *Ex post* individuals who make identical contributions are going to be rewarded very differently.

We have already seen how the job-competition and random-walk models alter individual and social investment decisions, but they also have implications for the relative weight that should be placed on tax-transfer policies in any effort to alter the distributions of earnings and wealth. Changes in individual background characteristics and the elimination of statistical discrimination have an important role to play in altering the distribution of positions (minorities, etc.) upon the overall distributions of earnings and wealth, but tax-transfer policies must bear a major weight in any effort to change the overall distributions themselves. The conditional lotteries simply are not different enough to make major changes in the overall distributions of earnings and wealth by moving individuals from one conditional lottery to another.

Originally, the war on poverty started with President Johnson's requirement that anything could be tried except direct tax-transfer programs of redistributing income from the rich to the poor. Although such a condition is feasible, even if not desirable, from a standard neoclassical point of view, it is completely unfeasible from a job-competition and random-walk point of view. To rule out direct tax-transfer programs is to rule out any possibility of significantly changing the distributions of earnings and wealth.

Stochastic processes also have implications for how we assess the economic justice or injustice of the existing distributions of earnings and wealth. They force us to confront the problem of whether the distributions of earnings and wealth are equitable or inequitable not just once, but at every point in time.[15] With stochastic processes it is not possible to argue that the distributional mechanism automatically creates economic justice by rewarding each individual in relation to his productive inputs. It doesn't. Each individual is not paid in accordance with what he produces, and equals do not have equal *ex post* incomes.

It is possible to argue that lottery processes are fair or just, just as it is possible to argue that marginal productivity is fair or just, but being willing to call a lottery fair is only a partial solution to the justice problem. Even if a lottery is just, there still is the subsidiary problem of determining the distribution of prizes that the lottery ought to produce. Should it be a widely dispersed distribution of economic prizes or a narrowly concentrated distribution of economic prizes? The same lottery process can create both.

Conclusions

In the end the reader must decide whether the do-it-yourself distributional mechanisms that he or she has constructed are better or worse than the job-competition model for distribution earnings and the random-walk model for distributing physical wealth. Hopefully, there is a net gain from this book even if you decide that your own models of distribution are superior. You will at least have been forced to outline your own theory of distribution more completely and perhaps to have refined them. The ultimate aim of this book is not to create a new orthodoxy that will completely supplant the existing amorphous marginal-productivity theories, but to reopen the process of investigating the actual mechanisms by which earnings and wealth are distributed.

APPENDIX A

A DO-IT-YOURSELF GUIDE
TO MARGINAL PRODUCTIVITY

IF marginal productivity is to be used as a functional theory of distribution, it is necessary to make a series of judgments as to what is meant by the marginal-productivity theory of distribution. Once these determinations are made, it then becomes possible to test the theory against actual data to see whether the theory does or does not explain what occurs.

The purpose of this appendix is to outline the judgments that anyone would have to make if they were to actually apply the marginal-productivity theory of distribution. Each person can make these determinations for himself or herself, construct his or her own version of marginal productivity, and then see whether their versions explain the actual distribution of economic prizes better than the theories outlined in this book.

Level of Applicability

Marginal-productivity factor payments could exist on a number of levels. Depending upon the level at which the theory holds, different types of evidence would be relevant to proving or disproving the hypothesis.

In its most rigorous form, marginal productivity states that each individual factor of production is paid his, her, or its marginal product at each instant of time. From this position there exists a continuum of possibilities where individual factors are paid their marginal products but only over longer and longer periods of time. At the other end of this continuum, factors are paid their marginal products, but only over the course of their entire lifetimes.

QUESTION: *What is the time period over which marginal products are paid?*

The importance of this question can be seen in seniority wage payments. Seniority wage schedules are not evidence contrary to the lifetime marginal-productivity hypothesis, but they are evidence contrary to the instantaneous marginal-productivity hypothesis.

Instead of being a theory of individual-factor payments, marginal productivity can be interpreted as a theory of group-factor payments. Individuals are not paid their marginal products, but groups are paid their average marginal products. Skill differences provide the most obvious groupings. Plumbers, for example, are not judged on the basis of their individual productivity, but are instead paid in accordance with the average marginal productivity of plumbers as a group. Individual plumbers who are below average will be paid more than their marginal productivity would warrant, whereas plumbers who are above average will be paid less than their marginal productivity would warrant.

QUESTION: *Are groups or individuals paid their marginal products?*

If groups are paid their marginal products, common wages for large groups of individuals is not evidence contrary to marginal productivity even if there are productivity differences among the members of the group. If individuals are supposed to be paid their marginal products, it is damaging evidence.

If the group interpretation of marginal productivity is used, a set of subsidiary questions must be answered. What grouping theory determines which individuals will be lumped together and paid a common wage? Does the economy generate large groups of hetergeneous skills or small groups of homogeneous skills? Obviously, as the groups grow smaller and smaller the skill group theory of marginal productivity gradually approaches the individual theory of marginal productivity.

QUESTION: *What is the theory that determines whether marginal-productivity groups are large or small, heterogeneous or homogeneous?*

Skill groups are not the only dimension upon which a group theory of marginal productivity could be constructed. Other possible groupings exist along industrial rather than skill lines. In this interpretation the relevant group is not the skill class to which an individual factor belongs, but the industrial group in which the individual factor is employed. Factors of production employed in the automobile industry, for example, are paid in accordance with the average marginal productivity of factors of production in automobiles. The same individual factor employed in textiles would be paid less because that factor is playing on a less productive team, but both factors are being paid in accordance with industrial marginal productivity.

QUESTION: *Do groups exist along skill or industrial lines?*

If marginal productivity exists along industrial lines, different skill-factor payments across industries are not evidence against marginal productivity; if marginal productivity exists along skill lines, however, different factor payments across industries are contrary evidence.

Once again there is a subsidiary question of how industrial groupings are formed and the level on which they apply. Do they exist at the level of the plant, the firm, or the industry?

Whatever the level of applicability, what causes these particular groups rather than some other particular groups to come about?

With industrial marginal productivity it is also necessary to subscribe to some subsidiary theory of distribution. The whole industrial team may be paid in accordance with its average marginal product. But what determines wage differences among different members of the same team? What is the theory of distribution that applies within the industrial group?

Another possible grouping exists across geographic areas. In this variant the geographic region in which the factor is employed is relevant to determining its marginal product. Does marginal productivity hold at the level of the world, the nation, the state, the city, or at even more narrowly circumscribed geographic regions? Clearly, the problem is to determine the geographic extent of the market for factors of production. If the market is less than worldwide, what are the explanations for geographically circumscribed markets for factors of production?

QUESTION: *What is the geographic area over which marginal productivity applies?*

If the area is the nation, geographic wage differences within the nation constitute evidence that is contrary to the theory, but if marginal productivity exists only within local areas, interarea wage differentials are obviously easy to explain.

In its most aggregate form the marginal-productivity theory of distribution simply means that an average unit of capital is paid in accordance with the average marginal productivity of capital and that an average laborer is paid in accordance with the average marginal product of labor. Individual units of capital and labor may not be paid their marginal products, but the pluses and minuses cancel out.

QUESTION: *What is the level of aggregation at which capital and labor are paid their marginal products?*

As this particular variant of marginal productivity clearly

indicates, the more aggregate the theory, the more necessary it is to have some subsidiary theory of distribution to explain how differences are distributed within group earnings. As marginal-productivity theories become more and more aggregate, they come closer and closer to a tautology. At the most aggregate level, factors in general must be paid in accordance with the productivity of factors in general. Factors produce the GNP and factors receive the GNP. At this level marginal productivity exists by definition if economies or diseconomies of scale do not exist (see below).

Subsidiary distribution theories are necessary in every variant except the strict interpretation in which every individual factor is paid his marginal product at every instant of time. If factors are paid lifetime marginal products, what determines the distribution of payments over a lifetime? If factors are paid in accordance with average group-skill marginal products, how are individuals assigned to groups? If factors are paid in accordance with industrial marginal products, how are intragroup earnings differences determined? If factors are paid in accordance with regional marginal products, what determines the geographic extent of the market for factors of production? If marginal productivity exists at the level of capital and labor aggregations, how are intragroup payment differences explained?

Obviously, it is also possible to argue that marginal-productivity factor payments are some combination of these different variants of marginal productivity. A factor's payments depends upon its own productivity, its skill's productivity, its industry's productivity, its region's productivity, and the productivity of the factor class to which it belongs. In this case it is necessary to determine the weights of the different components and then explain why these particular weights come about.

The Problem of Economies and Diseconomies of Scale

If either economies or diseconomies of scale exist within an economy, factors of production *cannot* be paid in accordance with the marginal-productivity theory of distribution. With economies of scale, marginal products exceed average products and paying marginal products would more than exhaust total output. There simply is not enough output to pay each factor its marginal product since the last factor adds more to output than the first factor. Similarly, if diseconomies of scale exist, average products exceed marginal products and paying marginal products leaves an unclaimed residual. Output is left over since the last factor adds less to output than the first factor. Technically, marginal productivity is only applicable when there are constant returns to scale.

If there are increasing or decreasing returns to scale, the marginal-productivity theory of distribution does not say what should be done about the positive or negative residuals. Who is to be paid less than his marginal product; who is to be paid more than his marginal product? There are no answers within the marginal-productivity theory. What is the answer?

Whether economies or diseconomies of scale are or are not a problem depends upon the level at which marginal productivity is to be applied. If marginal productivity means paying marginal products to capital and labor, then the only question is whether there are economies or diseconomies of scale at the level of the entire economy. If marginal productivity applies at the level of the individual, the skill, the industry, or the region, the problem exists if there are economies or diseconomies of scale at the appropriate level. Although the U.S. economy seems to exhibit constant returns to scale as a whole, there are many industries with economies or diseconomies of scale.

QUESTION: *What theory of distribution exists when marginal productivity cannot be applied because of economies or dis-economies of scale?*

The Impacts of Market Imperfections

Since marginal productivity flows from perfect competition, it is necessary to specify how different real world imperfections influence it. Are the imperfections so large and important that they require major modifications in the marginal-productivity theory of distribution, or do they only cause minor deviations?

MONOPOLY AND MONOPSONY

If monopolies or monopsonies exist, there are monopoly profits that must be allocated to those that control them and sub-tracted from those that are controlled by them. The monopolist receives more than his equilibrium marginal revenue product, and the factors controlled by the monopoly receive less than their equilibrium marginal revenue product.

In the case of a product market monopoly, the monopolist sets its price at the point where the marginal cost curve (supply curve) crosses the marginal revenue curve rather than the demand curve. Less output is sold at a higher price. The result is a variety of real income changes from those dictated by marginal productivity. Monopoly profits exist and are allocated to the owners of the monopoly. Since less output is produced and sold at higher prices, real incomes fall for the consumers who purchase the monopolized goods. With less output being produced, the derived demand curves for factors of production shift inward, lowering equilibrium factor prices. Relative factor prices are also affected since the supply curves for different factors of products do not have identical elasticities and since the industry may not use the economy's average mix of land, labor, and capital.

Assume, for example, that the monopolized industry has a

higher than average capital labor ratio and that supply curves for capital and labor have similar elasticities. With cuts in output the derived demand curves for both capital and labor fall, but the curve for capital falls more than that for labor. The result is a greater reduction in the price of capital than in the price of labor, with consequent income distribution effects.

Any student of micro-economics can quickly work out the income changes that occur under different assumptions about the characteristics of the product market monopoly and the changes that would occur in the case of a monopsony in the product market, a monopoly in the factor markets, or a monopsony in the factor markets. The changes are predictable, but the distribution of real incomes that emerges in these cases is not a marginal-productivity distribution of economic resources. QUESTION: *To what degree does the economy fit the competitive model and to what degree does it fit the monopoly model? The actual economy is a mixture, but what are the relevant proportions?*

To apply marginal productivity it is necessary to specify the extent to which the distribution of economic prizes is a marginal-productivity distribution and the extent to which the distribution of economic prizes reflects monopolies.

Although there is a perfectly adequate theory of monopoly income determination, the real world is marked more by oligopolies than pure monopolies. The literature on oligopolies does not contain a well worked out theory of distribution but generally depends upon a complicated unspecified bargaining process in which there is a range of possible outcomes. In the long run a oligopoly will never rationally charge more than a monopolist in the same position, and it will never charge less than a competitive firm. But within this range what is the relevant theory of distribution?

Monopoly profits also have an impact on the distribution of income long after the actual monopolies have disappeared. To the extent that they have made someone permanently wealthy, they influence the structure of demand in all later periods. With different demand curves different equilibrium marginal products emerge.

TIME LAGS AND DISEQUILIBRIUM

How fast do markets reach equilibrium? Do they reach equilibrium quickly or only after a long period of time? Consider the problem posed by a sudden expansion of the derived demand curve for medical doctors as the result of Medicaid or Medicare. There is a long-run equilibrium supply curve of medical doctors that depends upon the rate of return on a medical education, but there is also a short-term disequilibrium supply curve that may be much more inelastic. Over time, the economy's supply curve gradually shifts from this short-run disequilibrium supply curve to the more elastic long-run equilibrium supply curve. But in the interval before the long-run equilibrium is attained, there are short-run disequilibrium quasi-rents. These quasi-rents are necessary to efficiently allocate a limited supply of doctors, but they are payments over and above what would be necessary to guarantee the appropriate long-run supply of doctors.

Disequilibrium conditions are apt to be even more prevalent than those implied by the time lags necessary to get from one set of equilibrium conditions to another. If the basic factors that determine equilibrium are changing rapidly in relationship to the time necessary to achieve equilibrium, the economy may never be in equilibrium—even if it is always rapidly heading toward equilibrium. Equilibrium marginal products are never being paid, and quasi-rents play an important role in determining the distribution of income at all points in time.

In this case both the short-run and long-run distributions of factor payments are marginal-productivity distributions, but the short-run distribution is a disequilibrium marginal-productivity distribution, whereas the long-run distribution is an equilibrium marginal-productivity distribution.

QUESTION: *To what extent is the actual distribution of economic prizes a long-run equilibrium distribution and to what extent is it a short-run disequilibrium distribution? Rate of return on different investments must be equal in the first case but can be unequal in the second case.*

Quasi-rents are important not only because they influence the current distribution of income but also because they influence and alter the economy's equilibrium conditions. Whenever quasi-rents exist, they influence demands and hence the derived demand curves for factors of production. As a result of the induced alteration in demands, the economy's equilibrium conditions change. Disequilibrium quasi-rents do not disappear. Through their long-run impact on demand, they have a long-run impact on the economy even if the economy should ultimately attain an equilibrium position. An economy with a history of quasi-rents will have a different equilibrium position than an economy without such a history.

What this means is that comparative statics—the analysis of two periods of equilibrium without regard to the disequilibrium conditions in between—is fundamentally in error. The disequilibrium quasi-rents incurred in moving between two equilibrium positions will alter the final equilibrium. The disequilibrium path can never be ignored. It always makes a difference. The distribution of economic prizes will be different with and without periods of disequilibrium.

QUESTION: *To what extent is the current distribution of economic prizes determined by past disequilibriums and to what extent is it determined by current disequilibriums?*

KNOWLEDGE AND IGNORANCE

The marginal-productivity theory of distribution depends heavily on the existence of perfect, low-cost, widely dispersed knowledge. To reach a marginal-productivity distribution of factor payments in either the short run or the long run, each buyer and seller in both the product markets and the factor markets must know where he can find the best price. Knowledge is never prefect in the sense of having perfect foresight of future conditions, but substantial ignorance can also exist about current conditions. Here, the problem has not only to do with a lack of knowledge but with the distribution of existing knowledge.

Some informational differences spring from the competence of individual buyers and sellers in different markets, but much of it springs from the costs of acquiring the relevant information. In some markets information is simply expensive to acquire. The expected costs in terms of both time and money may exceed the expected value of the information to be acquired. In this case the market can be perfect in the sense that each individual is acquiring the optimum (costs-benefits) amount of information, yet very imperfect in the sense that all of the relevant information is not at hand and the market is not in equilibrium.

Either ignorance or high costs information will lead to a system in which identical factors of production are not paid identical amounts and in which the same goods and services cost different amounts. The market is reacting perfectly to what the players know, but the outcome is not a marginal-productivity outcome. The individual lucky enough to be at the right place at the right time will sell at above-equilibrium prices, and the individual unlucky enough to be at the wrong place at the wrong time will sell at below-equilibrium prices with obvious consequences for the distribution of income.

QUESTION: *To what extent does the level and distribution of ignorance cause deviations from the marginal-productivity distribution that would be expected in the case of perfect knowledge?*

Once again the question is not the existence of ignorance and high-cost information, but the extent to which the ultimate distribution of economic prizes is determined by the distribution of information and luck rather than the distribution of marginal products.

CONSTRAINTS AND IMPERFECTIONS IMPOSED BY GOVERNMENT

All economies work within a framework of rules and regulations laid down by society and enforced by government. This framework provides a set of constraints within which marginal productivity operates. If governments enforce private property rights, a different set of economic prizes will emerge than if governments do not enforce private property rights. Imagine the resources that each individual would need to be devoted to property defense if society did not attempt to enforce and inculcate a respect for private property. The distribution of real earnings and wealth would surely be substantially different.

Similarly, programs like truth in lending or advertising all serve to influence the demand for goods, services, and factors of production. Demand with subliminal advertising might be quite different from demands without subliminal advertising. The distribution of income that emerges within a framework of governmental regulations is still a marginal-productivity distribution, but the outcome of the process can be quite different depending upon what framework is in effect.

One of the basic changes in the U.S. framework was the abolition of slavery. Private property rights in other human beings were abolished. This meant that it was not possible for one person to appropriate the factor earnings of another, but it also had consequences for human-capital investment. Since an individual could sell himself into slavery or servitude, lending institutions could not obtain mortgages on human-capital investments as they could on physical investments. As a result, private human-capital loans were extremely rare before recent government programs to guarantee these loans. The loans could be defaulted, and the lending institutions had nothing that they could claim as theirs.

With limited human-capital loans, such investments must be self-financed. Each individual invests to the point at which his investments earn a rate of return equal to his rate of time preference. If his rate of time preference exceeds the market interest rate, he does not make the investments that perfect capital markets would indicate. The result is a different distribution of income than what would occur if individuals could mortgage themselves.

The examples are endless, but the basic point is that marginal productivity works within a framework that is prescribed by governmental regulations. The shape of the frame helps define the nature of the picture within the frame. But once again the question is to what extent.

QUESTION: *Which, if any, government actions cause major changes in the distribution of factor payments? Do governments, for example, pay their employees in accordance with the dictates of marginal productivity?*

Governments are not under the profit maximization dictates of the private economy, but cost-benefit maximization would lead to the same need to have marginal-productivity wage payments to insure efficiency.

The Maximization Hypothesis

The marginal-productivity theory of distribution depends upon an underlying assumption of maximization. Everyone in the economy is trying to maximize his or her money income. Analytically, it is possible to apply the maximization calculus of economics in either money or utility terms, but to be a valid explanation of money prizes, individuals must maximize their money prizes and not their utility prizes. Questions about money maximization arise with respect to both capital and labor, but they are most acute in the labor area.

When discussing work-leisure choices, economists quickly slip from money-income maximization postulates to utility or psychic-income maximization postulates. (As the social sciences are becoming less utilitarian and more Freudian, the jargon is gradually shifting from utility to psychic income, but the two refer to exactly the same phenomenon.) The shift is natural since a laborer must personally accompany his labor or human capital, whereas he does not need to accompany his physical capital. Since he must be personally present, he is interested in a range of nonmoney benefits that may spring from work. Some jobs are dirty; some jobs are clean. Some jobs provide prestige and power; some jobs do not. Some jobs provide enjoyable working conditions and friends; some jobs do not. The possibilities of being interested in nonmonetary factors are endless and real. An individual might, for example, be perfectly willing to be an absentee slum landlord or to loan money to a slum landlord yet be unwilling to manage or live in a slum apartment house. In the first two instances, he does not need to enter the slum in question; in the latter two cases, he must work or live there.

As a result, we quite naturally swing into talking about psychic-income maximization when we start talking about job choices. The problem springs from the fact that an individual who is a psychic-income maximizer is not a monetary-income maximizer. He maximizes a combination of money earnings plus nonmonetary benefits and costs. He works on a psychic-earnings supply curve rather than on a money-earnings supply curve.

When nonmonetary factors enter the maximization process, the distribution of total income (psychic benefits and costs plus monetary earnings) is a marginal-productivity distribution but the distribution of money earnings is not a marginal-productivity distribution. The money results are conditioned by a whole set of psychic benefits and costs. These psychic benefits and costs can easily dominate the distribution of money income and lead to a distribution of money income that does not resemble the distribution of total income (monetary plus psychic). To explain the distribution of money incomes, it would be necessary to know the distribution of the factors that create psychic incomes as well as the workings of the marginal-productivity mechanism. Each person's nonmonetary psychic income would be subtracted from his marginal product to obtain his money earnings.

Suppose, for example, that we were dealing with a job with substantial net nonmonetary benefits. Because of these benefits, the actual supply curve of labor falls to the right of the supply curve that would exist if the job provided nothing but money earnings. This leads to a lower monetary wage than would have existed if the psychic-income benefits had not existed. Ramifications also occur in other markets. The labor supplies to other industries decrease since more labor is now used in the industry or job with positive net nonmonetary benefits. Thus, the distribution of monetary prizes—the prize distribution that we measure and seek to explain—could be very different depending upon the extent and distribution of nonmonetary psychic-income benefits.

QUESTION: *To what extent do psychic-income benefits and costs alter the actual distribution of monetary prizes? Are they so large or distributed in such a manner as to noticeably alter the distribution of monetary rewards? Alternatively, is the marginal-productivity theory of distribution meant to apply in monetary space or in utility space? If marginal productivity applies only in utility space, then there is a need to have a subsidiary theory to explain the distribution of nonmonetary rewards before it is possible to explain the distribution of monetary rewards.*

In the capital area, maximization disputes revolve around the extent to which firms (capitalists?) are long- or short-run profit maximizers and the extent to which they are growth maximizers rather than profit maximizers. The first has to do with the quantity of quasi-rents that exist in the system at any one moment. A long-run profit maximizer may not set prices at the short-run disequilibrium level even if these prices could be charged and collected. The second has to do with the extent to which firms are willing to accept below-equilibrium rates of

225

return on capital in order to promote more growth than would occur if they insisted on market rates of return. In this case the distribution of factor payments is still a marginal-productivity distribution, but it is a disequilibrium as opposed to equilibrium distribution. The problem, as before, is that to actually use the marginal-productivity theory of distribution to explain economic prizes, it is necessary to specify the extent to which these two situations occur.

The Initial Conditions

In addition to specifying the mechanism of marginal productivity itself, it is necessary to specify the initial conditions from which the mechanism starts if actual distributions of economic prizes are to be explained. These conditions can be treated as exogenous events that do not need to be explained by economic theories—they simply need to be determined—or they can be treated as economic phenomena that need an explanation in any systematic theory of income and wealth determination.

THE INITIAL DISTRIBUTIONS OF WEALTH AND EARNINGS

Two neglected but important initial conditions have a large impact on the actual distributions of earnings and wealth that will be produced in competitive markets. These are the *initial* distributions of earnings and wealth. They have a double-barreled impact on the distribution of economic rewards, since they represent both the initial distribution of potential purchasing power and the initial distribution of ownership claims.

The initial distribution of purchasing power is critical, since it determines each individual's demand curves for goods and services and hence the derived demand curves for factors of production. As the distribution of purchasing power shifts, derived demand curves shift and different equilibrium marginal-revenue products emerge in the factor markets. Two economies with identical wealth and earnings, but different distributions of purchasing power, will generate different distributions of earnings and wealth.

The distribution of ownership claims is important since it determines to whom the marginal revenue products will be paid. Altering the distribution of ownership rights (human or physical) leads to different distributions of income, since marginal revenue products are paid to the owners of factors of production. An economy in which all factors of production are owned by one person will have a very different distribution of income than an economy in which all factors of production are equally owned even if the equilibrium marginal revenue products are identical in the two economies.

As a consequence, the competitive distribution of earnings and wealth is a function of the initial distribution of earnings and wealth. Neither the immediate distribution of earnings and wealth nor the latter distributions of earnings or wealth is independent of the starting conditions. The distributions generated in the economy do not necessarily replicate the initial conditions of the economy, but they are always dependent upon these initial conditions. Different initial distributions of wealth and purchasing power will generate different historical sequences of income as the economy moves along. These might become more or less unequal as time passes, but they are not independent of the initial conditions. The economy does not move toward the same outcome regardless of its starting point.

The process can be easily visualized if the economy is thought of in terms of discrete rounds of purchases, production, and generation of incomes. The distribution of incomes at the end of the first round may differ from the initial conditions and will in turn lead to yet a new distribution of income at the end of the second round, but the income in each round depends upon the initial starting point. The economy always achieves "equilibrium," but the actual equilibrium depends upon where the economy starts. As a result, actual distributions of earnings and wealth are partly dependent upon the functioning of marginal productivity and partly dependent upon the initial conditions. Since marginal productivity does not explain the initial conditions, an explanation must be found for these conditions if one is to have a complete theory of distribution.

THE DISTRIBUTION OF KNOWLEDGE

The spectrum of technical knowledge is an important determinant of the distribution of income since it ultimately influences both the level and variance in incomes. The marginal physical productivity of any factor of production depends upon the state of technical knowledge. Profit-maximizing economic substitutions can only occur within the economic space created by the spectrum of technical knowledge. To take the extreme case, if the world were in fact an input-output world with fixed coefficients, technology would completely determine the distribution of income with no room for any economic substitutions of one factor for another. Although the world is probably not a rigid input-output world, it also is not a world characterized by complete knowledge and unlimited technical substitutions.

Technology and changes in technology thus join the initial distributions of wealth and purchasing power as exogenous factors that impinge on the distribution of income even if marginal productivity is fully operational. The relevant question becomes one of the range within which marginal productivity and economic substitutions can take place. Is it a wide range or a narrow range? Depending upon the answer to this question, marginal productivity becomes more or less important vis-à-vis technology as an explanation of the actual distribution of income.

EXOGENOUS INGREDIENTS IN FACTOR SUPPLIES

There are also a variety of exogenous factors that affect the distribution of earnings and wealth from the factor supply side of the market. Factor supply curves are to some extent created by economic incentives and factor payments, and they are to some extent exogenously given. To the extent that they are exogenously given, these factors will have an independent influence on the final equilibrium marginal products and on the distribution of economic prizes.

The basic problem is most easily seen in the case of land. To a great extent the supply curve for land is exogenously given. Land either exists or it does not exist; it is not supplied in the economic sense of that term. Economic incentives are not necessary to bring it into existence and cannot in fact bring it into existence. The price of land simply serves to allocate the exogenously given supply efficiently. (Remember, however, that land is not a synonym for space. Space is augmentable, using labor and capital in conjunction with land—high-rise buildings, draining the sea, etc.) As a result, that part of income that is composed of land rents will be heavily dependent upon the exogenous supply of land.

A similar problem exists in the human-capital area, where the supply of human capital is to some extent dependent upon the exogenously given supplies of unaugmentable human skills (natural talent). In this case the distribution of economic prizes contains human rents as well as land rents. As before, the importance of these human rents depends partly upon the exogenously given supplies. Marginal products are being paid, but their sizes depend upon the initially given supplies. To explain the distribution of earnings, it is necessary to know the extent of these supplies as well as the mechanism of marginal productivity.

STOCHASTIC VERSUS DETERMINISTIC

Regardless of which variant of marginal productivity is being applied, there is still a problem of whether the model is supposed to be a deterministic model or a stochastic model. In the first case the model determines *ex post* factor payments, and in the second case it only determines *ex ante* factor payments.

Ex post factor payments are composed of an expected *ex ante* payment plus or minus some random disturbance term.

QUESTION: *Is the marginal-productivity model a deterministic model or a scholastic model? If the marginal-productivity model is a stochastic and not a deterministic model, then there is a problem of determining the stochastic process that augments marginal productivity. What is it?*

Conclusions

Although it would be possible to go on at greater length examining the judgments that must be made if marginal productivity is to be used to explain actual distributions of earnings and wealth, the previous question illustrates the kinds of specifications that must occur. Fortunately or unfortunately, each reader is going to have to construct his or her own marginal-productivity model. Many of the necessary judgments have not been examined in the literature of economics, and others are subject to little, if any, consensus.

I urge the reader to make a serious effort to spell out his own version of marginal-productivity theory since only then is it possible to think about the relative merits of different alternatives. As long as marginal productivity is left as a general amorphous theory, it can neither be used nor criticized. Technically, it is not a theory of distribution until it has been spelled out in sufficient detail to be testable.

APPENDIX B

THE RICHEST OF THE RICH

AND A CACHE

OF MULTIMILLIONAIRES

$1 Billion to $1.5 Billion

J. PAUL GETTY, seventy-five; Californian living in England; Getty Oil Co.

HOWARD HUGHES, sixty-two; Las Vegas; Hughes Aircraft, Hughes Tool, real estate.

$500 Million to $1 Billion

H. L. HUNT, seventy-nine; Dallas; independent oil operator.

DR. EDWIN H. LAND, fifty-eight; Cambridge, Massachusetts; Polaroid.

Reprinted from "America's Centimillionaires," *Fortune,* May 1968, p. 152. Courtesy of *Fortune* magazine.

DANIEL K. LUDWIG, seventy; New York; shipping.
AILSA MELLON BRUCE, sixty-six; New York.
PAUL MELLON, sixty; Upperville, Virginia.
RICHARD KING MELLON, sixty-eight; Pittsburgh.

$300 Million to $500 Million

N. BUNKER HUNT, forty-two; Dallas; independent oil operator; son of H. L. Hunt.

JOHN D. MACARTHUR, seventy-one; Chicago and Palm Beach; Bankers Life & Casualty.

WILLIAM L. McKNIGHT, eighty; St. Paul, Minnesota; Minnesota Mining & Manufacturing.

CHARLES S. MOTT, ninety-two; Flint, Michigan; General Motors.

R. E. (Bob) SMITH, seventy-three; Houston; independent oil operator, real estate.

$200 Million to $300 Million

HOWARD F. AHMANSON, sixty-one; Los Angeles; Home Savings & Loan Association.

CHARLES ALLEN JR., sixty-five; New York; investment banking.

MRS. W. VAN ALAN CLARK SR. (Edna McConnell), eighty; New York and Hobe Sound; Avon Products.

JOHN T. DORRANCE JR., forty-nine; Philadelphia; Campbell Soup.

MRS. ALFRED I. DU PONT, eighty-four; Jacksonville.

CHARLES W. ENGELHARD JR., fifty-one; Newark, New Jersey; mining and metal fabricating.

SHERMAN M. FAIRCHILD, seventy-two; New York; Fairchild Camera, I.B.M.

LEON HESS, fifty-four; New York; Hess Oil & Chemical.

WILLIAM R. HEWLETT, fifty-four; Palo Alto; Hewlett-Packard.

DAVID PACKARD, fifty-five; Palo Alto; Hewlett-Packard.

AMORY HOUGHTON, sixty-eight; Corning, New York; Corning Glass Works.

JOSEPH P. KENNEDY, seventy-nine; Palm Beach.

ELI LILLY, eighty-three; Indianapolis; Eli Lilly & Co.

FORREST E. MARS, sixty-four; Washington; Mars candy.

SAMUEL I. NEWHOUSE, seventy-three; New York; newspapers.

MARJORIE MERRIWEATHER POST, eighty-one; Washington and Palm Beach; General Foods.

MRS. JEAN MAUZE (Abby Rockefeller), sixty-four; New York.

DAVID ROCKFELLER, fifty-two; New York.

JOHN D. ROCKEFELLER III, sixty-two; New York.

LAURANCE ROCKEFELLER, fifty-seven; New York.

NELSON ROCKEFELLER, fifty-nine; New York.

WINTHROP ROCKEFELLER, fifty-six; Little Rock, Arkansas.

CORDELIA SCAIFE MAY, thirty-nine; Pittsburgh; Mellon family.

RICHARD MELLON SCAIFE, thirty-five; Pittsburgh.

DEWITT WALLACE, seventy-eight; Chappaqua, New York; *Reader's Digest*.

MRS. CHARLES PAYSON (Joan Whitney), sixty-five; New York.

JOHN HAY WHITNEY, sixty-three; New York.

$150 Million to $200 Million

JAMES S. ABERCROMBIE, seventy-six; Houston; independent oil operator, Cameron Iron Works.

WILLIAM BENTON, sixty-eight; New York; *Encyclopaedia Britannica.*

JACOB BLAUSTEIN, seventy-five; Baltimore; Standard Oil of Indiana.

CHESTER CARLSON, sixty-two; Rochester, New York; inventor of xerography.

EDWARD J. DALY, forty-five; Oakland; World Airways.

233

CLARENCE DILLON, eighty-five; New York; investment banking.

DORIS DUKE, fifty-five; New York.

LAMMOT DU PONT COPELAND, sixty-two; Wilmington.

HENRY B. DU PONT, sixty-nine; Wilmington.

BENSON FORD, forty-eight; Detroit; Ford Motor.

MRS. W. BUHL FORD II (Josephine Ford), forty-four; Detroit; Ford Motor.

WILLIAM C. FORD, forty-three; Detroit; Ford Motor.

HELEN CLAY FRICK, seventy-nine; Pittsburgh; daughter of Henry Clay Frick.

WILLIAM T. GRANT, ninety-one; New York; W. T. Grant variety stores.

BOB HOPE, sixty-four; Hollywood.

ARTHUR A. HOUGHTON JR., sixty-one; New York; Corning Glass Works.

J. SEWARD JOHNSON, seventy-two; New Brunswick, New Jersey; Johnson & Johnson.

PETER KIEWIT, sixty-seven; Omaha; construction.

ALLAN P. KIRBY, seventy-five; Morristown, New Jersey; Woolworth heir, Allegheny Corp.

J. S. MCDONNELL JR., sixty-nine; St. Louis; McDonnell Douglas, aircraft.

MRS. LESTER J. NORRIS (Dellora F. Angell), sixty-five; St. Charles, Illinois; niece of John W. (Bet-a-Million) Gates.

E. CLAIBORNE ROBINS, fifty-seven; Richmond; A. H. Robins, drugs.

MRS. ARTHUR HAYS SULZBERGER (Iphigene Ochs), seventy-five; New York; New York *Times*.

S. MARK TAPER, sixty-six; Los Angeles; First Charter Financial Corp.

ROBERT W. WOODRUFF, seventy-eight; Atlanta; Coca-Cola.

In compiling this list of sixty-six individuals whose wealth is estimated at $150 million or more, *Fortune* included the holdings of spouses and minor children, of trusts, and of foundations established by the individuals or their spouses. Only thirty-three of those listed—precisely half—appeared on a list of the seventy-six richest Americans published in the November, 1957, *Fortune.*

The thirty-nine individuals listed below all became extraordinarily wealthy during the past five years. Most of them are entrepreneurs who built fortunes from relatively small bases. Others climbed onto the list by making their privately held companies public, thus capitalizing the value of their holdings. Excluded are individuals who were worth more than $50 million five years ago, or who became wealthy merely by inheriting established fortunes. The estimates of wealth include not only the individual's personal holdings, but also those of spouses and minor children, of trusts benefiting the immediate family, and of foundations. When two or more people are listed together, e.g., the Levy brothers, each has a net worth qualifying him for the category.

Combined with the compilation of individuals who were worth more than $100 million five years ago (see "America's Centimillionaires," *Fortune*, May, 1968), this list provides a broad survey of personal wealth in the U.S. But neither should be considered definitive. The most striking omission from both lists is Ray A. Kroc, chairman of McDonald's Corp., the fast-food chain. He was worth more than $50 million five years ago and didn't qualify as a centimillionaire. Today he is one of the richest Americans, with holdings of around $500 million.

$500 Million to $700 Million

LEONARD N. STERN, thirty-five, pets, pet foods, accessories, real estate; heads Hartz Mountain Corp., Harrison, New Jersey.

Reprinted from "The New Rich," *Fortune*, September 1973, p.170. Courtesy of *Fortune* magazine.

$300 Million to $500 Million

H. Ross Perot, forty-three, computer services, securities brokerage; founder of Electronic Data Systems, Dallas; principal owner of duPont Walston Inc., New York.

Edwin C. Whitehead, fifty-four, medical equipment; chairman and cofounder of Technicon Corp., Tarrytown, New York.

$200 Million to $300 Million

Roy J. Carver, sixty-three, tire retreads and equipment; chairman and founder of Bandag, Inc., Muscatine, Iowa.

Leonard Davis, forty-nine, low-cost insurance; founder of Colonial Penn Group, Philadelphia.

Milton J. Petrie, seventy-one, women's clothing stores; founder of Petrie Stores Corp., Secaucus, New Jersey.

$150 Million to $200 Million

Arthur G. Cohen, forty-three, real estate; chairman of Arlen Realty & Development Corp., New York.

Jack M. Eckerd, sixty, drugstores; founder of the Jack Eckerd Corp., Clearwater, Florida.

Leo Goodwin Jr., fifty-eight, insurance; a director of Government Employees Insurance Co., Washington, D.C.

Henry S. McNeil, fifty-six, drugs; headed McNeil Laboratories, Philadelphia, now an affiliate of Johnson & Johnson.

Galen J. Roush, eighty-one, trucking; chairman of Roadway Express, Akron, Ohio.

$100 Million to $150 Million

Curtis L. Carlson, fifty-nine, trading stamps (Gold Bond), hotels, and other privately held enterprises, Minneapolis.

ARTHUR S. DEMOSS, forty-seven, insurance by mail; founder of National Liberty Corp., Valley Forge, Pennsylvania.

JOHN K. HANSON, sixty, motor homes; chairman and founder of Winnebago Industries, Forest City, Iowa.

ALEX MANOOGIAN, seventy-two, faucets and other metal products; founder of Masco Corp., Taylor, Michigan.

$75 Million to $100 Million

EDWARD J. FREY, sixty-three, and RICHARD E. RIEBEL, fifty, insurance, primarily for mobile homes, cofounders of Centennial Corp., Grand Rapids, Michigan.

WILLIAM W. GRAINGER, seventy-eight, electric motors; founder of W. W. Grainger Co., Chicago.

ROBERT H. KRIEBLE, fifty-seven, sealants and adhesives; heads Loctite Corp., Newington, Connecticut.

WILLIAM N. LANE, fifty-six, office machines, supplies; chairman of General Binding Corp., Northbrook, Illinois.

IRVIN L. LEVY, forty-four, LESTER A. LEVY, fifty, MILTON P. LEVY JR., forty-eight, industrial cleansers, paints. They are respectively president, chairman, and chairman of the executive committee of National Chemsearch, Irving, Texas.

JOSEPH M. LONG, sixty-one, and THOMAS J. LONG, sixty-three, self-service drugstores. The brothers founded Longs Drug Stores, Walnut Creek, California.

GEORGE P. MITCHELL, fifty-four, oil and gas exploration, real estate; founder of Mitchell Energy & Development, Houston.

THOMAS H. ROBERTS JR., forty-nine, hybrid seed and oil exploration. Son of the late founder of DeKalb AgResearch, Inc., DeKalb, Illinois; he is chairman of the company.

CHAPMAN S. ROOT, forty-eight, bottling and distribution; chairman, Associated Coca-Cola Bottling, Daytona Beach, Florida.

DANIEL J. TERRA, sixty-two, inks and resins for printing; founder of Lawter Chemicals, Northbrook, Illinois.

SAM M. WALTON, fifty-four, discount and variety stores; founder of Wal-Mart Stores, Bentonville, Arkansas.

$50 Million to $75 Million

CURTIS L. BLAKE, fifty-six, and S. PRESTLEY BLAKE, fifty-eight, restaurants; the brothers founded Friendly Ice Cream Corp., Wilbraham, Massachusetts.

ELI BROAD, forty, homebuilding; chairman and cofounder of Kaufman & Broad, Los Angeles.

WILLIAM M. DAVIDSON, fifty, safety glass, photographic services; heads Guardian Industries, Novi, Michigan.

MANNY FINGERHUT, fifty-eight, mail-order sales of consumer products; cofounder of Fingerhut Corp., Minneapolis.

THOMAS E. LEAVEY, seventy-six, insurance; chairman and cofounder of Farmers Group, Los Angeles.

HARVEY M. MEYERHOFF, forty-six, insurance, real estate; heads real-estate operations of Monumental Corp., Baltimore.

EDWARD B. OSBORN, sixty-six, cleaning and sanitation products; chairman and son of the founder of Economics Laboratory, New York and St. Paul.

ANTHONY T. ROSSI, seventy-two, fruit juices; chairman and founder of Tropicana Products, Bradenton, Florida.

NOTES

Chapter 1

1. The attention on family income has, however, led to the neglect of unrelated individuals.

2. Not too long ago it was common for wages to be set in accordance with family characteristics (i.e., marital status, number of children, etc.), but wage scales of this type have almost completely vanished from the American economy.

3. See James D. Smith and Stephen D. Franklin, "The Concentration of Personal Wealth," *American Economic Review* 64 (May 1974): 166.

4. Capitalizing earnings does not change the shape of the distribution of earnings as long as all earnings are capitalized at the same interest.

5. For a discussion of the implications of this factor, see Lester C. Thurow, *Investment in Human Capital* (Belmont, Calif.: Wadsworth Publishing Co., 1970), chaps. 5 and 8.

Chapter 2

1. John Rawls, *A Theory of Justice* (Cambridge: Harvard University Press, 1971).

2. In this case the individual

$$U = f (Y, X_1 \ldots X_n)$$

    where U = individual utility

        Y = personal income and the economic goals that it can purchase

    $X_1 \ldots X_n$ = all of those noneconomic goods and services

3. $W = f\ (u_1, \ldots U_m)$
    where W = social welfare
    $U_1 \ldots U_m$ = utility of all individuals from 1 to m
4. $W = U_1 + U_2 + \ldots U_m$
5. $W = (U_1)\ (U_2) \ldots (U_m)$
6. The individual is simply asked to specify the lottery that would make him indifferent between the initial prize and some new prize. See John Von Neumann and Oskar Morgenstern, *Theory of Games and Economic Behavior* (New York: John Wiley, 1944).
7. Kenneth Arrow, *Social Choice and Individual Values* (New York: John Wiley, 1951).
8. In this case the utility function would be:
    $$U = f\ (Y, G, X_1, \ldots, X_n)\ U = ((Y - G), G, X_1, \ldots, X_n)$$
    where Y = personal income
    G = gifts
9. In this case the utility function would be
    $$U^1 = f\ (Y, X_1, \ldots X_n, U^2)$$
    where U^1 = utility of individual 1
    U^2 = utility of individual 2

    For analysis along this line see M. Pauly, "Efficiency in the Provision of Consumption Subsidies," *Kylos* 23 (1970): 33–57; H. Hockman and J. Rodgers, "Pareto Optimal Redistributions," *American Economic Review* 59 (September 1961): 542–557.

    If the individual is interested in the consumption of some particular good rather than in the utility of individual 2, the utility function would have the following form:
    $$U^1 = f\ ((Y, X\ k \ldots X_n, Z^2)$$
    where Z^2 = individual 2's consumption of some particular good or series Z

    For analysis along this line see E. A. Olsen, "A Competitive Theory of the Housing Market" *American Economic Review* 59 (September 1969): 612

10. In this case the utility function would be:
    $$U = f\ (Y-T, X_1, \ldots, X_n)$$
    where T = the transfer payments that can be used to purchase one of the nonmarket economic goods $(x_1 \ldots X_n)$

    Because transfer payments are used to purchase the nonmarket social good, the distribution of income will differ pre- and post-transfer.

11. In this case the utility function would be:
    $$U = f\ (Y-T, D, X \ldots X_n)$$
    where D = some measure of the distribution of income

    For analysis along this line see Lester C. Thurow, "The Income Distribution as a Pure Public Good," *The Quarterly Journal of Economics* 85 (May 1971): 327–336.

12. Victor E. Smith, *Electronic Computation of Human Diets,* M.S.U.

Business Studies (E. Lansing: Michigan State University, 1964), chap. 2, p. 20.

13. Lee Rainwater, "Poverty, Living Standards and Family Well-Being," Joint Center for Urban Studies of M.I.T. and Harvard Working Paper No. 10. Prepared for Sub-Committee on Fiscal Policy, Joint Economic Committee U.S. Congress, June 1972.

14. For a more recent confirmation of the same results see Daniel M. Holland, "The Effect of Taxation on Effort," *Proceedings of the Sixty-second National Tax Association Conference,* October 1969, pp. 428–524.

15. Harold Watts, Glen G. Cain, "Basic Labor Responses from the Urban Experiment," *Journal of Human Resources* 9 (Spring 1974): 156–278.

Chapter 3

1. Council of Economic Advisers, *1974 Economic Report of the President,* January 1974, p. 102.

2. Not all economists who work in labor economics are labor economists in this sense of the word. Some are micro-economists who work on the labor market.

3. To prevent competitive erosion these impediments usually must have some legal basis by which the state uses its police power to keep them in place.

4. John Maynard Keynes, *The General Theory of Employment, Interest and Money* (New York: Macmillan, 1936).

5. Wage data from 1960 and 1970 Decennial Censuses:

$$\frac{\text{Occupational Earnings 1969}}{\text{Average Earnings 1969}} = \underset{(.0242)}{-.0733} + \underset{(.0220)}{1.0399} \left[\frac{\text{Occupational Earnings 1959}}{\text{Average Earnings 1959}} \right]$$

$R^2 = 0.94$ d.f. $= 146$ Se. $= 0.093$

6. Herman P. Miller, *Income Distribution in the United States* (Washington, D.C.: Bureau of the Census, 1966), p. 21.

7. For an illustration of such an interaction see Jacob Mincer, "On-the-Job Training," *Journal of Political Economy* 70 (October 1962), supplement.

8. Bureau of the Census, *Statistical Abstract, 1973* (Washington, D.C.: Government Printing Office, 1973), p. 114.

9. See Bureau of the Census, *U.S. Census of Population: 1970* (Washington, D.C.: Government Printing Office, 1972), vol. 7A, *Occupational Characteristics.*

10. For a recent example see Sheldon Danziger and Michael Weinstein, "The Effects of Employment Location on the Wage Rates of Poverty Area Residents," mimeographed (Cambridge: M.I.T., 1973).

11. Christopher Jencks, *Inequality* (New York: Basic Books, 1972).

12. George Hildebrand and Ta-Chung Liu, *Manufacturing Production*

Functions in the United States, 1957 (Ithaca, N.Y.: Cornell University Press, 1965), p. 187; Lester C. Thurow, "Disequilibrium and the Marginal Productivities of Capital and Labor," *The Review of Economics and Statistics* 45 (February 1968): 25.

14. Franklin M. Fisher, "The Existence of Aggregate Production Functions," *Econometrica*, 53 (1971): 553.

15. Peter B. Doeringer and Michael J. Piore, *Internal Labor Markets and Manpower Analysis* (Lexington, Mass.: D.C. Heath, 1971), chap. 6.

16. (a) Estimates of elasticities of substitution between college and non-college labor differ radically depending upon the estimation technique. Indirect techniques based upon relative wages and relative factor proportion indicate zero elasticities or even elasticities with the wrong signs—relative usage goes up as relative wages go up. Direct production function estimation techniques yield substitution elasticities substantially in excess of 1.

(b) Direct estimates of output elasticities with respect to different types of labor are not consistent with the relative wages for different types of labor.

(c) Rate of return calculations for education imply implausible aggregate production functions.

For a discussion of these and other problems see Lester C. Thurow, "Measuring the Economic Benefits of Education," in *Higher Education and the Labor Market*, ed. Margaret S. Gordon (New York: McGraw-Hill, 1974), pp. 373–413.

Chapter 4

1. U.S. Department of Labor, *Formal Occupational Training of Adult Workers*, Manpower Automation Research Monograph No. 2 (Washington, D.C.: Government Printing Office, 1964), pp. 3, 18, 20, 43.

2. At the extreme, the two may be joint products and inseparable. This is clearly the case when unique equipment exists.

3. Although direct wage and employment competition may not be pervasive, strong indirect wage and employment competition may occur if the product market is marked by high price elasticities of demand. If an industry or firm is marked by above-equilibrium wages, consumers force them back into line by shifting to alternative goods and services. The only comprehensive study of price elasticities, by Hauthakker and Taylor, found that out of eighty-two exhaustive consumption categories, fifty-four had price elasticities of demand that were not significantly different from zero, nine had price elasticities between zero and one, eight had price elasticities between one and two, and eleven had price elasticities in excess of two. There is thus some scope for indirect wage and employment competition through the product market, but it is limited. In many areas it does not seem to exist.

4. See "Vocational Education," *Journal of Human Resources,* 3 (1963): 1–140, supplement.

5. For a more extensive discussion of internal labor markets see Peter B. Doeringer and Michael J. Piore, *Internal Labor Markets and Manpower Analysis* (Lexington, Mass.: D. C. Heath, 1971).

6. Individuals could be ranked in terms of their potential economic ability by looking at that job for which they exhibit the highest benefit cost ratio. The costs would be the training costs for that job and the benefits would be the discounted lifetime earnings for the same job. The individual might not, however, be able to realize his potential if he is unable to win the competition for his best jobs. His actual economic ability will be given by the benefit cost ratio of the best job that he is actually able to get.

7. See Peter B. Doeringer, ed., *Programs to Employ the Disadvantaged* (Englewood Cliffs, N.J.: Prentice Hall, 1969).

8. For the basic discussion on general versus specific skills in a wage competition framework see Gary S. Becker, *Human Capital* (New York: Columbia University Press, 1964).

9. This was a common student complaint during the 1969–70 riots at universities.

Chapter 5

1. At the aggregate level, elasticities of substitution between capital and labor are thought to be less than 1 but greater than 0. Most studies place the elasticity of substitution near 0.6. For an example see Ronald G. Bodkin and Lawrence R. Klein, "Nonlinear Estimates of Aggregate Production Functions," *The Review of Economics and Statistics* 49 (February 1967): 28–44.

If wage competition exists, it is also possible to estimate elasticities of substitution between different types of labor. Using the standard econometric estimating techniques, by which relative factor proportions are regressed on relative wages, leads to low estimates for labor substitution elasticities. For an example see Lester C. Thurow, "Measuring the Economic Benefits of Education," in *Higher Education and the Labor Market,* ed. Margaret S. Gordon (New York: McGraw-Hill, 1974), p. 587.

Low estimates for elasticities of substitution would lead to the conclusion that technical knowledge heavily conditions actual distributions of factor payments.

2. For the last in a series of articles see Paul A. Samuelson, "A Theory of Induced Innovation Along Kennedy-Weisacker Lines," *The Review of Economics and Statistics* 47 (November 1965): 343–356.

3. In the case of complete ignorance, a research director might be told to investigate cost-reducing innovations in proportion to that factor's importance in the current production processes, but this would not lead to the

utilization of factors becoming relatively more abundant. It would lead to reduced utilization of factors that are now widely used. Widely used factors could, for example, be becoming relatively more abundant.

4. The degree to which this would happen depends upon the price elasticity of demand for those goods produced by the workers in question. In general U.S. price elasticities of demand seem to be low. See H. S. Houthakker and Lester D. Taylor, *Consumer Demand in the United States* (Cambridge: Harvard University Press, 1970).

5. Lee Rainwater, *Poverty, Living Standards and Family Well-Being.* Joint Center for Urban Studies of MIT and Harvard, Working Paper No. 10, p. 45.

6. Ibid., p. 49.

7. Richard Esterlin, "Does Money Buy Happiness?" *The Public Interest,* no. 30 (Winter 1973): 3–10.

8. See Edward E. Lawler III, *Pay and Organizational Effectiveness: A Psychological View* (New York: McGraw-Hill, 1971).

9. For a good discussion of relative deprivation and the source of the following few paragraphs see Walter Garrison Runcimen, *Relative Deprivation and Social Justice* (London: Routledge and Kegan Paul, 1966).

10. John Dunlop, *Wage Determination Under Trade Unions* (New York: Kelley, 1950).

11. If, for example, hiring policies use educational degrees as a selection procedure, equitable structure of wages will probably begin to take these requirements into account. They become part of the costs to be considered. Higher wages must be paid for higher requirements.

12. Changes in the distribution of background characteristics will not, however, increase the range of possible job opportunities. What was the highest potential marginal productivity job before the change will be the highest marginal productivity job after improvements. To expand the range of job opportunities, it would be necessary to create a new background characteristic that lowered the absolute level of training costs.

13. This assumes that the distribution of earnings is being measured by the coefficient of determination—the variance divided by the mean.

14. All of the data in this section came from the U.S. Bureau of the Census, *Current Population Reports: Consumer Income 1969* (Washington, D.C.: Government Printing Office, 1970), p. 101; and U.S. Bureau of the Census, *U.S. Census of the Population: 1950* (Washington, D.C.: Government Printing Office, 1953), pp. 5B–108.

Chapter 6

1. Richard Austin Smith, "The Fifty-Million Dollar Man," *Fortune,* November 1957, p. 176.

2. Arthur Louis, "America's Centimillionaires," *Fortune,* May 1968, p. 152.

3. Arthur Louis, "The New Rich," *Fortune,* September 1973, p. 170.

4. Earnings from raw labor are those earnings that could be generated when the individual had no marketable skills other than a willingness to give up his time.

5. This phenomenon can be modeled either as a rising rate of time preference with age or as a probability problem in which the expected value of next year's consumption is next year's consumption expenditures multiplied by the probability of being alive next year. In either case the value of next year's consumption gradually falls with age.

6. See U.S. Department of Labor, *Survey of Consumer Expenditures,* BLS Report 237 (Washington, D.C.: Government Printing Office, 1965), p. 11.

7. See Howard Tuckman, *The Economics of the Rich* (New York: Random House, 1973), p. 66; Carl S. Shoup, *Federal Estate and Gift Taxes* (Washington, D.C.: The Brookings Institution, 1966), p. 17; Joseph A. Pechman, *Federal Tax Policy* (Washington, D.C.: The Brookings Institution, 1971), p. 195.

8. The type of annuity under consideration here is the type in which the individual buys a lifetime income based on his actuarial life expectancy. This insurance company takes the risk of an uncertain death. Some individuals will die early, and the insurance company will make large profits. Other individuals will live well beyond their actuarial life expectancies, and on these individuals insurance companies will lose money.

9. Economic power is not simply a matter of wealth since the heads of General Motors and AT&T are economically powerful regardless of their own personal wealth.

10. *Fortune,* May 1974, p. 230.

11. U.S. Department of Commerce, "National Income and Product Accounts," *Survey of Current Business* 53 (1973): 38.

12. Short-term loans are made since each firm wants to manage its cash efficiently and invests in short-term paper.

13. Technically, price-earnings ratios reach infinity when dealing with a company with zero or negative returns gets a positive value.

14. Two excellent survey articles are Eugene F. Fama, "Efficient Capital Markets: A Review of Theory and Empirical Works," *Journal of Finance* 25 (May 1970): 383–417; and Michael C. Jensen, "Capital Markets: Theory and Evidence," *The Bell Journal of Economics and Management Science* 3 (Autumn 1972): 357–398.

15. $E(r_i) = E(r_j)$ where $E(r_i)$ = expected rate of return on investment i

$\qquad\qquad\qquad\qquad E(r_j)$ = expected rate of return on investment j

16. Risk is given by the variance in the expected returns.

17. $E(r_i) = a + b\,E(R_m)$

$\qquad$ where $E(r_m)$ = the average market rate of return

$\qquad\qquad$ a, b = measures of the risk class r_i and "a" is thought not to differ significantly from zero.

18. $E(r_i) = E(r_i|I)$

where $E(r_i|I)$ = the expected rate of return on investment i given all information, I, on that investment.

19. See Benoit Mendelbrot, "The Variation of Certain Speculative Prices," *Journal of Business* 36 (October 1963): 394–419.

20. They have in fact underperformed relative to market averages. The usual explanation for this is the transaction costs of buying and selling stocks.

21. There are, however, illegal sources of information (insider information) that can be used to design decision rules that will outperform the market averages.

22. Edwin Land has certainly demonstrated his ability to make more than one invention, but his more recent inventions do not seem to have added to his wealth in the manner of his initial invention of the Polaroid camera.

23. If the probability of winning a lottery once is one in a million, the probability of winning twice is one in a trillion.

Chapter 7

1. Gary S. Becker, *The Economics Discrimination* (Chicago: University of Chicago Press, 1957).

2. One of the central conclusions of Becker's book is that "when actual discrimination occurs, he (the discriminator) must, in fact, either pay or forfeit income for this privilege." Ibid., p. 6. This was an incorrect conclusion that forgot about changes in the terms of trade. Whites can raise their money incomes by practicing discrimination.

3. More precisely:

(A) $$\Delta P(N_0 - \Delta N) \geq < \tfrac{1}{2}N(DP_0 - \Delta P)$$

where

ΔP = change in the price of Negro labor

N_0 = initial quantity of Negro labor exported

ΔN = change in the quantity of Negro labor exported

N = Negro labor

D = discrimination coefficient

P_0 = initial price of Negro labor.

Substituting the relevant demand and supply elasticities into (A) yields

(B) $$\frac{De_0P_0}{e_s + e_d}\left[N_0 - \frac{N_0De_se_d}{e_s + e_d}\right] \geq < \tfrac{1}{2}\frac{N_0e_se_dD}{e_s + e_d}\left[DP_0 - \frac{De_0P_0}{e_s + e_d}\right]$$

or

(C)
$$1 - \frac{De_s e_d}{2e_s + e_d} \geq < \frac{e_s D}{2}$$

where

e_d = white elasticity of demand for Negro labor

e_s = supply elasticity for Negro labor.

When e_s = o, white losses are zero and when e_s = ∞, white gains are zero. Generally, white losses do not exceed white gains unless both e_s and e_d are large.

4. Marvin Kosters, "Effects of Income Tax on Labor Supply," in *The Taxation of Income from Capital*, ed. Arnold Harberger and Martin Bailey (Washington, D.C.: The Brookings Institution, 1969), p. 301.

5. Harry G. Johnson, "Optimum Tariffs and Retaliation," *International Trade and Economic Growth* (London: George Allen & Unwin, 1958), p. 31.

6. Ibid., p. 35 ff., for a proof of this proposition. Johnson finds that the discriminator (retaliator) benefits even in the face of retaliation (discrimination) when his elasticity of demand for imports is roughly more than two and one-half times as large as the elasticity of demand of the retaliator (discriminator). When the elasticities of demand are approximately equal, both countries lose, and between there is a range of indeterminacy.

For a formal application of these principles to Becker's model, see Anne O. Krueger, "The Economics of Discrimination," *Journal of Political Economy* 71 (October 1963): 481–486.

7. Kenneth J. Arrow, "Models of Discrimination," in *Racial Discrimination in Economic Life*, ed. Anthony H. Pascal (Lexington, Mass.: Lexington Books, 1972), p. 83.

8. Lester C. Thurow, *Poverty and Discrimination* (Washington, D.C.: The Brookings Institution, 1969), chap. 7.

9. In each type of discrimination, the monopolist attempts to maximize an objective function. For the specific objective function, see Ibid.

10. U.S. Department of Labor, *Employment and Earnings* (Washington, D.C.: Government Printing Office, 1974), p. 141.

11. Ibid., p. 145.

Chapter 8

1. The returns may accrue to either the employer or the employee, depending upon who pays for training costs.

2. The significant factor is the extent to which earnings rise on the margin between high-school and college jobs when the job shifts from being a high-school job to a college job.

3. If the individual is an expected-value investor, these expected benefits are given by:

$$EB = \left[\left[\left[\begin{array}{c} n \\ \Sigma \\ c = i \end{array} \; (P_i) \; \begin{array}{c} m \\ \Sigma \\ k = 1 \end{array} \; (P_k)(Y_k) \right]_i \right] \;\middle|\; j \right]$$

where EB_j = expected benefits of background characteristic j
$i = i \ldots n$ = job ladders for which j characteristics are eligible
P_k = probability of achieving job ladder i
Y_k = incomes within job ladder
P_k = probability of achieving Y_k income within job ladder.
If the individual is risk-averse, something will be subtracted from EB_j to allow for risk when making investment decisions.

4. In theory, inheritances over $10 million are supposed to be taxed at 77 percent. See Joseph A. Pechman, *Federal Tax Policy* (Washington, D.C.: The Brookings Institution, 1971), p. 267.

5. For a discussion of the technical problems of wealth taxation see Lester C. Thurow, *The Impact of Taxes on the American Economy* (New York: Praeger, 1971), chap. 7.

6. See C. T. Sandford, J. R. M. Willis, and D. J. Ironside, *An Accessions Tax* (Washington, D.C.: Institute for Fiscal Studies, 1973).

7. The most notorious example of this phenomenon was a Du Pont that declared bankruptcy while at the same time being the future recipient of over 200 trusts.

8. See Nicholas Kaldor, *An Expenditure Tax* (London: George Allen & Unwin, 1955).

9. If society does have different goals, one tax cannot be used to achieve both.

10. The corporation income tax and retained earnings constitute a tax loophole for any stockholder in the 48 percent or above bracket.

11. Realized capital gains are taxed at one-half of an individual's normal rates up to a maximum rate of 25 percent, but capital gains of over $50,000 per year are taxed at 35 percent. If gains are not realized until death, they completely escape income taxation.

12. Edward E. Lawler, *Pay and Organizational Effectiveness* (New York: McGraw-Hill, 1971), chap. 3, p. 37.

13. This may be impossible if contributions depend upon inherited wealth or talents. Contributions still determine outcomes, but individuals cannot change their contributions.

14. This individual merely moves from one conditional lottery to another. The expected value of the second lottery may be higher than that of the first, but the individual may end up with a lower income.

15. It is necessary to judge the justice of an initial distribution of income and wealth in order to get a marginal productivity game started.

INDEX

Accessions tax, cumulative lifetime, 198

Accumulation of wealth, xv, 130–142; consumption and, 131–142; economic power as motivation for, 141–142; initial inequalities and, 133–136; time constraints on, 134–136

Affirmative action programs, 205–206

Aggregation of preferences, equity and, 33–43

Allocation of skills, xiv

Annuities, 140, 141

Arrow, Kenneth, 36, 42, 247n

Assets, see Wealth

Automobile industry, dispersion of rates of return in, 143, 145, 146

Background characteristics: distribution of job opportunities and, 101, 114–115, 121–122; distribution of training costs and, 113–117; labor queue and, 91–97, 103; rates of return on investments in, 182–188; relative position with respect to, 95–97; statistical discrimination and, 171–175, 177–178, 181, 205, 206; training costs and, 86–88, 183; see also Education; On-the-job training

Banks, discrimination by, 168–169

Becker, Gary S., 243n, 246n

Blacks: differentials in earnings for, 7, 10, 63, 65, 155–156; discrimination against, see Discrimination; education and income gaps between whites and, 63, 65; labor queue and, 87–88

Bodkin, Ronald G., 243n

Budget constraints, accumulation of wealth and, 132–135, 137–139

Cain, Glen G., 241n

Capital, see Wealth

Capital income, 11

Capital market: discrimination in, 166; financial, rates of return for investments in, 148–154; real, see Real capital markets

Census Bureau, income as defined by, 11

Charity, private, 38, 40

Children: economic-power motivation and reluctance to transfer wealth to one's, 141; wealth accumulation and consumption of one's, 137–140

Choice: analysis of, 36–37; see also Individual preferences

College education: distribution of earnings and, 68–70, 116–119; distribution of training costs and job opportunities and, 115–118; rates of return from investment in, 185–186

Common good, equity and, 23, 47–50

Competition: economic power missing in neoclassical view of perfect,

DATE DUE